JUSTICE PERVERTED

JUSTICE PERVERTED

SEX OFFENDER LAW, PSYCHOLOGY, AND PUBLIC POLICY

CHARLES PATRICK EWING

OXFORD
UNIVERSITY PRESS

Oxford University Press, Inc., publishes works that further
Oxford University's objective of excellence
in research, scholarship, and education.

Oxford   New York
Auckland   Cape Town   Dar es Salaam   Hong Kong   Karachi
Kuala Lumpur   Madrid   Melbourne   Mexico City   Nairobi
New Delhi   Shanghai   Taipei   Toronto

With offices in
Argentina   Austria   Brazil   Chile   Czech Republic   France   Greece
Guatemala   Hungary   Italy   Japan   Poland   Portugal   Singapore
South Korea   Switzerland   Thailand   Turkey   Ukraine   Vietnam

Published by Oxford University Press, Inc.
198 Madison Avenue, New York, New York 10016

www.oup.com

Oxford is a registered trademark of Oxford University Press

Library of Congress Cataloging-in-Publication Data

Ewing, Charles Patrick, 1949-
   Justice perverted : sex offender law, psychology, and public policy / Charles Patrick Ewing.
      p. cm.
   Includes bibliographical references.
   ISBN 978-0-19-973267-8
   1. Sex offenders—Psychology.   2. Sex offenders—Legal status, laws, etc.—United States.
3. Sex offenders—Government policy—United States. I. Title.
   HV6556.E95 2011
   364.15'3—dc22

                                                        2010028074

9 8 7 6 5 4 3 2
Printed in the United States of America
on acid-free paper

To Sharon:
from your rock to my rock.

PREFACE

New York State's Sex Offender Management and Treatment Act (SOMTA) became effective April 13, 2007. The major purpose of SOMTA was to create a system under which some convicted sex offenders who had completed their prison sentences could be retained in state custody indefinitely. According to the state, the statute "establishe[d] an elaborate process for evaluating the mental condition of certain sex offenders who are scheduled to be released... to determine whether the individual is a 'sex offender requiring civil management.'"[1] A "sex offender requiring civil management" was defined as one having "a mental abnormality which predisposes him or her to sexual offending."[2] Under the law, such offenders are deemed by the court to be "either (1) a dangerous sex offender requiring civil confinement (who would be confined to a secure treatment facility operated by OMH [the Office of Mental Health]), or (2) a sex offender requiring strict and intensive supervision and treatment (who would be supervised by a Parole Officer in the community)."[3]

Having followed the legislative process leading to enactment of SOMTA and having read the entire legislative history of the statute, I was aware that this law, though opposed by organized psychology and psychiatry, was a veritable "full employment for psychologists act." SOMTA not only required OMH to hire a large cadre of psychologists and other mental health professionals to screen incarcerated sex offenders who were about to be released and also to conduct initial evaluations of these inmates. The law also mandated that each offender petitioned under the new law be entitled to an independent, court-appointed and state-paid psychological expert, who would examine the offender, prepare a report for the court, and, if requested, provide expert testimony. Moreover, given the adversarial nature of the complex legal proceedings provided for in the statute, it was obvious that the state's attorney general's office (which would prosecute these cases) would also hire psychological experts of its own to evaluate these offenders and testify against them in court.

As a forensic psychologist with over three decades of experience evaluating both victims and perpetrators of sex crimes, I was intrigued by the new law and immediately became involved in its administration by serving as an independent, court-appointed "psychiatric examiner."

As I began this work, it became immediately evident to me that almost none of the players (whether judges, lawyers, or psychologists or other mental health professionals) in the newly created system had much experience or knew much about sex offenses, sex offenders, or the victims of these offenses. Experts from out of state were brought in at great taxpayer expense to teach brief crash courses for the newly minted state psychologists and other mental health professionals hired by OMH under SOMTA. Some of these experts brought with them a handful of checklists they claimed could help differentiate dangerous from non-dangerous sex offenders.

Soon, New York's courts were humming with hearings and trials under the new law, and judges and attorneys on both sides were being told by psychologists, equipped with the *Diagnostic and Statistical Manual of Mental Disorders, Fourth Edition* (DSM-IV) and these recidivism checklists, that they were able to diagnose "mental abnormality" and determine which offenders were "predisposed to sexual offending."

As of March 12, 2010, the total number of sex offenders confined under SOMTA was 209; 119 had been adjudicated as "dangerous sex offenders requiring civil confinement"; 90 were confined with these offenders while awaiting trial under SOMTA.[4] The basic annual cost of confinement (i.e., keeping these offenders in a locked, secure facility) at that date was $175,000 per offender.[5] As of the same date, 70 offenders had been found to require "strict and intensive supervision and treatment" (SIST) in the community at an annual cost of $42,000 per offender.[6] Other costs, including those related to the legal process, experts, and specialized treatment of some offenders, have yet to be calculated.

While the numbers of released sex offenders committed to secure facilities or placed on SIST under SOMTA were mounting steadily, and the costs of administering the law were rapidly rising, New York State was hit with the worst fiscal crisis since the Great Depression and was facing an annual budget deficit in excess of $8 billion. At one point, in 2008, the Governor announced that the state's budget deficit had grown by $1.4 billion in just 90 days.[7] As this book is written, the state is teetering on the verge of bankruptcy and the Governor and members of the state legislature are considering imposing draconian cuts in state funding for public schools, health care, and the state university system as well as closing many state parks and even a number of prisons.[8]

Though my interest in New York's new sex offender law was sparked by my training and experience as a forensic psychologist, the more work I did on cases under SOMTA, the broader my interest became. Having also been trained in law and social policy, I quickly became fascinated with the legal and policy implications of this law, particularly given the state of government finances in New York and other states and at the federal level. I began examining the sex offender commitment laws in 19 other states as well as one recently passed by the U.S. Congress. Before long, I found myself immersed in a study of not only sex offender commitment laws like SOMTA, but all laws dealing with these offenders at the federal, state, and local levels. As a psychologist, I was struck by the extent to which sex offender laws relied upon psychologists and other mental health experts, who often appeared to be making judgments and offering opinions with little if any empirical basis. As a lawyer and law professor, I was troubled by the extent to which many courts, including the U.S. Supreme Court, appeared willing to strain longstanding legal and constitutional doctrines to uphold some of these laws. Finally, as a social policy analyst, specifically trained in program evaluation, I wondered whether the benefits of these laws justified their costs.

Soon my study of these laws became the basis for this book. Realizing that tackling the multitude of laws dealing with sex offenders would be impractical, I decided to focus on four particularly intriguing aspects of American sex offender law: civil commitment statutes such as SOMTA; sex offender registration, notification, and restriction laws; child pornography laws; and laws against using the Internet to sexually entice minors.

From the outset I realized that any effort to analyze these laws from a psychological, legal, or public policy perspective would be difficult and that trying to do so from all three perspectives would be a daunting task. I also realized that the results of any such effort, when reduced to the written word in a book such as this, would likely be controversial and open to criticism.

Although I fully anticipate that what I have written in this book will generate controversy and criticism from some quarters, I have strived to look at these issues with the open mind of a social scientist trained to understand and critically interpret empirical data and a lawyer trained to see all sides of every question.

To that end, readers are warned that I have relied heavily upon empirical data and have cited many statistics and research findings, often specifying them in great detail or even quoting them at length rather than simply summarizing them. My goal in that regard is to allow the reader to see the data for himself or herself, rather than through my eyes, however wide open they may be. Similarly, I have presented the legal reasoning of many courts, the precise language of which I frequently quote. Because I expect that many readers of this volume will not be lawyers, I want them to have the opportunity to read directly what the courts have said about their reasoning on these issues, rather than simply read my summaries of that reasoning. Additionally, in many instances I have quoted applicable statutory law at length so that readers can appreciate the full impact and meaning of these laws. Also, at numerous points in this book, I have quoted, at varying lengths, actual transcripts from trials and, in one chapter, online "chats" between sex offenders and "decoys" the offenders believed were minors. While I could have summarized some of this information, I chose to provide readers with (sometimes extensive) direct quotes from which they can make their own judgments. In that regard, another warning is in order: many accounts of sex offenses in this volume are graphic and some readers may find them unpleasant or offensive. I chose not to censor or sanitize these accounts because I believed doing so might reasonably have been perceived as minimizing the repulsive, often horrific, nature of some of these offenses.

Finally, while I have tried to be as open, objective, and informed as possible, I have also not shied away from offering my own conclusions and recommendations with regard to the future of these laws. Readers may be interested to know, however, that in the course of researching these laws and the empirical data related to them, my thinking about some of them changed significantly. I hope that what I have written here may lead some readers to question, if not change, their positions as well.

ACKNOWLEDGMENTS

For over 30 years I have been asked what it takes to write a book. My response has often been peppered with words and phrases such as inspiration, discipline, persistence, and willingness to be publicly criticized by others. But the more I have written, the clearer it has become that the most important asset any author has is the help of others.

This book could not have been written without a lot of help from a lot of people. Among those to whom I am most grateful are:

Regan Hofmann of Oxford University Press, who saw the value in this book well before it was written and encouraged me to write it;

My friend, Minsuk Kim, who immersed himself in the project from the start and helped shape my thinking with both data and arguments;

My research assistants, Bryant Cherry-Woode and Christopher Moran, both former students of mine who left no stone unturned in their efforts to give me access to all the material I needed, no matter how obscure or difficult to obtain;

My colleagues, attorneys Margot Bennett, Kevin Doyle, Keith Fehrer, Diane Gastle, Jim Gormley, Jeff Lacey, John Nuchereno, and Vicky Valvo, who all helped educate me as to many of the legal issues regarding sex offenders; and

My wife, Dr. Sharon Harris-Ewing, whose love, support, encouragement, and tolerance contribute to every word I write.

CONTENTS

INTRODUCTION

> The last great criminal war, the War on Drugs, resulted in an erosion of civil liberties, mass incarceration, and a fundamental reorientation of American criminal justice. As the War on Drugs loses momentum, there is an opportunity for a war against sex offenders to replace it. If such an eventuality takes place based only upon the body of laws currently targeting sex offenders, the likely social effects will be similar to the War on Drugs. If, as occurred during the drug war, the laws are expanded to further restrict sex offenders, the social and financial costs to America could be enormous. – Corey Rayburn Yung (2010)[1]

Sex offenses have a unique status among crimes in the United States and many other countries. Not without good reason, aside from homicides, these offenses are often regarded as the most heinous of all crimes. The victims of rape and other forms of sexual abuse frequently suffer devastating short-term and long-term physical and psychological consequences. These consequences may be especially severe for sex crime victims who are children.

Fortunately, for roughly the past two decades, the number of reported sex offenses in the United States has been declining steadily. For example, in 2008, the most recent year for which complete national data are currently available, the Federal Bureau of Investigation (FBI) reported that the "estimated number of forcible rapes (89,000)" represented "the lowest figure in the last 20 years"—a decrease of 1.6 percent from the 2007 estimate and 6.4 percent lower than the FBI's 2004 estimate.[2]

Because the FBI data include only reported crimes, and many crimes (especially sex offenses) are never reported, the U.S. Bureau of Justice also calculates criminal victimization statistics through its National Crime Victimization Survey (NCVS). The NCVS is "an ongoing survey of a nationally representative sample of residential addresses [and] is the primary source of information on the characteristics of criminal victimization and on the number and types of crimes not reported to law enforcement authorities."[3] The NCVS defines rape as follows: "Forced sexual intercourse including both psychological coercion as well as physical force. Forced sexual intercourse means vaginal, anal or oral penetration by the offender(s). This category also includes incidents where the penetration is from a foreign object such as a bottle. Includes attempted rapes, male as well as female victims and both heterosexual and homosexual rape. Attempted rape includes verbal threats of rape."[4] According to the NCVS, the number of rapes (so defined) "per 1,000 population age 12 or older" decreased from 2.8 in 1979 to 0.5 in 2008—an 82 percent drop.[5]

The decline in sex offenses against children in roughly the same time period was almost as dramatic. According to the NCVS, the number of rapes and sexual assaults committed against juveniles 12 to 17 years old decreased from 4.0 per 1,000 in 1993 to 2.2 per 1,000 in 2003—a 45 percent drop.[6]

Also, as Finkelhor and Jones reported in 2006, the annual number of substantiated cases of child sexual abuse "started to decline in the early 1990s, after at least 15 years of steady increases" and between 1990 and 2004 the annual number of such cases decreased 49 percent.[7] Finkelhor and Jones acknowledged that "Because the sexual abuse (and other child maltreatment) figures are based on reported cases known to and substantiated by state child protection agencies, observers have speculated that the decline might… simply reflect changed standards for investigation, decreased reporting to agencies, reduced funding, staff and interest, or statistical or other artifacts."[8] These researchers, however, rejected such speculation and noted that "after considerable efforts to study the CPS data in context, we have concluded that they probably reflect at least in part a real decline in sexual abuse."[9]

Meanwhile, other data gathered by the federal government regarding sex offenses were describing sex offenders and their relationships to their victims. To begin with, the NCVS and other data confirmed that, contrary to common belief, most sex offenses are not committed by strangers but rather by individuals known to their victims. For example, the 2002 NCVS found that non-strangers committed 69 percent of all sexual assaults against female victims; 57 percent were committed by a friend or acquaintance, 10 percent by an intimate partner, and 2 percent by one whose relationship to the victim was unknown.[10] The 2002 NCVS also found that non-strangers committed 52 percent of all sexual assaults against male victims, who were seven times less likely than females to be sexually assaulted.[11] The 2004 NCVS determined that only 26 percent of rapes and sexual assaults on female victims were committed by strangers; 38 percent were committed by a friend or acquaintance of the victim; 20 percent by an intimate partner, 7 percent by some other relative; and 2 percent were committed by perpetrators whose relationship to the victim was unknown.

Additionally, a 2000 report from the U.S. Bureau of Justice Statistics dealing with reported cases of child sexual abuse revealed that, at all ages, children were very unlikely to be sexually victimized by people they did not know.[12] Family members were the perpetrators in 51.1 percent of the cases involving girls 0 to 5 years old, 43.8 percent of those involving girls 6 to 11, 24.3 percent of those involving girls 12 to 17, 42.4 percent of those involving boys 0 to 5, 37.7 percent of those involving boys 6 to 11, and 23.7 percent of those involving boys 12 to 17. Acquaintances were the perpetrators in 45.9 percent of the cases involving girls 0 to 5 years old, 51.4 percent of those involving girls 6 to 11, 65.7 percent of those involving girls 12 to 17, 54.1 percent of those involving boys 0 to 5 years old, 57.7 percent of those involving boys 6 to 11, and 68.7 percent of those involving boys 12 to 17. Strangers were the perpetrators in only 3.0 percent of the cases involving girls 0 to 5 years old, 4.8 percent of those involving girls 6 to 11, 10 percent of those involving girls 12 to 17, 3.5 percent of those involving boys 0 to 5, 4.6 percent of those involving boys 6 to 11, and 7.6 percent of those involving boys 12 to 17.

Around the same time—the 1990s to mid-2000s—other data collected and published by federal and state agencies were revealing that, contrary to popular and political perception, sex offenders were rather unlikely to recidivate. For example, one federal study found that among all sex offenders (i.e., those convicted of rape, sexual assault, statutory rape, and child molestation) released from prison in 15 states in the same year, only 5.3 percent were re-arrested for a sex offense within 3 years of their release.[13] Published data from other states found similarly low rates of recidivism among convicted sex offenders, ranging from 3.21 percent to roughly 7 percent.[14]

Despite these data suggesting that sex crimes were dramatically decreasing in number, that most sex offenses were being committed by relatives and acquaintances rather than strangers, and that only a small percentage of convicted sex offenders were recidivating, the past two decades have been marked by an unprecedented spate of tough and expensive state and federal legislation that has recently been referred to as an "emerging criminal war on sex offenders." [15]

To date, this "war on sex offenders" has included a wide variety of federal, state, and local laws. For example, every state has now adopted its own version of "Megan's Law," requiring convicted sex offenders to register with the state and to have their photographs, names, addresses, and other information about them made readily available to the public on Internet websites and through other media. Registration is generally required on an annual basis, and failure to register is itself a serious crime, punishable by imprisonment. Many offenders are required to register for the rest of their lives. Moreover, many states and municipalities have passed residency restriction laws prohibiting convicted sex offenders from living, working, or even being in certain geographical areas such as 2,500 feet from a school, day care center, park, or other place where children may congregate.

The "war" on sex offenders has also included the imposition of lengthy prison sentences for those who utilize the Internet for criminal sexual purposes. For example, recently enacted federal laws mandate a minimum sentence of 10 years in prison for anyone convicted of using the Internet to attempt to entice a minor (or an adult posing as a minor) to engage in sexual acts. Additionally, under federal and some state laws, many individuals convicted of receiving and possessing child pornography are now routinely incarcerated for one or more decades.

Finally, this "emerging criminal war on sex offenders" now includes the "sexually violent predator" laws that have been enacted between 1990 and 2008 in 20 states and the federal jurisdiction. Under these statutes, convicted sex offenders who have fully served their criminal sentences may be indefinitely committed to secure prison-like treatment facilities if they are found to have a "mental abnormality" that makes them likely to reoffend.

All of these laws are aimed at reducing the incidence of sexual offending, especially against children. All are predicated on psychological assumptions about sex offenders. And all of them raise significant legal and public policy questions.

This book examines these laws from three perspectives: psychology, law, and public policy. Are these laws supported by, or consistent with, psychological and other empirical data? Are court decisions upholding the constitutionality of these laws consistent with such data and the ability of psychologists and other experts to predict future dangerousness? Finally, given their costs and benefits, do these laws represent sound public policy and a wise investment of increasingly limited taxpayer dollars in the government's efforts to reduce the incidence of sex offenses?

Chapter 1 deals with sexually violent predator (SVP) laws. The chapter begins by looking at the historical roots of these laws, which lie in what were once known as "sexual psychopath" laws—long-abandoned statutes that similarly attempted to reduce sex offending by a special commitment and treatment process aimed at certain sex offenders. This chapter also reviews the various SVP statutes and the major court decisions that have upheld these laws; presents and analyzes statistics on the implementation of these laws; explores the significant controversy these laws have engendered among psychologists and other mental health experts, especially with regard to the concept of "mental abnormality" and the ability of mental health experts to predict sexual recidivism; reviews the data regarding the efficacy of psychological and other treatment modalities that are critical to the constitutionality of SVP laws; and weighs the economic and other costs and benefits of the nation's current SVP statutes.

Chapter 2 examines sex offender registration, notification, and restriction laws. As in the preceding chapter, the analysis begins by looking at the historical roots of these laws, now long-defunct efforts by a number of states to monitor the whereabouts of convicted sex offenders. This chapter also traces the legislative and judicial history of these laws from 1990 to the present and examines this body of law in light of empirical data regarding sex offender recidivism and the deterrent efficacy of sex offender registration, public notification, and restrictions on where convicted sex offenders may live, work, or travel. Finally, this chapter details and then weighs the economic and other costs and benefits of these laws.

Chapter 3 deals with laws criminalizing the possession of child pornography and mandating lengthy prison terms for many of those convicted of this offense, particularly those sentenced in federal courts. The chapter begins with a historical overview of child pornography laws in the United States. This chapter then details current laws and penalties, with particular emphasis on the relationship of the U.S. Federal Sentencing Guidelines to the increasing length of incarceration for those convicted of possessing child pornography. This chapter also reviews current psychological data and understanding with regard to child pornography and those who possess it, paying particular attention to the question of whether these individuals are (or are likely to become) "hands-on" child sex offenders. Finally, this chapter looks at U.S. child pornography laws and sentencing from a comparative law perspective, estimates the cost of lengthy prison terms for child pornography offenders, and considers alternative methods to reduce the production, distribution, and possession of child sexual abuse images.

Chapter 4 examines laws, sentences, and law enforcement methods applicable to individuals who use or attempt to use the Internet as a means of arranging sexual encounters with minors, mostly teenagers. After reviewing the law and federal sentencing structure related to this offense, this chapter presents empirical data on the nature and scope of this crime and reviews psychological research on those who commit this offense and the danger they pose to minors. These analyses are followed by an examination of so-called sting operations used by law enforcement and private organizations in which Internet sex offenders are led to believe that they are attempting to sexually lure a teenager but are instead communicating online with an adult "decoy."

Included in this discussion is an analysis of the legal doctrines of entrapment and impossibility, explaining why these defenses usually fail. Finally, this chapter attempts to reconcile the punishment meted out to these offenders (i.e., a minimum of 10 years in prison) and the usually much lower criminal sentences prescribed for statutory rapists (adults who engage in sexual relations with minors who are willing but legally incapable of consent).

1

CIVIL COMMITMENT OF SEX OFFENDERS

In 1955, when Leroy Hendricks was 20 years old, he exposed his genitals to two young girls and asked if they wanted to join him in his car and play with his penis. A first-time offender, he pleaded guilty to indecent exposure. Two years later, he was convicted of lewd conduct for playing strip poker with a 14-year-old girl and incarcerated briefly. Three years later, in 1960, Hendricks fondled the genitals of two boys, ages 7 and 8, while working at a carnival. After serving 3 years of his sentence for those offenses, he was released on parole and befriended the parents of a 7-year-old girl. Hendricks fondled the girl's genital area and placed his fingers in her vagina. Hendricks testified that he knew this conduct was wrong but that he had been unable to control himself. These offenses led to Hendricks being adjudicated a "sexual psychopath" and civilly committed to a state mental institution.[1]

Released in 1965, Hendricks was in the community for 2 years before being convicted and imprisoned for repeatedly performing oral sex on an 8-year-old girl and fondling an 11-year-old boy over a period of about 2 months. This time, Hendricks stated that the crimes were the result of urges he did not even try to control. Imprisoned in 1967, Hendricks refused sex offender treatment, remained incarcerated until 1972, and then attended outpatient sex offender treatment for a few months before dropping out.[2]

The following year, 1973, he began sexually abusing his stepdaughter and stepson. He performed oral sex on his stepdaughter several times a month from the time she was about 9 until she was 14 years old. Hendricks secured her cooperation by threatening to tell her mother of her sexual involvement with a boy and by bribing her with favors, such as allowing her to drive his car. Hendricks also performed oral sex on his stepson and fondled his genitals approximately once a week from the time the boy was 9 until he was 14 years old. Additionally, Hendricks had his stepson perform oral sex on him, induced by favors such as giving him chewing tobacco.[3]

In 1984, after his stepchildren were grown, Hendricks was convicted of taking indecent liberties with two 13-year-old boys, after telling police he was unable to control his urge to touch the boys' penises.[4] Hendricks served a decade in prison for these offenses and, when he was up for release in 1994, became the first person indefinitely civilly committed under Kansas's newly enacted sexually violent predator law. The then-new Kansas law provided that once an offender such as Hendricks finished his prison sentence he could be civilly committed (i.e., detained for treatment in a secure psychiatric facility against his will) for an indefinite period of time if a jury found that, as the result of a "mental abnormality" or "personality disorder," he was likely to engage in "predatory acts of sexual violence."[5]

At trial, Hendricks, then 60 years old, told the jury that he had spent roughly half of his adult life in prisons or psychiatric institutions and that when he experienced stress, he was unable to control his urge to have sexual contact with children. As he testified, "I can't control the urge when I get stressed out."[6] Hendricks also testified that he understood that he was a pedophile and that his conduct caused serious harm to the children he victimized. Yet he further testified that he believed that at least some of his victims enjoyed what he did to them. Moreover, Hendricks offered his view that sex offender treatment was "bullshit" and that he had not been cured of pedophilia.[7] Finally, asked whether he could promise the jury that he would stop offending if released, he testified candidly that "the only way to guarantee that is to die."[8]

A state psychologist who examined Hendricks prior to his trial court proceeding testified that Hendricks was a pedophile and likely to commit further sexual offenses against children if released. The doctor testified that he based his opinion on his "belief that past behavior is a good predictor of future behavior, the fact that pedophilia commonly involves repeated behavior, Hendricks' failure to demonstrate that he can or desires to control his behavior, Hendricks' lack of understanding of the seriousness of his behavior, and Hendricks' lack of interest in treatment."[9] He also testified that, in 1985, Hendricks reported to another mental health professional that he acted on his sexual impulses at least "once per month, twice a month."[10]

A forensic psychiatrist called by Hendricks' attorney as an expert witness testified that treatment for sex offenders generally was ineffective, but that some studies showed that recidivism rates for sex offenders were reduced "from the 10–40% range to a 3–37.5% range with treatment" and that recidivism rates for child molesters were affected by a number of factors, including "whether he's been treated or not."[11] This doctor also testified that "psychiatrists and psychologists cannot accurately predict whether a sex offender is likely to engage in sexual predation in the future."[12]

The jury unanimously agreed, beyond a reasonable doubt, that Hendricks was a "sexually violent predator" as defined by the new Kansas law.[13] Then, pursuant to the Kansas law, the judge ordered Hendricks committed to a state hospital until a court found him no longer suffering from "a mental abnormality rendering him unable to control his dangerousness."[14]

After his commitment in 1994, Hendricks remained confined for over a decade, despite a lengthy legal battle that took his case all the way to the U.S. Supreme Court, which ruled against him. It appears that Hendricks' commitment cost the state roughly $1 million, exclusive of legal costs.[15]

By 2004, Hendricks had successfully completed all five stages of inpatient treatment offered under the Kansas law. State mental health officials resisted his discharge from civil confinement despite his having completed all phases of the inpatient program, but a judge ordered Hendricks released into the community, making him just the third offender (out of a total of 157) to be released from civil confinement under the 1994 Kansas law.[16] Hendricks, who was then 70 years old, barely ambulatory, and suffering from numerous physical impairments resulting from diabetes and a stroke, was to be placed in a specially devised group home that would eventually house him and other sexual offenders released from civil confinement in the state. During this sixth stage of the civil commitment process, as contemplated by the Kansas law, Hendricks would be on 1:1 supervision 24 hours a day, 7 days a week at an estimated cost of $278,000 for the first 15 months.[17] The extremely high cost of this placement appeared to be a function of the security under which Hendricks was to be kept:

> [T]he Phase 6 transition does not contemplate or suggest that Hendricks will be "at large" at any time. In fact, the placement provides for 24 hours a day, 7 days a week of supervision in which an observer is designated to be physically present or monitor Hendricks at all times. The facility sits on a remote 2-acre lot in rural Leavenworth County. There are alarms on all interior and exterior doors of the facility. Daily activities, such as food preparation, laundry, housekeeping, and hygiene, are all supervised and monitored. Hendricks cannot go out onto the porch or patio of the premises without an escort. All television, reading materials, and mail are monitored and screened. There is no computer access.[18]

Before this court-ordered statutory treatment plan could be implemented, however, local officials objected to the placement of Hendricks in their community. They petitioned a local court for an injunction against the operators of the group home where Hendricks was to live.

At a hearing on the issue, a state psychologist testified that Hendricks was still a pedophile, continued to be a "sexually violent predator," and would be a danger to others if allowed to be at large in the community, but was nevertheless ready to be placed in a supervised setting in the community and would not present a danger while living in a highly structured group home.[19] Medical reports at the time also indicated that Hendricks had poor eyesight and hearing and could not walk down the home's 120-foot-long driveway without falling.[20]

The trial court granted a permanent injunction preventing operation of the group home in which Hendricks was to live unless the operators first obtained a special-use permit from the county. The court's decision, affirmed on appeal by the Kansas Supreme Court, effectively killed the plan for a group home for sex offenders released from civil commitment.[21] With no legally acceptable place to live in the community, Hendricks was placed in a state hospital where he remained, at last report, at an annual cost to the state of $185,000 a year, eight times what it would have cost the state to imprison him.[22]

To explain why Hendricks ended up essentially committed to a mental institution for life requires an analysis of the history of American sex offender commitment laws leading up to his initial civil commitment and the role that his own case played in shaping sex offender commitment laws thereafter.

Inventing The Sexual Psychopath

The Kansas sexually violent predator (SVP) law under which Leroy Hendricks was committed in 1994 is one of roughly 20 on the books today in the United States. Other states with SVP laws include Arizona, California, Florida, Illinois, Iowa, Kansas, Massachusetts, Minnesota, Missouri, Nebraska, New Hampshire, New Jersey, New York, North Dakota, Pennsylvania, South Carolina, Texas, Virginia, Washington, and Wisconsin. These SVP laws were all enacted in a roughly two-decade span from 1990 to 2007.[23] But these laws are not the first of their kind in the United States: In an earlier span of approximately two decades, 26 states enacted what were known as sexual psychopath laws.[24]

Apparently spurred by a handful of brutal sex crimes against children, the American news media began to vastly increase and sensationalize their coverage of child molestation, rape, and other sex crimes in the late 1930s. As Freedman, an historian, would later write:

> Between 1937 and 1940, and again during the postwar decade, the
> *New York Times,* previously silent on the subject, averaged over
> forty articles per year on sex crimes. In 1937, magazines ranging

from *Science* and the *Christian Century* to the *Nation* and the *New Masses* reported on the sex crime panic. After World War II news and family magazines, including *Time, Newsweek,* and *Parents' Magazine,* carried articles titled "Queer People," "Sex Psychopaths," and "What Shall We Do About Sex Offenders?" In its 1950 series on "Terror in Our Cities," *Collier's* magazine summarized the newspaper headlines in St. Louis ("The City that DOES Something About Sex Crime") in a representative composite: KINDERGARTEN GIRL ACCOSTED BY MAN— CLERK ACCUSED OF MOLESTING 2 GIRLS IN MOVIE— MAN ACCUSED BY 8-YEAR-OLD BOY OF MOLESTING HIM IN THEATRE—6-YEAR-OLD GIRL AT ASHLAND SCHOOL MOLESTED—LABORER ARRESTED FOR RAPE OF 10-YEAR-OLD GIRL—FINED FOR MOLESTING 2 BOYS, AGED 8 AND 10—ARRESTED ON SUSPICION OF MOLESTING 4-YEAR-OLD GIRL—YOUTH WHO MOLESTED BOY, 4, IS FINED $500—9 CHARGES AGAINST MOLESTER OF GIRLS.[25]

At the same time media sources were trumpeting cases such as these, American psychiatrists were beginning to tout the notion that persistent sex offenders were "psychopaths" with "no control over their sexual impulses,"[26] who, if simply incarcerated and left untreated, would "prey again upon women and children."[27] According to the growing psychiatric point of view, these offenders could be readily diagnosed, treated, and perhaps even cured under the proper medical regimen.

Together, the media and the psychiatric profession swayed not only public opinion but also the minds of many legislators. In 1937, Michigan passed the nation's first state "sexual psychopath" law and, within two decades 25 other states followed suit. The idea behind these laws was simple in theory if not execution:

> [A] man accused of rape, sodomy, child molestation, indecent exposure, or corrupting the morals of a minor if diagnosed as a "sexual psychopath" could receive an indeterminate sentence to a psychiatric, rather than a penal, institution. The laws defined the sexual psychopath as someone whose "utter lack of power to control his sexual impulses" made him "likely to attack . . . the objects of his uncontrolled and uncontrollable desires."[28]

Though purportedly oriented to treatment of "sexual psychopaths," all but one of these laws called for open-ended or indefinite, potentially lifetime commitments from which offenders could be discharged only if and when cured. Many of those committed were confined much longer than they would have been if they had been sentenced to regular prisons instead. As Tappan, a sociologist and technical consultant to the New Jersey Commission on the Habitual Sex Offender, observed:

> Psychiatrists have expressed their great reluctance to release the alleged "sex psychopath" at all on the ground of the public reaction should any such person prove not to have been cured. Even in instances where the individual is believed not to be a true deviate, there is always the possibility that he may again at some time violate the sex mores, with ruinous effect upon the reputation of an institution and its administrative officers.[29]

"Sexual psychopath" laws were also criticized for other reasons. To begin with, critics complained that the laws were ill conceived in that, while the laws were aimed at persistent offenders, most sex offenders were not recidivists. For example, one study of 2,022 sex offenders conducted in New York in the late 1930s found that only 353 (17.4 percent) had prior arrests and that, of that number, just 85 (4.2 percent of the entire sample) had prior arrests for sex offenses. Moreover, among those previously arrested for sex offenses, only 49 (57.6 percent) had prior convictions for such offenses.[30]

Psychiatric critics took aim at the vagueness and elasticity of the term "sexual psychopath" and noted that, as a result of a lack of agreed-upon definition in the profession, many of those committed were clearly not mentally ill, even by the broadest definitions. Indeed, a substantial minority were affirmatively diagnosed as "normal."[31]

Psychiatric critics also complained about the overly optimistic claims that offenders likely to re-offend could easily be sorted out from those unlikely to recidivate. These critics also derided the treatment supposedly provided to "sexual psychopaths" in the "hospitals" to which they were committed. Numerous psychiatrists explained that these "patients" were effectively being warehoused in facilities that, as one critic put it, "lacked the space, the personnel, the treatment methods, or even the desire to" offer meaningful treatment to sex offenders.[32]

Detractors from the bench, bar, and legal academia observed that these laws sometimes provided nothing more than a form of preventive detention as well as a way in which prosecutors could succeed in putting away alleged sex offenders, the evidence against whom was lacking to secure a criminal conviction but sufficient to establish "sexual psychopathy" under the more lenient civil standard of proof (i.e., preponderance of the evidence rather than proof beyond a reasonable doubt).

By the 1970s, America's experiment with "sexual psychopath" laws ended largely at the hands of many of those who helped initiate it decades earlier. Organized psychiatry, speaking through the American Psychiatric Association (APA), declared that "The optimism of earlier decades that psychiatry held the cure to sexual psychopathy no longer [shines] so brightly."[33] The Group for the Advancement of Psychiatry, whose Committee on Forensic Psychiatry had been an early champion of "sexual psychopath" laws, ultimately concluded that:

> First and foremost, sex psychopath and sexual offender statutes can best be described as approaches that have failed. . . . The notion is naïve and confusing that a hybrid amalgam of law and psychiatry can validly label a person a "sex psychopath" or "sex offender" and then treat him in a manner consistent with the guarantee of community safety. The mere assumption such a heterogeneous legal classification could define treatability and make people amenable to treatment is not only fallacious; it is startling.[34]

Re-Inventing The Sexual Psychopath

"Those who do not learn from history are doomed to repeat it."
George Santayana (1906)[35]

In September 1988, in Seattle, Washington, 29-year-old Diane Ballasiotes was abducted from a downtown parking lot, raped, stabbed to death, and then dumped in another part of the city, where her body was not found until a week later. Her assailant was Gene Raymond Kane, who had recently completed a full sentence of 13 years in prison for two earlier sex attacks on women and was in the community on a prison release program.[36]

In May 1989, in nearby Tacoma, Earl K. Shriner kidnapped, raped, strangled, and severed the penis of a 7-year-old boy who had been riding a bicycle near his own home. The boy survived and identified Shriner, who was known to the police for his previous offenses, including homicide, kidnapping, and the assault of two teenage girls. Shriner, who had an IQ of 67, had recently been released from prison because he had fully completed his latest sentence.[37]

Less than 4 months later, in Vancouver, Washington, two brothers were found stabbed to death in a city park. Both boys were tied up and one had been sodomized. About 2 months later, the body of another boy, age 4, was found by a lake in Vancouver. The boy had been repeatedly raped, strangled, and sexually abused after death. Neither of these cases was solved until another 2 months passed and Westley Dodd, a 28-year-old pedophile with a long record of sex offenses against boys dating back to his own teenage years, was arrested as he tried to abduct a 6-year-old boy from a theater. Questioned by the police, Dodd admitted to killing all three Vancouver boys and to previously molesting about 30 children.[38]

Public outrage over these rare but horrible crimes, committed within such a limited geographic area and short time span, led the Washington legislature to pass what would become the first of more than 20 modern laws aimed at allowing states (and, most recently, the federal government) to confine sex offenders believed to be dangerous even after they have served their full criminal sentences. Indeed, the Washington sex offender civil commitment law, enacted in 1990, has served as a model for many if not most of those to follow.

Washington's civil commitment statute, like most of those that have come after it, uses the term "sexually violent predator" instead of "sexual psychopath," but this law and the others it has inspired have much in common with the now long-defunct "sexual psychopath" statutes. The statute defines a "sexually violent predator" as an individual "who has been convicted of or charged with a crime of sexual violence and who suffers from a mental abnormality or personality disorder which makes the person likely to engage in predatory acts of sexual violence if not confined in a secure facility."[39] "Mental abnormality" is defined as "a congenital or acquired condition affecting the emotional or volitional capacity which predisposes the person to the commission of criminal sexual acts."[40] The term "personality disorder" is not defined.

While today's SVP statutes have much in common with the old "sexual psychopath" laws, a major difference lies in what La Fond, a legal scholar, has called a "punish first, treat later" mentality.[41] Under sexual psychopath laws, the state had to make an initial choice as to whether an offender should be punished or treated. SVP laws provide that treatment may be imposed upon offenders *after* they are punished. As La Fond further noted, unlike most sexual psychopath laws, with SVP laws "the government [does] not have to prove the offender suffered from a medically recognized mental illness, [only that] the person suffered from a *mental abnormality* (a phrase that has no common or authoritative definition generally understood by mental health professionals) or a *personality disorder*."[42] Finally, as La Fond also observed, most sexual psychopath laws required the government to charge or convict an individual of a sex crime before it could seek civil commitment of the offender, thus ensuring that there was "*recent* evidence indicating the offender was sexually dangerous."[43] With SVP laws, "the government does not have to prove deteriorating mental condition or any recent criminal conduct or inappropriate behavior that manifests sexual dangerousness before seeking possible lifetime confinement."[44] In other words, the state can wait until an inmate has nearly completed his prison sentence and then use his original and/or most recent offense(s), which may have occurred many years earlier, as evidence of the need for confinement.

In 1995, the constitutionality of the Washington SVP statute was challenged in federal court by David Weston, who had been convicted of rape three different times, found to be a sexually violent predator and committed for treatment following completion of his criminal sentence. In *Young v. Weston*, the federal district began its opinion by summarizing the pertinent parameters of the Washington SVP statute:

> The Statute allows the State to initiate the involuntary commitment process when a person's sentence for a sexually violent offense is about to expire, or when a person who was incompetent to stand trial on a charge of a sexually violent offense or who was found not guilty by reason of insanity of a sexually violent offense is about to be released. To initiate the commitment process, the county prosecutor or the attorney general files a petition alleging that the person is a "sexually violent offender." A judge determines whether there is probable cause to believe that the person is a sexually violent predator. If so, the judge directs that the person be taken into custody and transferred to a facility for evaluation "by a person deemed to be professionally qualified to conduct such an examination pursuant to rules developed by the department of social and health services."
>
> A person charged under the statute is entitled to a trial within 45 days after the filing of the petition. The detainee has the right to retained or appointed counsel and the right to retained or appointed experts. Both parties have a right to a jury trial. The Statute further provides that the court or jury shall determine whether, beyond a reasonable doubt, the person is a sexually violent predator. . . . If the court or jury determines that the person is a sexually violent predator, the person shall be committed to the custody of the department of social and health services in a secure facility for control, care and treatment until such time as the person's mental abnormality or personality disorder has so changed that the person is safe to be at large.[45]

After noting that detained sexually violent predators were entitled to annual judicial reviews in which the state had the burden of proving beyond a reasonable doubt that the detainee's mental condition "remains such that the petitioner is not safe to be at large and that if discharged is likely to engage in predatory acts of sexual violence,"[46] the court examined Young's claims that the statute was unconstitutional because it violated the substantive due process component of the Fourteenth Amendment, the ex post facto clause of Article 1, Section 10, of the Constitution, and the double jeopardy clause of the Fifth Amendment.

Analyzing Young's due process claim, the court reasoned that:

> As incarceration of persons is the most common and one of the most feared instruments of state oppression and state indifference, we ought to acknowledge at the outset that freedom from this restraint is essential to the basic definition of liberty in the Fifth and Fourteenth Amendments of the Constitution. For this reason, the Supreme Court has carefully circumscribed the instances in which the state may, for non-punitive reasons, detain or incarcerate an individual. For example, in times of war or insurrection, the government may detain individuals whom it believes are dangerous. And, under certain circumstances, individuals may be detained pending arraignment, trial, or deportation, on the grounds that such individuals are dangerous to the community, dangerous to witnesses, or that they present flight risks.
>
> The Supreme Court has also held that the state has authority to protect the community from the dangerous tendencies of some individuals who are mentally ill. Absent clear and convincing evidence of both mental illness and dangerousness, however, detention is impermissible.
>
> The State does not argue that the Sexually Violent Predator Statute is comparable to the pretrial detention schemes [approved by the Supreme Court]. Such an argument would, of course, fail: [Supreme Court precedents] authorize pretrial detention of dangerous persons for stringently limited periods of time. This is quite obviously not true of the Sexually Violent Predator Statute. Commitment pursuant to the Statute is indefinite. Indeed, given the State's open acknowledgement of the poor treatment prospects for detainees, prolonged incarceration is to be expected.
>
> The State argues, however, that the Statute passes constitutional muster as a traditional civil commitment scheme . . . This argument

also fails. The essential component missing from the Sexually Violent Predator Statute is the requirement that the detainee be mentally ill. Like the scheme rejected [by the Supreme Court], the Statute here permits indefinite incarceration based on little more than a showing of potential future dangerousness.

The absence of a mental illness requirement is apparent both in the statutory language and in its legislative history. First, the legislature's findings expressly disavow the notion that the targeted group of persons are [sic] mentally ill. As explained in [the legislative history], the target group is made up of individuals "who do not have a mental disease or defect that renders them appropriate for the existing involuntary treatment act." Unlike persons with serious mental disorders, the legislature concluded, sexual predators "have antisocial personality features which are unamenable to existing mental illness treatment modalities," and for which the prognosis of cure is poor.

The abandonment of a mental illness requirement is further revealed in the statutory definitions. As noted above, a "sexually violent predator," for purposes of the Statute, is a person who, among other things, "suffers from a mental abnormality or personality disorder." Amicus, the Washington State Psychiatric Association, explains that the term "mental abnormality" has neither a clinically significant meaning nor a recognized diagnostic use among treatment professionals. Even accepting the statutory definition of "a congenital or acquired condition affecting the emotional or volitional capacity which predisposes the person to the commission of criminal sexual acts in a degree constituting such person a menace to the health and safety of others," the term establishes an unacceptable tautology: a sexually violent predator suffers from a mental condition that predisposes him or her to commit acts of sexual violence. . .

Whatever doubt might remain after reviewing the Statute itself is resolved by the legislative history. The Governor's Task Force on Community Protection, whose proposed bill was substantially similar to that enacted, plainly intended to craft legislation to permit the involuntary commitment of persons who are not mentally ill: ["]Civil commitment under the involuntary treatment law allows indefinite commitment, but is quite restrictive in its definitions. Under current laws, sexually violent predators only qualify for civil detention when a mental illness or mental disorder

13

is present. The Task Force examined the histories of some individual violent predators who had been judged not to have a mental illness or mental disorder and therefore were not detainable[."]

Indeed, in testimony before the legislature, one member of the Task Force explained that Washington's traditional civil commitment law was inappropriate for Earl Shriner, the perpetrator of the highly publicized assault and mutilation of a young boy, because he was not mentally ill . . . Professor David Boerner . . . stated "Mr. Shriner is not mentally ill as that term is defined. He is clearly a problem, and clearly very dangerous, but he doesn't suffer from a classic mental illness . . ."

The Court concludes that the Sexually Violent Predator Statute, allowing as it does the indefinite confinement of persons who are not mentally ill, violates the substantive protections of the Due Process Clause. Predictions of dangerousness alone are an insufficient basis to continue indefinitely the incarceration of offenders who have completed their prison terms.[47]

The court then rejected the state's claim that the SVP statute did not violate the Constitution's ex post facto clause because the law was intended for purposes of treatment and not punishment. As the court concluded:

Two critical elements must be present for a criminal or penal law to be *ex post facto*: (1) "it must be retrospective, that is, it must apply to events occurring before its enactment," and (2) "it must disadvantage the offender affected by it." The debate here is not whether the sexually Violent Predator Statute is retrospective or disadvantageous in its application to Young. Rather, the debate concerns whether the Statute is penal or criminal in nature. . .

The Court concludes that the Statute cannot be classified as civil, considering the relevant factors. First, there is no dispute that Statute subjects individuals to an affirmative restraint. The Statute entails a complete loss of freedom for an indefinite period of time. . .

Second, the Statute applies to behavior that is already criminal. Indeed, it is expressly limited in its application to persons who have been convicted of a crime or who have been charged with a crime but found incompetent to stand trial or found not guilty by reason of insanity.

Third, the Statute, in its operation, will promote the traditional aims of punishment—retribution and deterrence. . . Washington's Sexually Violent Predator Statute requires that the convicted sex offender serve his sentence prior to commitment; the State has no power to initiate proceedings under the Statute until the sentence of the convicted offender "is about to expire, or has expired" . . .

Thus, despite the State's claims that the Statute is intended only to provide treatment . . . [t]he Statute is inextricably linked to the traditional goals of punishment, because it requires, on its face, that the detainee serve his entire criminal sentence before being committed or treated.

The punishment imperative also undermines the State's purported interest in treating violent sexual predators. The Statute forecloses the possibility that offenders will be evaluated and treated until after they have been punished. Of course, it defies reason to suggest that the mental abnormalities or personality disorders causing violent sexual predation surface only at the termination of a prison term. Common sense suggests that such mental conditions, if they are indeed the cause of sexual violence, are present at the time the offense is committed. Setting aside the question of whether a prison term exacerbates or minimizes the mental condition of a sex offender, it plainly delays the treatment that must constitutionally accompany commitment pursuant to the Statute. The failure of the Statute to provide for examination or treatment prior to the completion of the punishment phase strongly suggests that treatment is of secondary, rather than primary, concern.

The Court concludes that, although there is clearly an alternative purpose to which the Statute may be connected and although indefinite commitment is not necessarily excessive in relation to that purpose, these factors are greatly outweighed by factors favoring the conclusion that the Statute is criminal. As noted above, there is no dispute that, as to Young, the Statute is retrospective and disadvantageous. Accordingly, it stands in violation of the *ex post facto* prohibition of the Constitution.[48]

Finally, the court ruled that the SVP statute also violated the Constitution's double jeopardy clause:

"The Double Jeopardy Clause protects against three distinct abuses: a second prosecution for the same offense after acquittal; a second prosecution for the same offense after conviction; and multiple punishments for the same offense." The third of these abuses, multiple punishments, is at issue in this case. . .

As explained above, in the Court's analysis of the *Ex Post Facto* Clause, the Statute at issue here serves the traditional aims of punishment—retribution and deterrence. The analysis applies equally for purposes of the Double Jeopardy Clause. Having once been punished for the commission of a violent sexual offense, the offender is subject to further incarceration under the Statute's commitment scheme. The punishment imperative embodied in the statutory approach, in addition to the secondary nature of the treatment provisions, renders the Statute an unconstitutional second punishment.[49]

The Washington district court's decision proved to be short-lived. In 1997, an SVP law modeled on the Washington statute was considered by the U.S. Supreme Court in *Kansas v. Hendricks*.[50] The respondent in that case was Leroy Hendricks, whose crimes and involvement with the SVP civil commitment process were described at the beginning of this chapter.

Hendricks challenged his commitment under the Kansas SVP law, which was almost identical to the Washington statute. The Kansas Supreme Court held that the SVP law violated Hendricks' right to substantive due process and was thus unconstitutional. Relying upon reasoning similar to that of the Washington federal district court in *Young*, and quoting that court's decision at length, the Kansas high court held that:

> It is clear that the overriding concern of the legislature is to continue the segregation of sexually violent offenders from the public. Treatment with the goal of reintegrating them into society is incidental, at best. The record reflects that treatment for sexually violent predators is all but nonexistent. The legislature concedes that sexually violent predators are not amenable to treatment [under the state's civil commitment statute for the mentally ill]. If there is nothing to treat under [that law], then there is no mental illness. In that light, the provisions of the Act for treatment appear somewhat disingenuous. . .
>
> It is clear that the primary objective of the Act is to continue incarceration and not to provide treatment. Protecting the public is a legitimate exercise of the State's police power. Although the Act is a well-intentioned attempt by the legislature to accomplish that objective, it cannot be done in a constitutionally impermissible manner. Having said that, we need to point out that the legislature has provided the State with other options to achieve that objective and, in addition, has the authority to increase the penalty for sex crimes committed against children.

The record indicates that Hendricks had at least three felony convictions prior to being charged in the present case. Under the Habitual Criminal Act, Hendricks' sentence could have been tripled. Also, Hendricks could have been sentenced to the maximum rather than the minimum sentence. Additionally, the sentences could have been ordered to run consecutively rather than concurrently. The State chose not to pursue any of these options. Instead, the State opted to enter into a plea bargain with Hendricks. The State agreed to dismiss one count, to recommend the statutory minimum sentence of 5 to 20 years, and to not seek imposition of the Habitual Criminal Act.

The State now chooses to pursue the option under the Act to continue Hendricks' incarceration. The State contends that commitment under the Act requires "a finding of mental illness and dangerousness . . ."

We find no support in the Act that a finding of mental illness is required. As noted by the federal district court in *Young,* there is an absence of a mental illness requirement in the language of the Washington act. [The Kansas law at issue here] states that sexually violent predators do not have a mental illness which "renders them appropriate for involuntary treatment pursuant to the treatment act for mentally ill persons . . ." The statute then contrasts sexually violent predators with persons appropriate for civil commitment [of the mentally ill] in that they have "antisocial personality features which are unamenable to existing mental illness treatment modalities." By such language, the legislature recognizes that sexually violent predators are not mentally ill but, rather, have an "antisocial personality feature" or a "mental abnormality."

Hendricks takes the position that . . . the record in this case will not support a finding that the statutory requirement of a mental abnormality or a personality disorder is equivalent to the constitutional standard of mental illness. We agree. . .

In addition, the State's own evidence is that Hendricks was being committed even though he does not suffer from mental illness. Hendricks is not mentally ill, and the criminal offenses for which he was imprisoned were not the result of mental illness. Therefore, as applied to Hendricks, the constitutionality of the Act depends upon a showing of dangerousness without a finding of mental illness. Clearly, the due process standard [required by U.S. Supreme Court precedents] is not met by the Act as applied to Hendricks.

We conclude that the Act violates Hendricks' substantive due process rights. . .

Having so held, we need not consider the other issues raised by Hendricks [violations of the Ex Post Facto Clause and the Double Jeopardy Clause] in this appeal. . . [51]

Despite the cogent reasoning of these courts in *Young* and *Hendricks*, the U.S. Supreme Court soon overruled the Kansas Supreme Court's decision and rendered moot the Washington federal district court's ruling. The State of Kansas appealed the decision of its Supreme Court, and in a 5–4 decision the U.S. Supreme Court held that the Kansas SVP statute did not violate the Constitution's guarantee of substantive due process. As Justice Clarence Thomas wrote:

Kansas argues that the Act's definition of "mental abnormality" satisfies "substantive" due process requirements. We agree. Although freedom from physical restraint "has always been at the core of the liberty protected by the Due Process Clause from arbitrary governmental action," that liberty interest is not absolute. The Court has recognized that an individual's constitutionally protected interest in avoiding physical restraint may be overridden even in the civil context . . .

. . . States have in certain narrow circumstances provided for the forcible civil detainment of people who are unable to control their behavior and who thereby pose a danger to the public health and safety. We have consistently upheld such involuntary commitment statutes provided the confinement takes place pursuant to proper procedures and evidentiary standards. It thus cannot be said that the involuntary civil confinement of a limited subclass of dangerous persons is contrary to our understanding of ordered liberty.

The challenged Act unambiguously requires a finding of dangerousness either to one's self or to others as a prerequisite to involuntary confinement. Commitment proceedings can be initiated only when a person "has been convicted of or charged with a sexually violent offense," and "suffers from a mental abnormality or personality disorder which makes the person likely to engage in the predatory acts of sexual violence." The statute thus requires proof of more than a mere predisposition to violence; rather, it requires evidence of past sexually violent behavior and a present mental condition that creates a likelihood of such conduct in the future if the person is not incapacitated. As we have recognized, "previous instances of violent behavior are an important indicator of future violent tendencies." A finding of dangerousness, standing alone, is ordinarily not a sufficient ground upon which to justify indefinite involuntary commitment. We have sustained civil commitment statutes when they have coupled proof of dangerousness with the proof of some additional factor, such as a "mental illness" or "mental abnormality." These added statutory requirements serve to limit involuntary civil confinement to those who suffer from a volitional impairment rendering them dangerous beyond their control. The Kansas Act is plainly of a kind with these other civil commitment statutes: It requires a finding of future dangerousness, and then links that finding to the existence of a "mental abnormality" or "personality disorder" that makes it difficult, if not impossible, for the person to control his dangerous behavior. The precommitment requirement of a "mental abnormality" or "personality disorder" is consistent with the requirements of these other statutes that we have upheld in that it narrows the class of persons eligible for confinement to those who are unable to control their dangerousness.

Hendricks nonetheless argues that our earlier cases dictate a finding of "mental illness" as a prerequisite for civil commitment . . . He then asserts that a "mental abnormality" is not equivalent to a "mental illness" because it is a term coined by the Kansas Legislature, rather than by the psychiatric community. Contrary to Hendricks' assertion, the term "mental illness" is devoid of any talismanic significance. Not only do "psychiatrists disagree widely and frequently on what constitutes mental illness," but the Court itself has used a variety of expressions to describe the mental condition of those properly subject to civil confinement. . . e.g., . . . "emotionally disturbed"[,] "mentally ill"[,] "incompetency" and "insanity". . .

Indeed, we have never required State legislatures to adopt any particular nomenclature in drafting civil commitment statutes. Rather, we have traditionally left to legislators the task of defining terms of a medical nature that have legal significance. As a consequence, the States have, over the years, developed numerous specialized terms to define mental health concepts. Often, those definitions do not fit precisely with the definitions employed by the medical community. . . Legal definitions, however, which must "take into account such issues as individual responsibility . . . and competency," need not mirror those advanced by the medical profession.

To the extent that the civil commitment statutes we have considered set forth criteria relating to an individual's inability to control his dangerousness, the Kansas Act sets forth comparable criteria and Hendricks' condition doubtless satisfies those criteria. The mental health professionals who evaluated Hendricks diagnosed him as suffering from pedophilia, a condition the psychiatric profession itself classifies as a serious mental disorder. Hendricks even conceded that, when he becomes "stressed out," he cannot "control the urge" to molest children. This admitted lack of volitional control, coupled with a prediction of future dangerousness, adequately distinguishes Hendricks from other dangerous persons who are perhaps more properly dealt with exclusively through criminal proceedings. Hendricks' diagnosis as a pedophile, which qualifies as a "mental abnormality" under the Act, thus plainly suffices for due process purposes.[52]

Justice Thomas then went on to dismiss Hendricks' claim that the Kansas SVP law violated the Constitution's double jeopardy clause and its ban on ex post facto lawmaking, primarily based on his conclusion that confining sex offenders against their will in prison-like settings after they have completed their legally prescribed prison sentences is not "punishment." Thomas reasoned that since ordinary civil commitment of the dangerously mentally ill is not punitive, neither is civil commitment of sex offenders who, while not necessarily mentally ill, are predicted to pose a future danger to the public. As Thomas wrote:

> Because none of the parties argues that people institutionalized under the Kansas general civil commitment statute are subject to punitive conditions, even though they may be involuntarily confined, it is difficult to conclude that persons confined under this Act are being "punished."[53]

Five years after its decision in *Hendricks*, the U.S. Supreme Court clarified the constitutional standard for SVP civil commitment. In *Hendricks* the court rejected any technical definition of "mental illness," instead focusing on whether a mental impairment, whatever it might be called, rendered an individual "unable to control [his] behavior and thereby pose a danger to the public health and safety…"[54] In *Kansas v. Crane*, which arose out of controversy over the same SVP statute at issue in *Hendricks*, the Supreme Court held that states do not have unfettered discretion in defining the terms "mental abnormality" or "mental disorder" as they are used in SVP commitment statutes.[55] In *Crane*, the court held that such a "disorder" or "abnormality" was constitutionally adequate for SVP commitment purposes if it were capable of "distinguishing a dangerous sexual offender subject to civil commitment from other dangerous persons who are perhaps more properly dealt with exclusively through criminal proceedings."[56] Writing for himself and six other justices, Justice Breyer noted at least two indicia that a statutory definition of mental "disorder" or "abnormality" meets this requirement: (1) whether the disorder or abnormality was one the "psychiatric profession itself classified... as a serious mental disorder"[57] and (2) whether "the severity of the mental abnormality itself [was] sufficient to distinguish the dangerous sexual offender whose serious mental illness, abnormality, or disorder subjects him to civil commitment from the dangerous but typical recidivist convicted in an ordinary criminal case."[58]

Today's Sexually Violent Predator Laws

The U.S. Supreme Court's decision in *Hendricks* has been widely criticized by mental health and legal professionals but, as the conclusion of the nation's highest court, it has also been regarded as giving the constitutional green light to then-current and later adopted SVP commitment laws.

As of 2010, 19 states, the District of Columbia, and the federal government had enacted some form of SVP civil commitment statutes. These statutes vary from state to state, but nearly all of them (including the federal law) follow in large measure the model first adopted in the state of Washington. Sex offenders who are about to be released from prison, having served their entire terms of incarceration or having otherwise reached their maximum release dates, are screened by state employees who review their files and decide whether or not they should be considered for SVP status. Those found to merit further scrutiny are referred for follow-up, which often includes an in-person psychological or psychiatric evaluation. The results of that evaluation are used to determine whether the offender is to be petitioned—that is, ordered into court to face the charge that he is a sexually violent predator.

This petition, when it is proffered by the state, triggers a complex series of legal events, including but not limited to appointment of counsel, a probable cause hearing, examination by a court-appointed psychologist or psychiatrist, and ultimately a trial, usually by jury, to determine whether the offender is, in fact, a sexually violent predator.

Offenders found not to be sexually violent predators are generally released from custody altogether or on some form of parole. Depending on the state, those who are determined to be sexually violent predators will be indefinitely committed to a secure prison-like sex offender treatment center or conditionally released to the community under strict and intensive supervision that generally amounts to a form of super-parole. In only one state, Texas, is the latter disposition mandatory.[59]

All states with SVP statutes offer some form of treatment to those adjudicated as sexually violent predators. The form such treatment takes varies and is discussed in greater detail below. In all states, periodic judicial review of the offender's status as a sexually violent predator is required, and those found no longer to be SVPs must be released. It is generally expected, however, that to reach that point an offender must have successfully completed all stages of his prescribed treatment plan, a regimen that generally takes many years.

In most states, the vast majority of offenders appear to be held more or less permanently. Consider for example, Table 1.1, adapted from a report issued in 2007 (based upon 2006 data) by the Washington State Institute for Public Policy. This table specifies the year each SVP law took effect, the number of individuals who have been committed under the statute, the number and percent who have been released, and the number of those released who have had their releases revoked and been returned to civil confinement.

As this table indicates, between 1990 and 2006, 4,465 individuals were subjected to inpatient civil commitment as sexually violent predators, but only 494 (11 percent) were released or discharged. Moreover, of the 11 percent who were released or discharged, 89 (18 percent) had their releases or discharges revoked. Taking these revocations into account, these data indicate that only slightly more than 9 percent of those civilly committed as sexually violent predators were released and not returned to commitment status. Moreover, nationwide, about half of those who are released from confinement under SVP laws are "let go on legal or technical grounds unrelated to treatment."[61]

The rather low percentage of committed offenders who are released from SVP civil commitment appears to be largely the result of three factors: (1) the popular image, shaped by the application of certain psychiatric diagnoses, that such offenders are permanently mentally abnormal; (2) the popular but erroneous view, reinforced by the application of static, statistically generated predictions of risk, that these offenders are and always will be at a high risk of re-offending; and (3) unresolved questions about the efficacy of current treatment modalities for sex offenders and the practical concern that many committed SVPs are not receiving any treatment.

TABLE 1.1.   State Sexually Violent Predator Statutes and Those Committed
Under Them

State	Year Law Took Effect	Number Held Since Law Took Effect	Number (Percent) Discharged or Released from Commitment	Number Revoked After Release
Arizona	1996	414	87 (20.77%)	13
California	1996	558	96 (17.20%)	2
Florida	1999	942	28 (2.97%)	9
Illinois	1988	307	40 (13.03%)	6
Iowa	1998	69	15 (21.74%)	1
Kansas	1994	161	16 (9.94%)	0
Massachusetts	1998	121	5 (4.13%)	Not available
Minnesota	1999	342	43 (12.57%)	27
Missouri	1994	143	10 (6.99%)	0
Nebraska	2006	18	18 (100%)	0
New Jersey	1994	342	30 (8.77%)	2
North Dakota	1997	75	20 (26.67%)	0
Pennsylvania	2003	12	Not available	Not available
South Carolina	1998	119	32 (26.89%)	0
Virginia	2003	37	5 (13.51%)	2
Washington	1990	305	19 (6.23%)	4
Wisconsin	1994	500	30 (0.60%)	23
Total		4465	494 (11.06%)	89

Source of Data: Washington State Institute for Public Policy[60]

Diagnosing Mental Abnormality

Although no statute or court decision demands it, a finding that a sex offender
qualifies for SVP civil commitment requires, as a practical matter, a formal
diagnosis by a qualified mental health professional. Moreover, that diagnosis
must generally be one recognized in the field of mental health. Those diagnoses so recognized are specified in the APA's treatise, the *Diagnostic and
Statistical Manual of Mental Disorders, Fourth Edition*, generally referred to
in the mental health professions as the DSM-IV.[62] Currently undergoing
revision and soon to be released as the DSM-V, the DSM-IV has, de facto,
become part of every one of America's SVP laws.

Conscientious reliance upon the DSM-IV for this purpose, however, has
created numerous problems for experts and the courts. As Janus and Prentky
have neatly and succinctly observed:

> [T]he courts seem to assume that, though the mental disorder
> criterion is a legal creation, it must be grounded on a mental

disorder that has some medical legitimacy. The clearest and most obvious source for "medical legitimacy," the DSM, was never intended as a system for classifying criminal behavior, and consequently does not provide meaningful diagnoses for most of the individuals who are candidates for SVP commitments.[63]

Necessity, of course, is the mother of invention, so the lack of meaningful DSM diagnoses for most candidates for SVP commitment has caused many mental health experts to make creative use of the DSM, in some instances relying upon diagnoses that may or may not be accurate but are so common among sex offenders as to have little value separating ordinary offenders from those who cannot control their sexual impulses; stretching diagnoses to fit facts that otherwise would not support them; and simply making up diagnoses that are not in the DSM.

Antisocial Personality Disorder

Antisocial personality disorder is defined in the DSM-IV largely on the basis of criminal or antisocial behavior:

A. There is a pervasive pattern of disregard for and violation of the rights of others occurring since age 15 years, as indicated by three (or more) of the following:
    (1) failure to conform to social norms with respect to lawful behaviors as indicated by repeatedly performing acts that are grounds for arrest
    (2) deceitfulness, as indicated by repeated lying, use of aliases, or conning others for personal profit or pleasure
    (3) impulsivity or failure to plan ahead
    (4) irritability and aggressiveness, as indicated by repeated physical fights or assaults
    (5) reckless disregard for safety of self or others
    (6) consistent irresponsibility, as indicated by repeated failure to sustain consistent work behavior or honor financial obligations
    (7) lack of remorse, as indicated by being indifferent to or rationalizing having hurt, mistreated, or stolen from another
B. The individual is at least age 18 years.
C. There is evidence of Conduct Disorder with onset before age 15 years.
D. The occurrence of antisocial behavior is not exclusively during the course of Schizophrenia or a Manic Episode.[64]

Antisocial personality disorder is the most common diagnosis applied to sex offenders considered for SVP commitment.[65] That is not surprising given that, in all likelihood, most prison inmates would qualify for this diagnosis. In *Kansas v. Crane*, the U.S. Supreme Court noted that "40%–60% of the male prison population is diagnosable with Antisocial Personality Disorder."[66] Other authorities have estimated that 50 to 70 percent, even as many as 80 percent, of male prison inmates in the United States meet the DSM criteria for this disorder.[67]

There is great debate among mental health professionals in general over whether antisocial personality disorder is, in fact a mental disorder, or merely a description of behaviors associated with persistent criminality. There is, however, widespread agreement if not consensus that whatever antisocial personality disorder is, it is not likely to respond to any currently available treatment.

Among mental health experts who specialize in the evaluation and treatment of sex offenders, this debate has been sharpened to the question of whether this diagnosis is sufficient, by itself, to support a clinical conclusion that an individual is a sexually violent predator. Although all acknowledge that some courts appear to have answered this question in the affirmative, others note that:

> As most professionals know, research is mixed regarding the relationship between antisocial personality disorder and/or psychopathy and sexual recidivism. While ASPD is a very good predictor of future general and violent recidivism, it has not proved to be a consistent predictor of future sexual re-offending. The consensus is, however, that the behavior of the "more general personality disordered offender" would not be as predictable in the specific area of future sexual behavior. It is as a result of this non-specific criminal risk that the Supreme Court has suggested that antisocial personality disorder alone is an inadequate ground for civil commitment. The reason this is so is that, as noted in the *Kansas v. Crane* decision, it does not properly distinguish the subject "from other dangerous persons who are more properly dealt with through criminal proceedings."[68]

The rare commentator who argues that antisocial personality disorder alone is sufficient to support a finding that a person is a sexually violent predator seems to rely upon an argument that is more legal than clinical. The argument seems to be that legally, in some states, any mental abnormality or personality disorder, particularly any one found in the DSM-IV, may support SVP civil commitment; that antisocial personality disorder is a personality disorder and it is found in the DSM-IV; and, thus, that a diagnosis of antisocial personality disorder is by itself sufficient.

Those who oppose such a reductionist and legalistic viewpoint note, for example, that caffeine dependence is a condition listed in the DSM-IV, but that does not mean that this disorder has any relevance to future sex offending.[69] Those who assert that "antisocial personality disorder is not enough" also observe that:

> [T]here is nothing in the diagnosis [of antisocial personality disorder] related to, correlated with, or predictive of any sexual behavior. . . A repetitive pattern of violating social norms and laws does not inform the evaluator in any way about sexual orientation or deviant sexual interest. . .
>
> Also notably absent in the above referenced criteria is [sic] any diagnostic implications regarding the ability to control sexual behavior. The diagnostic criteria for an antisocial personality disorder presumes [sic] the person has volitional control, and that the criminal conduct on which the diagnosis is based generally can be explained by the person's conscious decisions, albeit bad ones. Indeed, a person with this diagnosis still can have volitional control and the capability to make conscious decisions even while the person has the tendency to be impulsive. A person with an antisocial personality disorder diagnosis, therefore, has chosen to break the law or disregard the rights of others, and simply has little or no concern for the consequences.[70]

Even the Association for the Treatment of Sexual Abusers, a national organization of individuals who assess and treat sex offenders, which had an obvious tangible stake in the outcome of *Kansas v. Hendricks*, informed the Supreme Court in its amicus brief in support of the Kansas SVP law: "The presence of an antisocial personality disorder in and of itself is not sufficient to meet the criteria for sexual predator laws."[71]

Pedophilia

One diagnosis that is clearly recognized by the DSM-IV and clearly relevant to the question of whether a sex offender is likely to re-offend is pedophilia. The DSM-IV describes the diagnostic criteria for pedophilia as follows:

A. Over a period of at least 6 months, recurrent, intense sexually arousing fantasies, sexual urges, or behaviors involving sexual activity with a prepubescent child or children (generally age 13 years or younger).

B. The person has acted on these urges, or the sexual urges or fantasies cause marked distress or interpersonal difficulty.

C. The person is at least age 16 years and at least 5 years older than the child or children in Criterion A.

Note: Do not include an individual in late adolescence involved in an ongoing sexual relationship with a 12- or 13-year-old.[72]

Unfortunately, this diagnosis, which clearly applies only to sexual attraction to prepubescent children, has been applied "indiscriminately to individuals who offend against children (anyone under the age of consent) whether or not they meet the rather specific diagnostic criteria."[73]

For example, to some evaluators, the age, sexual maturity, and duration requirements for this diagnosis seem to matter little. Consider *Commonwealth v. Connolly*, a 2009 Massachusetts SVP proceeding in which four psychologists testified.[74] The first found no evidence of pedophilia since the respondent's victim was over 13 and the sexual conduct took place over a 2-month period. A second doctor testified that "in her opinion the respondent did not meet the criteria for Mental Abnormality... based... on the fact that the only offense occurred in the context of a relationship with an adolescent who he had known for less than three months, the age of the victim was thirteen; that the victim was pubescent; and he was able to ejaculate. She opined **pedophilia** is defined as sexual attraction to prepubescent children, and that as such the respondent did not meet criteria for that diagnosis."[75] A third psychologist testified that the respondent's "presentation was not consistent with an identifiable mental disorder as recorded in the Diagnostic and Statistical Manual"[76] and added that his "behavior was consistent with a condition described as Hebephilia,"[77] a so-called "diagnosis" related to sexual attraction to older, pubescent teenagers (discussed in greater detail below). The fourth psychologist, although not of the opinion that the respondent was a "sexually dangerous person" as SVPs are referred to in Massachusetts, "concluded that he met the clinical diagnostic criteria for pedophilia..."[78]

Consider also *Commonwealth v. Meals*, a 2006 Pennsylvania SVP case in which a diagnosis of pedophilia appears to have been made with little regard for the DSM diagnostic criteria, accepted by the trial court, rejected by the intermediate appellate court, and then accepted by the state's highest court.[79]

Meals, the respondent, had pleaded guilty to sex offenses against two girls, a 13-year-old he sexually abused in October and November 1999 and a 9-year-old he abused in August 2000. Meals fondled the girls' genitals, digitally penetrated them, and performed oral sex on them. He had no prior reported sexual assaults.

A state-employed counselor with a master's degree, who did not interview Meals, testified based on the offender's records. The counselor told the court that Meals "met the profile for the mental abnormality of pedophilia."[80] The counselor, who "conceded that his diagnosis was based on limited information,"[81] was asked on direct examination why he made this diagnosis and his answer was clearly not one that satisfied the diagnostic criteria of the DSM-IV:

> Q. Mr. Loop, during the course of your evaluation of Mr. Meals, did any of the facts available to you lead you to the belief that this Defendant had any mental illness or mental abnormalities?
>
> A. Based on the behavior that was reported over time, that behavior being the sexual engagement of children, it appeared that he would present in a similar manner as those diagnosed with pedophilia.[82]

While finding as a matter of fact that Meals had no prior history of committing sexual offenses other than the two just described, the trial court accepted this diagnosis and allowed it to serve as the basis for a finding that Meals was a sexually violent predator.

Meals appealed, claiming that the evidence was insufficient to establish that he was a sexually violent predator. The appeals court agreed, holding that:

> [T]he record fails to reflect that the Commonwealth has proven by clear and convincing evidence that Appellant suffers from "a mental abnormality or personality disorder that makes the person likely to engage in predatory sexually violent offenses." Mr. Loop's diagnosis of pedophilia seems based entirely on the age of the victims. As this Court has noted, SVP status does not automatically apply to persons who commit sexual offenses against children. Indeed, were it otherwise, the offender would be subject to a presumption of SVP status. Our Supreme Court has held that such a presumption is unconstitutional. . . The Commonwealth has failed to meet its burden of proof . . .[83]

The Pennsylvania Supreme Court refused to resolve what it called "the dispute between the parties concerning whether reference to the DSM-IV, as a source for the criteria for assessing pedophilia, is appropriate."[84] As that court held, "We need not decide, and hence do not decide, the relevance of the DSM-IV criteria in determining the required proof, or sufficiency of proof, of a diagnosis of pedophilia in determining SVP status."[85]

"Hebephilia"

Many victims of sexual abuse, though young, are pubescent. Indeed, under statutory rape laws in some states, a youngster as old as 17 years, 11 months, and 31 days who willingly engages in sex with an adult is considered a sex crime victim. And certainly, in every state, anyone (child, adolescent, or adult) who is forced to have sexual contact against his or her will is a sex crime victim.

In a rather transparent effort to ensure that all otherwise eligible sex offenders (including those whose preferred sexual targets are pubescent teenagers rather than children) may be subject to a diagnosis for SVP commitment purposes, some mental health professionals have attempted to create the diagnosis of hebephilia. Hebephilia is a word that describes the sexual attraction of an adult to a pubescent (i.e., sexually mature) person who is under the age of consent. Hebephilia is not, however, a recognized diagnosis; indeed, it was specifically rejected as such by the authors of the DSM-IV.[86]

The fact that hebephilia was specifically excluded from the DSM-IV has not stopped some SVP evaluators from claiming that this is a recognized diagnosis. Nor has it stopped some mental health professionals from lobbying the APA to include hebephilia in the forthcoming DSM-V.[87] In fact, some have even gone so far as to attempt to parse out the differences among pedophiles, hebephiles, and ephebophiles. In such a classification, hebephiles are those sexually aroused by or attracted to pubescent children roughly from age 11 or 12 to about 14 or 15 years; those aroused by or attracted to younger, prepubescent children would continue to be known as pedophiles; and those aroused by or attracted to roughly 15- to 19-year-olds would be regarded as ephebophiles.[88]

While some courts have accepted as valid the purported diagnosis of hebephilia, others have not. Whatever legal or clinical fate awaits this proposed diagnostic category, it is not difficult to see why it is controversial at best and why its senior counterpart, ephebophilia, has virtually no chance of gaining either widespread legal or clinical recognition. Consider, for example, a recent federal district court decision dealing with the validity of hebephilia as a diagnosis in SVP civil commitment cases.

In *United States v. Shields*, in 2009, a federal district court was presented with a psychologist who wished to testify for the government that the respondent had "a mental disorder called hebephilia." The court held that:

> The government has not provided persuasive expert evidence that
> there is a mental illness, abnormality, or disorder named hebephilia.
> The peer-reviewed literature provided by the government defines
> hebephilia as "a sexual attraction to pubescent children." While
> this literature may establish that hebephelia is generally accepted
> in the field as a group identifier or label, it does not establish that

hebephilia is generally accepted as a mental disorder by professionals who assess sexually violent offenders. In fact, both sides agree that the attraction of an adult male to a pubescent adolescent is not, without more, indicative of a mental disorder. The government relies on Dr. Dennis Doren, who states that "a significant portion of adult men show sexual arousal to adolescents." In Dr. Doren's view, a person only shows the characteristics of "hebephilia" when he repeatedly seeks sexual contact with adolescents "despite the ongoing risk of legal consequences and inability to maintain such relationships on a long-term basis due to the adolescents' growing beyond the age range of interest." When Dr. Tomich made his diagnosis of "hebephelia," he defined the term as "a diagnostic term that is indicative of a deviant pattern of sexual arousal to adolescent individuals under the age of consent." However, the government does not point to any peer-reviewed literature recognizing either Dr. Doren's or Dr. Tomich's diagnostic definition of a mental disorder called hebephilia. Significantly, the American Psychiatric Association considered and rejected hebephilia as a diagnostic category for a mental disorder. Moreover, there is no expert testimony in this record that psychiatric experts generally accept this definition of hebephilia as a mental disorder.[89]

In *Shields*, the government also argued that even if hebephilia is not a legitimate diagnosis, it should nevertheless be allowed as part of the diagnosis "paraphilia not otherwise specified," which is included in the DSM-IV.[90] As is discussed in greater detail below, the court also rejected this "back door" effort to get the psychologist's "diagnosis" of hebephilia into evidence.

Paraphilia Not Otherwise Specified (NOS)

According to the DSM-IV, "[t]he essential features of a Paraphilia are recurrent, intense sexually arousing fantasies, sexual urges, or behaviors generally involving (1) nonhuman objects, (2) suffering or humiliation of oneself or one's partner, or (3) children or other nonconsenting persons that occur over a period of at least 6 months."[91] DSM-IV lists eight specific paraphilias: exhibitionism (deviant arousal to "public exposure of one's genitals to an unsuspecting stranger"), fetishism (deviant arousal involving the use of nonliving objects), frotteurism (deviant arousal "involving touching and rubbing against a non-consenting person"), pedophilia (deviant arousal "involving sexual activity with a prepubescent child or children"), masochism (deviant arousal "involving the act [real not simulated] of being humiliated, beaten, bound, or otherwise made to suffer"), sadism (deviant arousal "involving acts [real, not simulated] in which the psychological or physical suffering [including humiliation] of the victim is sexually exciting"), transvestic fetishism (deviant arousal involving "cross-dressing"), and voyeurism (deviant arousal to "observing an unsuspecting person who is naked, in the process of disrobing, or engaging in sexual activity").[92]

DSM-IV also includes a diagnostic category called "paraphilia not otherwise specified (NOS)." According to the diagnostic manual, "This category is included for coding Paraphilias that do not meet the criteria for any of the specific categories. Examples include, but are not limited to, telephone scatologia (obscene phone calls), necrophilia (corpses), partialism (exclusive focus on part of body), zoophilia (animals), coprophilia (feces), klismaphilia (enemas), and urophilia (urine)."[93]

As noted above, some sex offenders who are the subject of SVP civil commitment proceedings are diagnosed with the paraphilia known as pedophilia. Exhibitionism, frotteurism, sadism, and voyeurism are also paraphilias that have been used to satisfy or partially satisfy the mental abnormality requirement for SVP civil commitment.

From the perspective of the government, a major problem in many cases is that the individual recommended for SVP civil confinement does not have a mental disorder or personality disorder, including one or more of the paraphilias recognized in DSM-IV or by most mental health professionals. For example, many rapists, while violent criminals and perhaps perverted in the lay sense of that term, are not mentally ill, personality disordered, or even sexual sadists, as that term is defined by the DSM-IV.

In many instances this "problem" has been addressed through the attempted use of the residual diagnosis of paraphilia NOS. For example, In *U.S. v. Shields*, the 2009 federal case just mentioned, although the court rejected the government's claim that hebephilia was a mental disorder, "[t]he government argue[d] that, in some circumstances, hebephilia falls within a category within the DSM-IV: Paraphilia Not Otherwise Specified (Paraphilia-NOS)."[94] The court was unconvinced:

> As a threshold matter, [the government's expert witness] does not specifically diagnose Mr. Shields with Paraphilia NOS; his diagnosis is limited to pedophilia and hebephilia. While the government's position may be true in some circumstances, this Court has an inadequate record for determining how the psychiatric community determines what may properly be included within the Paraphilia NOS category. The government never submitted Dr. Doren's book,

which is apparently not peer-reviewed. This book is the lone source cited by the government for the proposition that some kinds of hebephilia fall within Paraphilia NOS. It does not suffice.[95]

Experts testifying for the government in SVP civil commitment cases have also tried to expand the concept of paraphilia NOS to include forcible rape as evidence of mental illness. For example, in *United States v. Graham*, a federal SVP commitment proceeding, three mental health experts testified. The first, a psychiatrist appointed by the court to examine the respondent, "diagnosed Respondent with Antisocial Personality Disorder ('ASPD'), though he explained that, in his opinion, ASPD is not a serious mental illness, abnormality or disorder [and] also testified that he did not believe Respondent met the criteria for any paraphilia diagnosis."[96] A psychologist retained by the defense, who also examined the respondent, "concluded that Respondent did not meet the criteria for a paraphilia diagnosis [but] acknowledged that 'by his record' the Respondent 'could' meet the criteria for an ASPD diagnosis..."[97] A second psychologist retained by the government, who had never examined or interviewed the respondent, "diagnosed Respondent as suffering from Paraphilia Not Otherwise Specified Nonconsent ('Paraphilia NOS: Nonconsent'), a disorder [she] also referred to as 'paraphilic Rapism.'"[98] This doctor also concluded that the respondent did not meet the criteria for a diagnosis of sexual sadism. Finally, she "concluded that Respondent suffers from ASPD" but opined "that, standing alone, an ASPD diagnosis was not sufficient to justify indefinite commitment in this case."[99]

DSM-IV does not contain a specific diagnosis for sexual arousal to non-consensual sex. Indeed, such a diagnosis has been rejected for inclusion in the DSM. In the 1980s, some mental health professionals lobbied unsuccessfully to add the diagnosis of paraphilic coercive disorder to the DSM.[100] Nevertheless, in *Graham*, "the Government maintain[ed] that it is appropriate to consider such behavior as a Paraphilia Not Otherwise Specified ('NOS')."[101]

In *Graham*, the court held that the government failed to prove by clear and convincing evidence that the respondent suffered from any paraphilia, including paraphilia NOS. The court indicated that "[t]his finding is not based on a ruling as to the legitimacy of a Paraphilia NOS: Nonconsent diagnosis, though the court heard significant testimony at trial on the vigorous debate in the medical community over the soundness of such a diagnosis."[102]

As the court further explained: "[T]his court has the task of attempting to determine, from the totality of expert testimony and the other record evidence, whether Respondent satisfies the 'essential features' of a Paraphilia NOS diagnosis." The court acknowledged that "[r]ead broadly... all repeat rapists would seemingly satisfy this feature of a paraphilia, as they exhibit 'behaviors involving... nonconsenting persons.'"[103] The court, however, declined to adopt this "expansive interpretation," noting that to do so would essentially characterize all repeat rapists as mentally disordered, a position that even the government's psychological expert was unwilling to take.[104] As the court further noted, that witness "stat[ed] that she did not agree that if an individual 'has multiple rapes he must be paraphiliac' because there are 'typologies of sex offenders going back 30 years' demonstrating that 'some rapists are motivated by anger' and '[s]ome rapists are antisocial only and simply want sex.'"[105]

The court did, however, bluntly reject this expert's opinion, affirmatively holding that she was "not a credible witness."[106] As the court explained: "It is difficult for the court to determine the ultimate significance, if any, of each mistake or ignored fact on [her] final diagnosis. Viewed in total, however, the court discerned a definite bias in her overall analysis towards a finding that Respondent suffers from Paraphilia NOS: Nonconsent, and that his condition is serious. This troubling bias detracted from her credibility as a witness for the Government."[107]

Predicting Recidivism

SVP laws require proof not only that a sex offender has a mental abnormality but also that he is likely to sexually re-offend if not civilly committed. In other words, these laws require courts to predict recidivism. Even offenders who are mentally abnormal are not to be committed unless they are also likely to engage in future sex offenses.

As was noted in the introductory chapter to this volume, contrary to common public opinion (as well as the beliefs of many legislators and public officials), the known recidivism rate for sexual offenders is remarkably low. In 2003, the U.S. Department of Justice released a 3-year follow-up study of the recidivism of all 272,111 prisoners released from prison in 15 states (Arizona, Maryland, North Carolina, California, Michigan, Ohio, Delaware, Minnesota, Oregon, Florida, New Jersey, Texas, Illinois, New York, and Virginia). These offenders—3,115 of whom had been convicted of rape, 6,576 of sexual assault, 4,295 of child molestation, and 443 of statutory rape—were all released in 1994.[108]

The Justice Department reported that during the 3 years after their release, only 1.3 percent of released non-sex offenders (3,328 of 262,420) were arrested for a sex offense. Although sex offenders released that same year were four times more likely than released non-sex offenders to be rearrested for a sex crime in the same 3-year period, their rate of re-arrest for a sex offense was just 5.3 percent (517 of 9,691). During that 3-year period, 5.0 percent of convicted rapists (155 of 3,115), 3.3 percent of child molesters (141 of 4,295), 5.5 percent of sexual assaulters (362 of 6,576), and 2.5 percent of statutory rapists (11 of 443) were arrested for new sex offenses.

Data from other states appear to support the Justice Department's figures on sex offender recidivism. For example, among 232 male sex offenders released by the Alaska Department of Corrections in 2001, just 3.4 percent were arrested for a sex offense in the next 3 years.[109] And an Illinois study found that within 1, 3, and 5 years after their release from custody, less than 4 percent of convicted child molesters, and only about 7 percent of convicted rapists, were re-arrested for a sex offense.[110]

Two more recent studies of the recidivism of released sex offenders relied upon convictions rather than arrests but extended the follow-up period to 5 years and 10 years, respectively. The studies, conducted in parallel, by the California Sex Offender Management Board and reported in 2008, found that among a cohort of 4,204 paroled sex offenders, 3.21 percent were convicted of a new sex offense within 5 years of release, and that 3.38 percent of a cohort of 3,577 released sex offenders were convicted of a new sex offense within 10 years of release.[111]

Interestingly, data from countries other than the United States appear to show a much higher rate of sex offender recidivism. In a 1998 meta-analysis (including 61 studies from six different countries—United States, Canada, United Kingdom, Australia, Denmark, and Norway—with information on 28,972 sexual offenders), Canadian researchers reported that "On average, the sex offense recidivism rate was 13.4% (18.9% for 1,839 rapists and 12.7% for 9,603 child molesters). The average follow-up period was 4 to 5 years."[112] The higher rates of sexual recidivism found in this meta-analysis may be due, in large degree, to the varying ways in which the analyzed studies measured that variable. As the authors note, "The most common measures of recidivism were reconviction (84%), followed by arrests (54%), self reports (25%) and parole violations (16%). Forty-four percent of the studies (27 of 61) used multiple indices of recidivism."[113] Indeed, as these authors observed, "These averages should be considered cautiously... since they were based on diverse studies..."[114]

A 2004 Canadian study limited to released sex offenders in that country and the American states of California and Washington also reported sexual recidivism rates much greater than those reported generally in the United States. This study examined a diverse sample of 4,724 sex offenders who had been released from federal, state, or provincial prisons or from a Canadian maximum security psychiatric facility. In most but not all cases, both charges and convictions for sexual offences were used as recidivism criteria.[115]

Using a statistical technique known as "survival analysis," the authors estimated recidivism rates for 5, 10, and 15 years after release. Use of this technique meant that offenders who died or were re-incarcerated were removed from the data pool, so that only those who were at risk of re-offending were considered at any given time period. The authors summarized their findings as follows: "The overall recidivism rates (14% after 5 years, 20% after 10 years and 24% after 15 years) were similar for rapists (14%, 21% and 24%) and the combined group of child molesters (13%, 18%, and 23%)."[116]

While these estimates greatly exceed the sexual recidivism rates described above in American studies, it is interesting to note how they were interpreted by the Canadian researchers:

> Most sexual offenders do not re-offend sexually over time. This may be the most important finding of this study as this finding is contrary to some strongly held beliefs. After 15 years, 73% of sexual offenders had not been charged with, or convicted of, another sexual offence. The sample was sufficiently large that very strong contradictory evidence is necessary to substantially change these recidivism estimates.[117]

Obviously, none of the studies described here are fully accurate in their assessments of sexual recidivism since neither convictions, charges, or even arrests are perfect proxies for crimes committed because many sex crimes are never reported. Still, the best available data suggest that sexual recidivism rates for released sex offenders, especially in the United States, are rather low.

Psychologists and other social scientists have long recognized that predicting any kind of future behavior is fraught with difficulty and uncertainty, but especially so when the behavior one is trying to predict has a low base-rate. Given that an overwhelming majority (looking at the literature, probably somewhere between 73 and 94 percent) of released sex offenders do not appear to commit new sex crimes, trying to predict whether a given offender will do so or not is a profoundly difficult, perhaps impossible, task.

Nevertheless, that is exactly the task that legislators and judges have prescribed for the SVP civil commitment process. In response to this demand, psychologists and others have attempted predictions of recidivism in one or both of two ways: clinical judgment and statistical inference. Unfortunately, as is widely recognized, clinical predictions of future dangerousness, including sexual recidivism, are notoriously subjective and prone to bias and are frequently wrong. Given the unimpressive track record of such clinical predictions, coupled with the high stakes in the SVP civil commitment context, some social scientists have attempted to develop statistical methods to predict the likelihood that a given sexual offender will recidivate sexually.

Although often referred to as actuarials, actuarial risk assessment instruments, or actuarial risk tools, in reality these methods are simple paper checklists of a relatively small number of factors research has found to be associated with sex offender recidivism in large groups of known recidivists. As Janus and Prentky have explained:

> [A]ctuarial scales are developed using statistical analyses of groups of individuals (in the present case, released sex offenders) with known outcomes during a "follow-up" period (either arrested for or convicted of a new sexual offense, or not identified as having committed a new sexual offense). These analyses tell us which items ("predictor variables") do the best job of differentiating between those who reoffended and those who did not reoffend within a specified time period. Since some of these variables inevitably do a better job than others, these analyses also help us to determine how much weight should be assigned to each item. The variables are then combined to form a scale, which is tested on many other groups of offenders (cross-validation). When the scale has been used on many samples with a sufficiently large number of offenders, the scores derived from the scale may be expressed as estimates of the probability that individuals with that score will reoffend within a specified time frame.[118]

Numerous such checklists have been devised and used in the SVP context over the past couple of decades, but by far the most commonly used and most widely studied is the Static-99,[119] which is generally used by SVP evaluators and the courts to assign a recidivism risk level to a particular sex offender (low, moderate-low, moderate-high, or high).[120] According to the authors of the Static-99, "[i]t is the most widely used sex offender risk assessment instrument in the world, and is extensively used in the United States, Canada, the United Kingdom, Australia, and many European nations."[121] Interestingly, however, according to these authors, only 19 people in the entire world (including the two of them) are "certified" by them to train others to use this 10-item checklist.[122]

The authors of the Static-99 used data from four samples of offenders in Canada and the United Kingdom to develop their checklist.[123] Offenders in these samples included 344 sex offenders from a Canadian maximum security psychiatric hospital, followed up for an average of 4 years with a sexual recidivism rate of 15.4 percent; an "extreme"[124] group of 191 child molesters ("most [of whom] had been referred for treatment because of their persistent sexual problems"[125]) released from an Ontario maximum security prison, who were followed up for an average of 23 years with a recidivism rate of 35.1 percent; 142 sex offenders released from another maximum security psychiatric facility, followed up for an average of 10 years with a recidivism rate of 35.1 percent; and 531 sex offenders, released from prison in England and Wales, followed up for an average of 16 years with a recidivism rate of 25 percent.

On the Static-99 checklist, each offender evaluated is scored (according to complex procedures described in a scoring manual) on each of 10 items, including age (18 to 25 vs. 25 or older), having lived with a lover for at least 2 years, current and prior nonsexual violence convictions, prior sex offense charges and convictions, prior criminal sentences, convictions for non-contact sex offenses, unrelated victims, stranger victims, and male victims.[126] Offenders who "score" 0 or 1 on this checklist are deemed to be at low risk for sexual re-offending; those "scoring" 2 or 3 are said to present a moderate-low risk; those "scoring" 4 or 5 are regarded as presenting a moderate to high risk; and those "scoring" 6 or higher are considered to be at high risk.[127]

Based upon the development samples just described, the authors of the Static-99 calculated the following recidivism rates for offenders in each of these categories.[128] After 5, 10, and 15 years, the rate for those with a score of 0 was 5 percent, 11 percent, and 13 percent; for a score of 1, 6 percent, 7 percent, and 7 percent; for a score of 2, 9 percent, 13 percent, and 16 percent; for a score of 3, 12 percent, 14 percent, and 19 percent; for a score of 4, 26 percent, 31 percent, and 36 percent; for a score of 5, 33 percent, 38 percent, and 40 percent; and for a score of 6 and over, 39 percent, 45 percent, and 52 percent.

More recently, in 2009, using a broader array of international data, the authors of the Static-99 and their colleagues published new norms that reflect much lower recidivism rates. These norms cover two time periods, 5 years and 10 years, and divide offenders into "routine" and "high risk," leaving it to those who fill out the checklist to use their clinical judgment to determine in which category a given offender belongs. These more recent norms are summarized in Table 1.2.

The authors of the Static-99 recommend that these newer norms be used by "those reporting absolute recidivism rates" as "we believe these new norms are better than the original because they are based on larger and more current

TABLE 1.2. Recidivism Rates Reportedly Associated with Static-99 "Scores"

Static-99 Score	5-Year Sexual Recidivism Rate for "Routine" Sex Offenders (Percent)	5-Year Sexual Recidivism Rate for "High-Risk" Sex Offenders (Percent)	10-Year Sexual Recidivism Rate for "Routine" Sex Offenders (Percent)	10-Year Sexual Recidivism Rate for "High-Risk" Sex Offenders (Percent)
0	2.3	8.3	1.8	13.0
1	3.2	10.3	2.6	15.8
2	4.3	12.8	3.9	19.1
3	5.7	15.7	5.7	23.0
4	7.7	19.1	8.2	27.3
5	10.2	23.1	11.8	32.1
6	13.4	27.7	16.7	37.3
7	17.4	32.7	23.0	42.8
8	22.3	38.2	30.8	48.5
9	28.2	44.0	39.8	54.3
10+	34.9	50.0	49.7	59.9

Source of Data: Leslie Helmus, R. Karl Hanson, and David Thornton (2009)[129]

samples, are derived from better statistical estimation procedures (logistic regression), and more accurately reflect variation in recidivism base rates."[130] Finally, they note that "this research project is ongoing and the absolute recidivism rates presented here will be updated."[131]

While the newer norms associated with the Static-99 bring the recidivism rates underlying the checklist closer to those found in the United States, they are still a great deal higher. Moreover, with the norms being reported for two separate groups of offenders ("routine" vs. "high risk"), clinicians using the Static-99 now must rely on clinical judgment of the sort this checklist and others like it were originally devised to help avoid.

The Static-99, while still widely used, continues to be the subject of harsh criticism by those from both the legal and psychological professions, and its use in SVP commitment cases, though allowed by many courts, is at best controversial.

Perhaps the most obvious and frequent criticism of the Static-99, coming from mental health professionals and social scientists in general, is that it relies almost solely on static factors, variables that will remain constant regardless of what changes may occur to the individual offender or his environment. Except by living with a lover for 2 years or turning 25 years old, there is nothing an offender ever can do to lower his Static-99 score and thus his purported level of risk as assessed by that checklist.

Consider, for example, the recent case of a 51-year-old man who was incarcerated but about to be released if not civilly committed under his state's SVP law. This man (referred to here as Mr. X to protect his identity) had raped a woman 25 years earlier, had been imprisoned almost continuously since, and had received extensive sexual offender counseling, training, and treatment, both in and out of prison. Mr. X had become so well versed in the tenets of sex offender treatment that he served as a treatment assistant to those providing such treatment in the penal institutions in which he was later incarcerated. As one of the court-appointed psychological experts in the case noted in his report:

> The Petitioner's social worker (who never met or interviewed Mr. X) scored Mr. X on an actuarial instrument known as the Static-99. Relying upon available Static-99 scoring criteria, she viewed Mr. X as presenting a Static-99 score of 6 largely because the Static-99 allows mere allegations to be used against a subject. Thus, the social worker completing the Static-99 in this case relied upon at least five charges for which Mr. X was arrested but never convicted. [W]hile Mr. X was accused of previous sex offenses he was never convicted of any sex offenses other than the instant offense, the rape . . . 25 years ago. Moreover, it should be noted that virtually all of the factors on the Static-99 were already in place in 1983 and no matter what Mr. X ever does from now on, his score on the Static-99 can never be reduced. Thus, unless incarceration and treatment are assumed to be of no rehabilitative value whatsoever, the Static-99 has no reliable predictive value in a case such as this.[132]

As this case also illustrates, the Static-99 does not take into account the offender's age. Mr. X was about 26 years old when he committed the rape that led to his SVP petition 25 years later at the age of 51. Research clearly indicates a decline in criminality, violence, and sexual recidivism as individuals grow older. Yet, the Static-99 uses a cut-off age of 25 years. Thus, an offender such as Mr. X, who is 51 years old, is regarded as in the same class as an offender who is just 25 years old. Should Mr. X live to be 100 years old, his Static-99 score and purported level of risk will remain the same.

Indeed, even if he became physically incapable of committing a sex crime, his Static-99 score and risk (as assessed by that checklist) would remain the same. As was reported by a court-appointed evaluator in another recent SVP case:

> It should also be noted that virtually all of the factors on the Static-99 contributing to [the offender's] score were already in place

when he was last convicted in 1993 and that no matter what [he] ever does from now on, his score on the Static-99 can never be reduced. Indeed, if, for example, [he] were to be fully castrated and become quadriplegic, his Static-99 score and purportedly high risk of recidivism based on that score would remain the same.[133]

Another frequent criticism of the Static-99 and other actuarial checklists is that while they may offer a relative ranking of risks based upon certain offender and offense characteristics in large samples, they can never specify the recidivism risk of any particular offender.

As a New York State trial court judge noted in 2009 in *State v. Rosado*:

As was made clear in the hearing testimony, the STATIC-99 has no predictive value for an individual. The STATIC-99 does not and cannot measure an individual's risk of reoffending. Rather, it ranks an individual with a group sharing certain characteristics. In other words, the STATIC-99 score only indicates that a respondent has characteristics which correlate with a group of individuals whose rate of recidivism is "x" percent. The offender's risk may be higher or lower than the probabilities estimated in the STATIC-99, depending on other risk factors not measured by the STATIC-99.[134]

And as psychologists Amenta, Guy, and Edens recently further explained:

Although this may seem like a trivial point, it nevertheless is the case that stating an individual is X% likely to reoffend is a direct inference from a group that entails certain simplifying assumptions that may not apply to a particular individual. Risk assessment tools may indicate the rate of reoffending (e.g., 50%) observed during a certain follow-up period in the normative or validation samples among individuals who received a score similar to or the same as the individual being evaluated. However, this information does not translate to the conclusion that a given individual with a particular score has that same probability of committing future crime . . .[135]

Actually, this is not a trivial point for at least two reasons. First, many courts have been misled into believing that the Static-99 is a "test," indeed a "psychological test." Second, many courts have been led by experts to believe that the Static-99 is able to predict the likelihood that a specific sex offender will re-offend sexually.

With regard to the erroneous notion that the Static-99 is a "test" or, worse, a "psychological test," consider, for example, the following excerpts from recent court decisions in SVP civil commitment cases in which the Static-99 has been used (emphasis is added):

The Static-99 *test* is widely used in SVPA cases.[136]

***

Benjamin was additionally given the Static-99 *test* to evaluate his rates of recidivism.[137]

***

Dr. Anderson did his own calculation of the Static-99 *test,* concluding that Evans's risk of reoffending was very low, less than 10 percent.[138]

***

Based on his evaluations, a review of McKee's prior history, and the results of a standard risk assessment *test* (i.e., Static-99), Romanoff believed McKee's mental disorders made it difficult for him to control his sexual behavior and he was likely to engage in sexually criminal behavior in the future.[139]

***

Dr. Hupka concurred that Evans would most likely reoffend, based on the Static-99 *test* that he administered. Evans received a high score of 8.[140]

***

After identifying the particular characteristics of the offender, the Static-99 *test* assigns a numeric score to them. The total score of the *test* is a percentage chance of the defendant's likelihood of being convicted for a future sexual offense.[141]

***

Dr. Phenix's application of the Static-99 *test* indicated a 52 percent chance that defendant will reoffend within 15 years. Dr. Paladino scored defendant one point higher on the Static-99 *test.*[142]

***

In evaluating whether it was likely that defendant would engage in sexually violent behavior, both Drs. Vognsen and Starr used the "Static 99" *test.*[143]

***

As additional behavioral factors to be considered, the trial court also considered . . . that the result of a *psychological test* (Static-99) showed him to be at a moderate to high risk to re-offend.[144]

***

Appellant's expert, Dr. Foley, reviewed the same material as Dr. Valliere, but he also used the Static 99 *test* and determined that Appellant would likely not be reconvicted.[145]

***

The "Static 99" test is a *psychological test* that predicts whether a male convicted of a sex offense is likely to reoffend.[146]

***

Four *psychological tests* were used to determine whether G.R.H. would have a likelihood of recidivism. Only one of the four *tests* indicated a recidivism rate that could logically be denoted as "likely" to re-offend. [T]he Static-99 showed a 39% chance of recidivism . . . [147]

The courts' misperception of the Static-99 as a kind of psychological test is perhaps most graphically and unjustly illustrated by the decisions of both the trial and the appeals courts in *State v. Thomas*, an Ohio case.[148] In *Thomas*, the offender's attorney sought a continuance of the trial and court funding for an expert when he received a copy of the report prepared by the state's expert. According to the court, counsel "submitted his motion in early June... In the trial court, defense counsel argued that he could not have filed the motion earlier because he did not receive Dr. Hopes' report until early June... He asserted that he was unaware of the need to hire an expert until after reviewing her work. In support, he noted Dr. Hopes' reliance on the MMPI and Static-99 tests and argued that he required an expert to review her findings about those tests."[149]

The trial court refused a continuance and refused to fund an expert to review the report by the state's expert. Finding no abuse of discretion in these rulings, the appeals court said:

> We discern no reason why defense counsel could not have sought to hire an expert before reviewing Dr. Hopes' report. Thomas underwent an examination by Dr. Hopes on May 8, 2004. On that date, *he obviously knew that he had been subjected to the MMPI and Static-99 tests* and that Dr. Hopes was evaluating him for purposes of the sexual-offender classification hearing. Thus, defense counsel could have sought, at that time, to hire an expert to review *Thomas' performance on the tests* or to conduct an independent examination [emphasis added].[150]

Of course, unlike the Minnesota Multiphasic Personality Inventory (MMPI), which is one of the most widely used psychological tests in the world and is filled out directly by the examinee, the Static-99 is not a test but rather a checklist filled out by the evaluator based on information contained in records. Thus, it would certainly *not* have been obvious to Thomas, or even known to him at all, that he "had been subjected to the... Static-99."[151]

Beyond having been led to believe that the Static-99 is a "test" or "psychological test," numerous courts have also been given the false impression that this "test" is able to specify the likelihood that a particular offender will sexually re-offend. Consider, for example, the following excerpts from recent judicial opinions dealing with expert testimony regarding the Static-99:

> Both Dr. Vognsen and defense expert Dr. Longwell testified that based upon a test called the "Static 99" appellant has a 19 percent chance of being reconvicted of a new sexual offense within 15 years following release.[152]
>
> ***
>
> Dr. Rackley also reviewed the results of two tests that assist mental health professionals in determining whether a sex offender is likely to commit another sex offense in the future: the "Static 99" test and the "Minnesota Sex Offender Screening Test, Revised" ("MNSOST-R") [The actual name of the checklist is the Minnesota Sex Offender Screening Tool, Revised]. These tests help determine the likelihood that a subject may commit a sexual offense in the future based on actuarial, historical and other data. Respondent had a score of 12 on the MNSOST-R test and a score of 7 on the Static-99 test. According to Dr. Rackley, respondent's score on the MNSOST-R test indicated that there was a 57% chance that respondent will commit a sexual offense in the next six years. Respondent's score on the Static 99 test indicates a 43% chance that he will commit a sexual offense in the next five years.[153]
>
> ***
>
> Nancy Schmidtgoessling, Ph.D, who administered the psychological testing to Morales, testified . . . that, according to the Static-99 test results, Morales's chances of recidivism were six percent within five years, seven percent within ten years, and seven percent within fifteen years. She described these percentages as "quite a low risk compared to others."[154]
>
> ***
>
> Korpi also used the STATIC-99 test to assess the risk that Ayala would reoffend. He considered [the] 10 factors [in the Static-99]. Based on these factors, Korpi determined that there was a 39 percent

likelihood that Ayala would reoffend within five years, a 45 percent likelihood that he would reoffend within 10 years, and a 52 percent chance that he would reoffend within 15 years.[155]

***

Dr. Paladino found that defendant's score on the STATIC-99 was 6, meaning that he had a 39 percent probability of reoffending within five years, a 45 percent probability of reoffending within 10 years, and a 52 percent probability of reoffending within 15 years.[156]

***

Dr. Phenix's application of the Static-99 test indicated a 52 percent chance that defendant will reoffend within 15 years.[157]

***

[Citing the testimony of a psychologist:] Petitioner scored a five on the Static-99 actuarial tool, which placed him in the medium to high risk category for committing another sexual offense if released from custody. Based upon his Static-99 score, the probability that he would commit a sexual offense if released from custody is as follows: (1) a 33 percent chance within five years; (2) a 38 percent chance within 10 years; and (3) a 40 percent chance within 15 years.[158]

In perhaps the most puzzling attempt to utilize the Static-99 to specify the likelihood of recidivism for a particular offender, the court appeared to have been misled and/or mistaken not only about the capacity of the Static-99 to make such individual conclusions, but also about the very nature of the Static-99. In *State v. Anderson*, a 2007 North Dakota case, the court reported:

Under the Static-99, Anderson scored a 5 on a scale of 11 or 12; however, Dr. Belanger testified that "the highest known score achieved in reality is about a seven." This test measures both paraphilia and antisocial personality disorder; therefore, "the strong loading on the antisocial factor is washed out to a degree by the low loading on the paraphilic factor," according to Dr. Belanger. According to Drs. Etherington and Belanger, even with this mitigation, Anderson's score translates to a 38 to 40 percent probability of recidivism over the next 15 years.[159]

Of course, not all courts have been so willing to simply take the word of an expert in assessing the validity and forensic use of Static-99. For example, in 2008, in United *States v. McIlrath*, Judge Richard Posner, writing for a panel of the U.S. Court of Appeals for the Seventh Circuit, undertook his own brief analysis of the Static-99. As Judge Posner wrote:

> [H]ow valid was Dr. Ostrov's prediction, a prediction of a specific person's likely rate of recidivism rather than an average rate across heterogeneous sex crimes? Has the algorithm that Ostrov used to derive the 9-to-13 percent estimate—Static 99—been validated by methods accepted in the psychological community? Would it satisfy the standard in *Daubert* [the leading U.S. Supreme Court case dealing with the admissibility of expert testimony] or in Rule 702 of the Federal Rules of Evidence? We are not told.
>
> We are not even told what "Static 99" is. Of course one can look it up, and when one does one finds that what it does is try to match a sex offender's characteristics to characteristics found in studies of convicted sex offenders to be correlated with recidivism, such as age (though only whether the offender is over 25), prior sexual offenses, and whether he has lived with someone for at least two years with whom he had a sexual relationship. Our defendant's characteristics matched those of offenders 9-to-13 percent of whom were found to have repeated their offense.
>
> The methodology employed by Static 99 to predict the probability of recidivism has been accepted in a number of cases. Not that it is perfect (what is?); even its advocates claim only "moderate predictive accuracy." It may be more accurate than clinical assessments, but that may not be saying much. Estimates of recidivism are bound to be too low when one is dealing with underreported crimes such as sex offenses. Static 99 treats as a recidivist only someone who is convicted of a further sex offense, but the recidivism concern is with someone who commits a further offense, whether or not he is caught—yet if he is not caught, his subsequent crime does not affect the data on which the Static 99 calibrations are based.
>
> These and other problems with efforts to predict recidivism from offenders' characteristics (such as the limited number of potentially relevant characteristics considered by the Static 99 algorithm— education and occupation, for example, or finer age gradations than just 25 or older, are excluded) have engendered skepticism.[160]

In 2009, in *State v. Rosado*, a New York SVP case mentioned earlier, State Supreme Court Justice Dineen A. Riviezzo also conducted her own inquiry into the Static-99, hearing from five different experts. After noting that the

Static-99 has no predictive value for an individual, Justice Riviezzo went on to observe:

> The hearing testimony revealed that there are other drawbacks and inadequacies in the STATIC-99. It is only moderately accurate for the use intended. Indeed, the STATIC-99 Coding Rules promulgated by Dr. Hanson and others, forthrightly indicates that, "The weaknesses of the STATIC-99 are that it demonstrates only moderate predictive accuracy (ROC = .71) and that it does not include all the factors that might be included in a wide-ranging risk assessment." Dr. Siegel defined "moderate predictive validity" as values ranging between .6 to .7 with 1 being "perfect" and .5 being "useless." One law journal opined that in predicting whether an individual is more likely than not to recidivate consistent with the group's percentage rate of recidivism, "the STATIC-99 cannot do much better than a coin flip."
>
> Moreover, "static" tests based exclusively on historical factors do not take into account dynamic (changing) factors in determining risk. The goal of actuarial risk assessment is to achieve an objective criteria for measuring risk, but there exists no accepted mechanism to take into account individual and dynamic factors before reaching a conclusion. For example, as Dr. Siegel testified, Jeffrey Dahmer, who was convicted of various sexual offenses and in fact consumed the body parts of his victims, would score only a 2 on the STATIC-99 (low risk), because the more deviant aspects of his crimes are not "risk factors" listed in the STATIC-99, and thus are not reflected by his score. For those individuals who were in long term relationships and therefore did not earn an extra point in that category, there is no accounting for a relationship that might have been violent or abusive. On the other hand, an offender who scored "high risk," but who suffered a stroke and is now paralyzed, would not present a heightened risk of reoffending. Other examples include "protective factors" that might decrease risk, such as the completion of sex offender treatment programs, advancing age, or the offender's use of drug therapy to reduce sexual appetite. Currently, there is no uniformly recommended methodology for altering an [actuarial checklist] score upward or downward to account for these factors. Consequently, "if the score from an [actuarial checklist] is simply incorporated into a clinical judgment, absent any systematic, transparent procedure for doing so that is

recommended by the authors of the scale, we run the risk of nullifying the advantage of objectivity by the use of the scale."

Nor does the STATIC-99 delineate recidivism rates by the type of offense committed. No mechanism exists to distinguish pedophiles and other persons with recognized deviancies from other sex offenders. For example, incest offenders recidivate at a significantly lower rate than offenders who target victims outside of the family. Child molesters who target male victims recidivate at a significantly higher rate than those targeting only female victims. As explained in one scholarly journal, "The current research of actuarial measures is highly reductionist, in collapsing most sex offenders into a single category. This profound disregard for the heterogeneity of sexual offenders may lead to serious errors in prediction. Even the most basic typologies (e.g., rapists and child molesters) are neglected. For example, child molesters are often motivated by sexual aspects of offending . . . in contrast, rapists are often motivated by anger and commit nonsexual offenses. Lumping together all paraphilias and sex offenses confounds any attempt at meaningful interpretation. Unquestionably, more focused methods are needed that take into account both clinical conditions (e.g., paraphilias) and offense types."[161]

Finally, it is worth noting that, regardless of whether experts and courts are confused about or ignorant of the limitations of the Static-99 and other similar actuarial tools, these checklists are problematic because of the great likelihood that the "scores" they provide will erroneously categorize individual offenders.

In a recently published study, psychologists Hart, Michie, and Cooke used a well-established statistical method to "evaluate the 'margins of error' at the group and individual level for risk estimates made using ARAIs" (actuarial risk assessment instruments), particularly the Static-99.[162] Hart et al. found that "at the individual level, they were so high as to render risk estimates virtually meaningless."[163] These researchers also reported that their analysis raised deep concern about the margin of error of these checklists, even at the group level: "[S]ome professionals argue that it is appropriate to use ARAIs to make relative risk estimates concerning individuals (e.g. 'Jones has a higher risk for violence than does Smith'). However, our findings indicate that the margin of error in group findings is substantial, leading to overlap among ARAI score categories. This means that it is perhaps difficult to state with a high degree of certainty that one individual's risk for future violence is higher than that of other individuals."[164] As a result of their findings, Hart et al. concluded: "The ARAIs cannot be used to estimate an individual's risk for future violence with any reasonable degree of certainty and should be used with great caution or not at all."[165]

Sex Offender Treatment

All SVP laws require—as they must in order to meet constitutional standards-- meaningful treatment of those offenders who are involuntarily confined. Although the U.S. Supreme Court upheld the constitutionality of SVP civil commitment laws in *Kansas v. Hendricks*, it did so by a 5–4 vote. Providing the fifth and decisive vote was Justice Anthony Kennedy, who wrote a separate concurring opinion that emphasized the requirement that committed sex offenders receive meaningful treatment, and appeared to hinge the constitutionality of the law on that factor: "A law enacted after commission of the offense and which punishes the offense by extending the term of confinement is a textbook example of an *ex post facto* law. If the object or purpose of the Kansas law had been to provide treatment but the treatment provisions were adopted as a sham or mere pretext, there would have been an indication of the forbidden purpose to punish."[166]

As Fitch, a legal scholar and state forensic mental health administrator, notes, "Should a case arise involving an offender for whom treatment were shown to be a 'sham or mere pretext,' there is little doubt that Kennedy's stand with the majority would change, possibly tipping the balance of the court."[167]

According to a 2009 statement by the U.S. Justice Department's Center for Sex Offender Management, "[t]he primary goal of sex offender treatment is to assist individuals to develop the necessary skills and techniques that will prevent them from engaging in sexually abusive and other harmful behaviors in the future, and lead productive and prosocial lives."[168]

Current treatment modalities for sex offenders may be characterized as biological or psychological. Biological treatments, which are almost always utilized conjointly with psychological treatments and are much less commonly used than psychological modalities, include surgical castration and so-called chemical castration. Chemical castration is a term used to describe the prescription of anti-androgens and other hormonal substances that help reduce an offender's sex drive, as well as the use of certain psychotropic medications that may have a similar effect.[169]

Psychological treatment programs often consist of individual and group counseling; didactic experiences aimed at increasing social skills, enhancing aggression management, and developing empathy for victims; homework assignments on these and other topics; and institutional behavior modification approaches such as the use of privileges and report cards to alter offender conduct.

For the most part, these psychological interventions may be characterized as forms of cognitive-behavioral treatment and/or relapse prevention. Cognitive-behavioral modalities are aimed at challenging and overcoming cognitive distortions and thinking errors sex offenders often use to justify or rationalize their offending behavior. Based on addictions theory, relapse prevention approaches seek to help offenders understand the psychological and situational triggers for their offending behavior, identify specific cues as precursors to offending, and utilize learned coping mechanisms to stop the progression toward re-offending.

Whatever their theoretical roots, many if not most sex offender treatment programs require participating offenders to make a complete disclosure of all sex offenses they have ever committed. This disclosure requirement appears to be based on the belief that owning up to one's entire offense history is crucial to both assessment and treatment. It is said that those who treat sex offenders will be handicapped in assessing risk and developing collaborative treatment plans unless they have this information. It is also said that offenders need to reveal this information in order to overcome denial, which limits treatment, and to facilitate their understanding of the patterns and cycles of their offending behavior.

Mandating full disclosure of all sex offenses as a treatment prerequisite places some treated sex offenders in the position of having to choose between cooperating with treatment and incriminating themselves with regard to crimes for which they may still be prosecuted. That concern led one convicted sex offender, Robert Lile, to refuse to cooperate with the Sexual Abuse Treatment Program (SATP) in a Kansas prison.[170]

A few years prior to Lile's scheduled prison release, it was recommended that he undergo sex offender treatment. One of the conditions of the program was filling out a sexual history form, detailing all prior sexual activities, including any that might be as yet uncharged criminal offenses. Offenders were required to undergo a polygraph examination to verify the accuracy and completeness of their disclosures. Under Kansas law, these disclosures were not privileged and thus could be used against an offender in future criminal proceedings. Also under the state's law, sex offender treatment staff were required to report to authorities any uncharged sex offenses involving minors.

When Lile balked at making such a disclosure, he was informed that if he refused to participate in the SATP, his "visitation rights, earnings, work opportunities, ability to send money to family, canteen expenditures, access to a personal television, and other privileges automatically would be curtailed" and he "would be transferred to a maximum-security unit, where his movement would be more limited, he would be moved from a two-person to a four-person cell, and he would be in a potentially more dangerous environment."[171]

Lile responded with a lawsuit seeking a federal injunction to prevent his transfer and loss of privileges. He claimed that requiring him to choose between making the disclosure and losing his privileges and being transferred was a violation of the Fifth Amendment privilege against self-incrimination.

The federal trial court agreed with Lile and granted summary judgment in his favor. The court noted that Lile had testified at his trial that his sexual intercourse with the alleged victim was consensual; thus a disclosure that the sex was not consensual would subject him to a potential charge of perjury. The court also concluded that the threatened transfer and loss of privileges "constituted coercion in violation of the Fifth Amendment."[172]

On appeal by the state, the U.S. Court of Appeals for the Tenth Circuit affirmed the trial court's decision. The appeals court observed that the reduction in privileges and housing was a penalty identical to the punishment imposed on inmates for serious disciplinary violations. That court also noted that the state's interests in "rehabilitating sex offenders and promoting public safety... could be served without violating the Constitution, either by treating the admissions of the inmates as privileged communications or by granting inmates use immunity."[173]

In 2002, however, in *McKune v. Lile*, the U.S. Supreme Court reversed the decision of the lower courts. The Supreme Court started from the unproven premise that sex offender treatment reduces sex offender recidivism—a question that is discussed in greater detail later in this chapter. Indeed, the court cited a guidebook published by the U.S. Justice Department in 1988 that set forth extraordinarily high and unsubstantiated recidivism rates for sex offenders in the United States, treated and untreated: "'The rate of recidivism of treated sex offenders is fairly consistently estimated to be around 15%,' whereas the rate of recidivism of untreated offenders has been estimated to be as high as 80%."[174] It should be noted that the guidebook itself acknowledged that both of these figures might be exaggerated.[175]

Justice Anthony Kennedy, writing for the 5–4 majority, then explained:

> An important component of [sex offender] rehabilitation programs requires participants to confront their past and accept responsibility for their misconduct. "Denial is generally regarded as a main

impediment to successful therapy," and "therapists depend on offenders' truthful descriptions of events leading to past offences in order to determine which behaviors need to be targeted in therapy." Research indicates that offenders who deny all allegations of sexual abuse are three times more likely to fail in treatment than those who admit even partial complicity.

. . . As the parties explain, Kansas' decision not to offer immunity to every SATP participant serves two legitimate state interests. First, the professionals who design and conduct the program have concluded that for SATP participants to accept full responsibility for their past actions, they must accept the proposition that those actions carry consequences. . . If inmates know society will not punish them for their past offenses, they may be left with the false impression that society does not consider those crimes to be serious ones. The practical effect of guaranteed immunity for SATP participants would be to absolve many sex offenders of any and all cost for their earlier crimes. This is the precise opposite of the rehabilitative objective.

Second, while Kansas as a rule does not prosecute inmates based upon information revealed in the course of the program, the State confirms its valid interest in deterrence by keeping open the option to prosecute a particularly dangerous sex offender. Kansas is not alone in declining to offer blanket use immunity as a condition of participation in a treatment program. The Federal Bureau of Prisons and other States conduct similar sex offender programs and do not offer immunity to the participants.

. . . If the State of Kansas offered immunity, the self-incrimination privilege would not be implicated. The State, however, does not offer immunity. So the central question becomes whether the State's program, and the consequences for nonparticipation in it, combine to create a compulsion that encumbers the constitutional right. . .

The SATP does not compel prisoners to incriminate themselves in violation of the Constitution. The Fifth Amendment Self-Incrimination Clause, which applies to the States via the Fourteenth Amendment, provides that no person "shall be compelled in any criminal case to be a witness against himself." The "Amendment speaks of compulsion," and the Court has insisted that the "constitutional guarantee is only that the witness not be compelled to give self-incriminating testimony." The consequences in question here—a transfer to another prison where television sets are not placed in each inmate's cell, where exercise facilities are not readily available, and where work and wage opportunities are more limited—are not ones that compel a prisoner to speak about his past crimes despite a desire to remain silent.[176]

Is effective treatment—treatment characterized by the federal government as likely to "assist individuals to develop the necessary skills and techniques that will prevent them from engaging in sexually abusive and other harmful behaviors in the future, and lead productive and prosocial lives"[177]— provided for those committed and confined under today's SVP laws?

In 2009, Levenson and Prescott succinctly summarized studies of contemporary sex offender treatment as follows:

> Early studies of sex offender treatment stirred skepticism about the benefits of rehabilitation, but more recently, some researchers have reported significant treatment effects. On the other hand, a 12-year follow-up of treated and untreated Canadian sexual offenders found no significant differences in recidivism between the groups. Outcome research from the Sex Offender Treatment and Evaluation Project (SOTEP; a methodologically rigorous long-term investigation conducted in an inpatient program in California) revealed that offenders who received treatment generally reoffended at similar rates as those who did not receive treatment. Of importance, however, is that SOTEP results indicated that offenders who successfully achieved treatment goals (as opposed to simply receiving treatment) sexually reoffended less often than those who did not seem to "get it". Debates persist regarding whether sex offender treatment is effective in preventing future sex crimes.[178]

It has often been observed that well-designed and -implemented sex offender treatment outcome studies are difficult to come by. As Barbaree, one of the early leading authorities in the field of sex offender treatment, has pointed out:

> Numerous recidivism studies have been reported but the interpretation of the findings remains controversial. The usual recidivism study has been conducted in the following way: A sample of men who have received treatment in a program, either institutional or community-based, have been studied some months or years after the completion of treatment. The recidivism in this

group, defined as rearrests or reconvictions for sexual or nonsexual violent crime, has been compared with the recidivism among men in a sample of convenience who did not receive treatment but were found to be equivalent in other important respects.[179]

As Hanson, Broom, and Stephenson further explain:

The central problem concerns potential differences between the treatment and comparison groups. The standard method for minimizing differences is to randomly assign offenders to treatment and no-treatment groups; such designs, however, are difficult to implement and sustain in criminal justice settings. . . When long follow-up periods are required, there is ample opportunity for the research design to be corrupted (e.g., "untreated" offenders receive treatment, administrative support collapses). Consequently, most sex offender treatment outcome studies were not initially designed as such; instead, they have taken advantage of "natural experiments."[180]

Added to these inherent problems in sex offender outcome research is the difficulty of establishing statistically significant effects when relying upon sex offender recidivism, a low base-rate phenomenon, as the criterion for success. As Prentky and Schwartz have put it:

When the proportion of non-treated sex offenders who re-offend is relatively small (for example, around 15%) the proportion of treated sex offenders who re-offend must be very small (around 8–10%) for there to be a statistically significant difference. At the present time, given current methods of treatment and conditions of treatment (typically in prison), reducing re-offense rates among treated sex offenders to 8–10% is rarely accomplished. The result is a mixed, and often confusing, message. Treatment often reduces re-offense rates but not enough to be statistically significant. This same "mixed message" has been trumpeted both by treatment advocates and treatment opponents to support their "causes."[181]

Some researchers have attempted to produce more optimistic results by conducting meta-analyses that combine the results of multiple outcome studies, most of which used small samples with no random assignment and many of which were unpublished and thus not subject to peer review.

Two of the largest and best-known of these meta-analyses were reported in 2002 and 2005. The 2002 meta-analysis was conducted by Hanson and six of his colleagues, who met through (and received logistical support from) the Association for the Treatment of Sexual Abusers, the organization mentioned earlier in this chapter.[182] Hanson et al. summarized data from 43 studies that included 9,454 sex offenders and reported that "Averaged across all studies, the sexual offence recidivism rate was lower for the treatment groups (12.3%) than the comparison groups (16.8%, 38 studies, unweighted average)."[183] The Hanson study also reported "a similar pattern" for "general recidivism" in a group comprising 30 studies—that is, a 27.9 percent rate for treated offenders and a 39.2 percent rate for comparison offenders.[184]

Harris and Rice, however, reviewed the same studies as Hanson et al. and reached a very different conclusion:

> The Association for the Treatment of Sexual Abusers recently supported a meta-analysis (Hanson et al., 2002) of the effectiveness of psychological treatment for sex offenders. It was concluded that current treatments for sex offenders reduce recidivism. . . [W]e reevaluate[d] the evidence. Whereas the random assignment studies yielded results that provided no evidence of treatment effectiveness, Hanson et al. reviewed approximately a dozen others (called "incidental assignment" studies), which yielded substantial positive results for treatment. Upon close inspection, we conclude that such designs involve noncomparable groups and are too weak to be used to draw inferences about treatment effectiveness. In almost every case, the evidence was contaminated by the fact that comparison groups included higher-risk offenders who would have refused or quit treatment had it been offered to them. We conclude that the effectiveness of psychological treatment for sex offenders remains to be demonstrated.[185]

The 2005 meta-analysis was conducted by Lösel and Schmucker and included 69 studies comprising 80 separate comparisons of 22,181 treated and non-treated sex offenders.[186] Lösel and Schmucker reported:

> The 74 comparisons reporting data on sexual recidivism revealed an average recidivism rate of 12% for treated groups and 24% for comparison groups (unweighted average). This is a 50% reduction. However, when we calculated the recidivism rates for treated and comparison participants taking the respective sizes of TG [treatment groups] and CG [comparison groups] in the 74 comparisons into account (i.e., when we calculated an n-weighted average for treated and comparison groups), the difference in recidivism rates vanished completely (11% each for treated and comparison participants).[187]

However, Lösel and Schmucker also reported that the mean rates of recidivism were 11.1 percent for the treated offenders and 17.5 for offenders in the comparison groups. They noted that this effect was larger than that found in the Hanson et al. 2002 meta-analysis of psychological treatment and stated that "Most probably this is due to our inclusion of both psychological and medical models of treatment. The average effect of physical treatment is much larger than that of psychosocial programs. The main source for this difference is a very strong effect of surgical castration..."[188]

Even the limited positive findings of this meta-analysis have not escaped significant criticism and doubt. For example, as DeClue notes: "Meta-analyses of sex-offender treatment that include studies with sub-optimal research designs tend to show that people who complete sex-offender treatment recidivate at slightly lower rates than people who were not treated (Lösel and Schmucker, 2005), but the difference could be explained by the markedly higher rates of recidivism for people who drop out of treatment or are kicked out (Lalumière et al., 2005)."[189]

Given the obvious methodological limitations on outcome research in this area, and the results of the limited research to date, it is no surprise that there remain serious doubts as to the efficacy of sex offender treatment, at least as its effects are measured by reduced recidivism. As LaFond has observed, there is an "agnostic view" (i.e., "that there is simply not enough high quality research to answer this question) and a "cautiously optimistic view" (i.e., that "the balance of available evidence suggests that current treatments reduce recidivism, but that firm conclusions await more and better research").[190] But, as DeClue has observed, there is also a "cautiously pessimistic" view. Citing Lalumière, Harris, Quinsey, and Rice, with whom he agrees, he writes:

> [They] have reviewed the treatment of sex offenders in great depth, and "believe that there are too few well-controlled studies of sex offender treatment to conduct an informative meta-analysis." [T]hey "conclude that the balance of available evidence suggests that current treatments do not reduce recidivism, but that firm conclusions await more and better research" and "there is no clarity about whether anyone has demonstrated a specific effect of treatment in lowering sexual offender recidivism. The situation is even worse with respect to rapists in particular. There is simply no convincing evidence that treatment has ever caused rapists to desist or even to reduce their offending behavior."[191]

One final concern must be noted with regard to sex offender treatment for those offenders civilly committed under SVP laws. Whether treatment "works" or not, it will certainly be of no avail to committed offenders unless they receive it.

In fact, many of those civilly committed under SVP laws receive no sex offender treatment at all. Many of these offenders go untreated because their mental and physical infirmities preclude their participation. For example, one national survey found that 12 percent of those committed under SVP laws suffered from severe, debilitating mental illnesses such as schizophrenia and bipolar disorder.[192] But most of those who remain untreated do so because they refuse treatment; they decline to participate because most sex offender treatment regimens (like that considered and constitutionally approved by the Supreme Court in *Lile*) require full disclosure of all past sex offenses, often enforced by polygraph testing, and many offenders fear the legal repercussions of such disclosure. For example, 80 percent of sexually violent predators in California, 75 percent in Wisconsin, and 70 percent in Florida refuse treatment, mostly on the basis of legal advice and/or concern that disclosing past offenses may hurt their chances of release or lead to additional charges against them.[193]

Moreover, one national media investigation found that civilly committed sex offenders who do participate in sex offender treatment "spend an average of less than 10 hours a week doing so."[194] According to the *New York Times*, many spend the rest of their time taking health and social improvement classes (such as Athlete's Foot, Lactose Intolerance, Male Pattern Baldness, Flatulence, and Proper Table Manners) as well as music and art classes.[195]

Costs, Benefits, And Public Policy

Are SVP statutes worth the expense they impose on government? In theory this question might best be answered by a straightforward comparison of costs and benefits. How much does it cost to implement SVP statutes and how much benefit is derived from the operation of these statutes? If the benefits outweigh the costs, these statutes may be worthwhile. If the costs outweigh the benefits, they probably are not worthwhile.

This kind of rudimentary cost–benefit analysis has been given surprisingly little attention by legislatures, bureaucrats, and scholars in the SVP context. In 1990, Prentky and Burgess observed:

> Given the unabating controversy over what to do with sex
> offenders in general and child molesters in particular, it is all
> the more remarkable that there have been no concerted efforts

to subject treatment programs for these offenders to cost-benefit evaluations.[196]

Now, more than two decades later, these words ring as true as ever.

There are likely several reasons for the dearth of cost–benefit analyses in this context. To begin with, it appears that many, perhaps most, of these laws have been enacted in response to a handful of horrifying cases. The political pressure to "do something" about sex offenders has been so intense that even ordinarily fiscally conservative legislators have taken a "no matter what it costs" approach to the problem. To put it perhaps more directly, legislators have not cared much, if at all, about the economic costs of implementing SVP statutes.

But politics and public concern engendered by a handful of awful cases is not the only reason few have given serious thought to undertaking a cost–benefit analysis with regard to SVP programs. Perhaps an even more compelling impediment has been the difficulty of determining what the costs and benefits of such programs are.

Even the economic costs of SVP laws are extremely difficult to specify. Perhaps the easiest costs to determine are those of the treatment programs. How much does it cost to house, feed, care for, and provide sex offender treatment in a secure, prison-like inpatient setting? Table 1.3 shows the economic costs of these items in the 18 states that had working SVP laws in 2006.

In total, these states spent $454.7 million, nearly half a billion dollars, in one year simply providing secure confinement (or, in the case of Texas, supervision) and treatment. Aside from Texas (which provides only outpatient supervision and treatment) and Pennsylvania (which provides inpatient care only for juvenile sex offenders who have "aged out" of the youth system by turning 21), states spent between $2.9 million and $147.3 million in 1 year on this aspect of their SVP programs alone. Moreover, these states spent an average of more than $94,000 per offender simply providing secure confinement, care, and treatment. The comparable annual cost of confining these individuals in prisons would have averaged about $26,000.

These data, of course, not only are outdated but do not come even close to fully detailing the economic costs of SVP laws. To begin with, New Hampshire, New York, the District of Columbia, and the federal system have all initiated SVP civil commitment programs since 2006. While comparable cost data are not available for all of these jurisdictions, in New York, for example, the cost of providing confinement, care, and treatment was recently estimated to be $100 million by the year 2012.[198] New York is currently spending approximately $175,000 per year per offender for these purposes.[199]

TABLE 1.3. State-by-State Annual Budgets for Sex Offender Civil Commitment and Average Cost of Civil Commitment vs. Incarceration in State Prison

State	2006 Civil Commitment Budget	2006 Average Cost Per SVP Resident	2006 Average Cost Per State Prison Inmate
Arizona	$11,300,000	$110,000	$20,564
California	$147,300,000	$166,000	$43,000
Florida	$23,300,000	$41,845	$19,000
Illinois	$25,600,000	$88,000	$21,700
Iowa	$5,000,000	$71,000	$23,002
Kansas	$10,900,000	$69,070	$22,630
Massachusetts	$30,700,000	$73,197	$43,026
Minnesota	$54,900,000	$141,255	$29,240
Missouri	$8,300,000	$75,920	$14,538
Nebraska	$13,500,000	$93,325	$26,031
New Jersey	$21,900,000	$67,000	$35,000
North Dakota	$12,700,000	$94,728	$27,391
Pennsylvania*	$1,800,000	$150,000	$32,304
South Carolina	$2,900,000	$41,176	$15,156
Texas**	$1,200,000	$17,391	$15,527
Virginia	$8,200,000	$140,000	$23,123
Washington	$40,500,000	$149,904	$29,055
Wisconsin	$34,700,000	$102,500	$27,600
Total	$454,700,000	$94,017 (mean)	$25,994 (mean)

*Pennsylvania confines only juveniles who have "aged out" at 21 years.
**Texas has outpatient commitment only.
[New Hampshire, New York, District of Columbia, and the federal SVP laws were not in force at the time these data were collected.]
Source of Data: Washington State Institute for Public Policy[197]

These confinement, care, and treatment costs also do not cover the capital outlays associated with building secure facilities to house and treat SVPs. Although national data are not available, figures from three states (California, Minnesota, and New York) make it clear that it costs a tremendous amount of money to create new (or even renovated) secure SVP facilities. For example, in 2006, California spent $388 million to construct a secure state hospital intended to house up to 1,500 civilly committed SVPs;[200] Virginia constructed a similar facility for 60 SVPs at a cost of $62 million.[201] Minnesota recently spent $45 million on a building to provide secure care for SVPs and is about to embark on the construction of another such building at a cost that will likely be between $45 million and $89 million.[202] New York recently spent $30 million to turn a building (formerly used to house civilly committed psychiatric patients) into a secure place of confinement for individuals committed under its new SVP law.[203]

These data also do not account for costs of items other than confinement, care, and treatment. As a matter of law, alleged SVPs have the right to a probable cause hearing and a full jury trial before being civilly committed. They also have the right to have their commitments reconsidered by a court every year or two. And they have the right to state-funded counsel and experts at all stages of SVP litigation, including annual or biennial retention proceedings.

These constitutional safeguards carry a heavy price for states with SVP laws. For example, as noted earlier, in New York the cost of simply confining and treating civilly committed SVPs has been estimated to reach $100 million by 2012. The state legislature has recently noted that in addition to these costs, there will be additional costs to state agencies, including the Department of Correctional Services, the Division of Criminal Justice Services, the Division of Parole, the Department of Law, the Office of Court Administration, the Mental Hygiene Legal Service, and the state's assigned counsel program, which provides legal, investigative, expert, and other services "necessary for an adequate defense."[204] Taking these additional costs into account, the legislature estimated that the annual costs associated with the state's SVP law will be "approximately $200 million" by the year 2012.[205]

To the extent that these figures from New York are representative, it seems fair to estimate that the true economic cost of a state's SVP civil commitment program is approximately twice what it pays for confinement, care, and treatment alone. That would mean that the above-quoted 2006 cost figure of nearly half a billion dollars a year for state SVP programs is actually closer to a billion dollars per year.

Of course, that was 2006. The costs of these programs have risen steadily over the years, partly due to the influx of newly committed offenders and the extremely low rate of release from SVP commitment facilities.[206] Thus, it seems reasonable to estimate that current costs of maintaining SVP programs in 20 states, now including New York and New Hampshire as well as the District of Columbia and the federal criminal justice system, are well in excess of a billion dollars a year and rising.

There are, in addition to these economic costs, other intangible costs associated with SVP statutes. Perhaps the greatest intangible cost of these laws is the harm many feel they have done to the fields of psychology and psychiatry, and the patients these professions normally serve.

As early as 1999, a task force of the APA argued that "sexual predator commitment laws represent a serious assault on the integrity of psychiatry."[207] The APA task force was referring to what it regarded as "bending civil commitment to serve essentially non-medical purposes," thereby "undermin[ing] the legitimacy of the medical model of commitment."[208]

Ironically, despite the objections of the psychiatric profession to SVP statutes, these laws have proven to be a financial windfall for many mental health professionals, especially psychologists. Many states have hired additional mental health professionals to staff the new institutions required by these laws and have offered them salaries well beyond those offered to their peers who work in other institutions in the same state.

Also, many states have contracted with independent psychologists and psychiatrists to conduct evaluations of offenders being considered for civil commitment and/or release from such commitment. In New York State, for example, these independent experts were, until recently, paid $300 per hour for their services, including review of documents, offender interviews, report writing, testimony, consultation with counsel, and travel. They are now limited to $250 per hour for all services and $100 per hour for travel time.[209]

In California, the state has paid such independent evaluators $3,500 for an initial evaluation plus $200 per hour for services thereafter. In one recent year, the state utilized the services of 79 psychologists and psychiatrists and paid them a total of $24 million.[210] Fourteen of these doctors billed the state in excess of $500,000 each and two earned more than $1 million each. The top earner, a psychologist, was paid $1.5 million. The second-highest-paid evaluator, a psychologist who earned $1.1 million, billed the state $17,500 for a single day's work. The third-highest-paid evaluator, a psychiatrist who billed the state almost $1 million for a year's worth of SVP evaluations, did so while maintaining a private practice, conducting other forensic evaluations and testifying in court, directing a laboratory, and supervising medical residents. The *Los Angeles Times* reported that this doctor conducted as many as 20 SVP evaluations a month and concluded that "[e]ven at 100 hours per week, he would have had no more than six hours to complete each of five evaluations."[211]

Although there is no evidence that these highly paid private SVP evaluators—or their peers in other states—have not earned the money they are paid by the states that hired them, the media (and some of their colleagues) have sometimes implied that there is something unseemly about what they are being paid, especially in times when many states are cutting essential services due to growing budget deficits.

On a related note, numerous critics, including some professional organizations, have complained that by labeling certain sex offenders "sexually violent predators" based upon whether they are "mentally abnormal" and "predisposed" to recidivate, legislatures not only have created the need for psychologists and psychiatrists to depart from standard, universally accepted, and evidence-based diagnostic practices, but have appropriated scarce mental health resources that would otherwise have been used to treat the truly mentally ill. Indeed, the National Association of State Mental Health Program Directors has argued that SVP civil commitment laws "disrupt the state's ability to provide services for people with treatable psychiatric illnesses [and] divert scarce resources away from people... who both need and desire treatment."[212]

A final cost of SVP laws worth noting is also one that lies in the eyes of the beholder and certainly cannot be quantified or valued in dollars and cents. The courts, including the U.S. Supreme Court by the narrowest of margins, have constitutionally authorized SVP civil commitment based on reasoning that is at best highly debatable, at worst disingenuous. They have justified a massive intrusion on individual liberty interests by holding that SVP commitment (being confined indefinitely in a prison-like setting until one is no longer sexually dangerous) is not punitive, even though it is clearly based not only on crimes the individual has committed, but crimes for which he has already been punished. They have then concluded that SVP statutes, which are retroactive by design, do not violate the Constitution's ban on ex post facto lawmaking because they are not punitive. The courts have abandoned generations of legal precedent that protects individuals from having their liberty interests curtailed solely on the basis of predictions of future criminality and explained this result by giving constitutional recognition to "mental abnormality," a term with no generally accepted meaning in either law or the behavioral sciences. Finally, the courts have made this infringement of liberty contingent on the state's obligation to provide committed individuals with sex offender treatment, a concept that is both amorphous and unproven. In so doing, they have, in the eyes of some, diminished the liberty interests of all and debased the Constitution.

The other side of the ledger, the benefits column, is similarly difficult to specify with any precision. If SVP laws do, in fact, reduce sexual recidivism, they have many benefits, tangible and intangible. As Donato and Shanahan have observed, "obvious" tangible benefits would include reduced "expenditures on police, social welfare services (possibly including foster care), and medical services such as specialist care by child protection units, doctors, psychologists, psychiatrists, and counselors, as well as offender-related costs such as incarceration and court costs, to name but a few."[213]

Reducing sex offender recidivism would also result in numerous "obvious" intangible but vitally important benefits, which, according to Donato and Shanahan, "include, but are not necessarily limited to [preventing] physical injury and illness, emotional and psychological pain and trauma, fear, anxiety and depression, and other psychiatric disorders" as well as "the potential for intergenerational costs when victims themselves become perpetrators, the continuing the cycle of sexual abuse."[214]

The fact that the tangible and intangible benefits that may accrue from a reduction in sex offender recidivism cannot be readily quantified, if calculated at all, does not detract from their reality, value, or significance. There can be little doubt that every violent sex offense causes substantial economic losses for both the victim and society. There also can be no doubt that every such act results in physical and/or psychological harm, often devastating and permanent injury, to the victim—indeed, harm that, in some instances, may spread as victims become victimizers.

In theory, at least some of the intangibles on both sides of this analysis could be assigned dollar values. For example, though not without controversy, tort law routinely assigns dollar damages for pain and suffering, physical and psychological injury, emotional trauma, and even predicted future lost wages. Of course, that is done on a case-by-case basis by judges or juries familiar with the particular facts in each case. It would be little more than rank speculation to assign dollar values to these intangibles on a general basis. Moreover, it would be almost futile to try to put a dollar value on items such as the feeling that the liberty interests of all citizens have been diminished by SVP laws, the perception that psychology and psychiatry have been tarnished by these laws and the roles some psychologists and psychiatrist play in their administration, and the increased stigma that attaches to every sex offender who, fairly or not, may now be regarded by the public as a "predator."

It may be, however, that a rough cost–benefit analysis can proceed in this context without explicitly valuing all or even any of these intangibles. SVP laws clearly carry heavy and reasonably well-defined economic costs, but even if those costs are significantly outweighed by the perceived benefits just discussed, the relevance of those benefits to this analysis is strictly a function of one assumption—namely that SVP laws reduce sex offender recidivism. If that assumption is false or unproven, there are no benefits to be weighed against the costs.

Also to be considered is whether there are less costly alternatives to SVP laws that would offer the same or greater benefits. If so, at the very least, any such alternative should be considered as a possible substitute for SVP laws.

With regard to the first of these issues—whether SVP laws reduce recidivism—sex offender treatment is the main, though perhaps not the only, component of SVP laws that might serve that function. It is possible, for example, that the mere presence of SVP laws has some as yet undocumented marginal deterrent effect on sex offender recidivism. And, of course, the confinement of committed sexually violent predators definitely limits their ability to recidivate while they are in secure, prison-like facilities. However, the only aspect of SVP laws that has been specifically purported to reduce recidivism and subjected to significant empirical scrutiny is sex offender treatment.

As has already been suggested, if not established, the research on sex offender treatment and recidivism is inadequate to answer the question of whether the former reduces the latter. As noted earlier, while some meta-analyses purport to find significant positive treatment effects, the vast majority of studies underlying these analyses suffer from serious methodological flaws. Even if the meta-analyses are to be taken at face value, the most they can fairly say is that, in general, sex offender treatment may have some positive, albeit marginal, effect on recidivism.

However, the vast majority, if not all, of these outcome studies dealt with sex offenders who *agreed to be treated*. No doubt some cooperated in order to secure an extra-therapeutic benefit such as a reduced sentence or an enhanced chance for early release. But it does not appear that any of them were offenders indefinitely committed to treatment against their will under SVP statutes. Thus, there simply are no data that would answer the question of whether sex offender treatment mandated under current SVP laws reduces recidivism.

There remains the question of alternatives: Even if SVP laws are effective in reducing sexual recidivism, are there less costly, viable alternatives to SVP civil commitment that would yield equal or greater benefits—that is, reduce such recidivism by an equal, if not greater, margin?

There are many possible alternatives to SVP civil commitment. One is the SVP statute in Texas, which is, in all major respects but one, nearly identical to other current SVP laws. Texas law provides that an offender determined to be a sexually violent predator is to receive outpatient treatment and supervision in the community. This includes, among other things, comprehensive case management, residential housing requirements, intensive sex offender treatment (including group, individual, and family sessions), 24-hour-a-day monitoring via global positioning satellite (GPS) tracking, polygraphs, penile plethysmography, anti-androgen medication (where appropriate), substance abuse testing, and biennial reassessments.[215] sexually violent predators who violate conditions of their supervision and treatment may be charged with a third-degree felony and, if convicted, face prison sentences ranging from 2 to 10 years.[216]

There is no question that the Texas SVP program is much less expensive than SVP programs in other states. As indicated earlier, the Texas program had a budget of $1.2 million in 2006 and was spending an annual average of $17,391 per sexually violent predator, as compared with the national average of $94,017.[217] Moreover, the average amount Texas was spending annually per committed sexually violent predator was only about $2,000 more per individual than the average amount that state was then spending per individual on incarceration, $15,527.[218]

If the Texas program were shown to be as effective as, or more effective than, inpatient SVP commitment laws in other states, it would certainly be preferable on economic grounds. It is not only much less expensive to operate but avoids the massive intrusion on committed individuals' liberty interests required by all other current SVP laws. Of course, commitment to outpatient care under the Texas statute, like its counterparts in other states, relies upon the clinically and scientifically dubious criteria of "behavioral abnormality"[219] (instead of "mental abnormality") and predicted likelihood of recidivism, both of which almost necessarily entail what the APA has decried "a serious assault on the integrity of psychiatry... bending civil commitment to serve essentially non-medical purposes [and] undermin[ing] the legitimacy of the medical model of commitment."[220]

To date there are no known direct comparisons between the Texas outpatient SVP approach and the SVP programs of other states. However, data reported in 2008 suggest that the Texas approach has been quite successful in preventing recidivism:

> When the program was created, it was estimated the length of
> time to work through the various stages of the program would take
> 5–10 years. To date, five years is the longest time a client has been
> in the program. This person is currently in Stage 3 of the 5 Stage
> (plus aftercare) program. As of July 29, 2008 there had been a
> total of 100 individuals committed to the program. Of those 100
> committed:
>
> - 28 were actively participating in the outpatient program—living
>   in the community.
> - 18 were in county jail awaiting trial for their violation of the
>   SVP commitment orders (3rd-degree felony or habitual
>   sentencing). They will either return to the community or be sent
>   back to prison.
> - 49 are in prison either awaiting release into the program or are
>   serving a sentence for their violation of the SVP commitment
>   order . . . Once they complete their sentence for their SVP
>   violation, they automatically are returned to the outpatient SVP
>   program.
> - 5 are no longer in the program, but were once committed:
>   1 - committed on to state mental health hospital

1 - committed on to state school (MR/DD)

2 - died

1 - absconded

Since the inception of the program, 35 participants have violated their outpatient treatment orders and were sent back to prison (seven of the 35 have been sent back twice). Of those 35, thirty-two were technical violations such as using drugs or alcohol, GPS violations. Three were new criminal charges, one related to failure to register as a sex offender and two related to assault on a law enforcement officer. None were new sex crimes.

To date, no one has successfully completed the program. In other words, no one has been released by the courts because their behavioral abnormality has changed and they are no longer likely to engage in acts of predatory sexual violence.[221]

Given the relatively small percentage of those committed under this "outpatient" SVP law who appear willing and/or able to comply with the extremely stringent conditions of their outpatient commitments and remain at large in the community, not to mention the zero release rate, it might be argued that Texas, like the other states with inpatient SVP programs, is in fact controlling recidivism largely by incarceration or the threat of incarceration. More cynically, the Texas approach might be viewed as little more than an inexpensive cosmetic twist on SVP laws that appears designed to avoid confinement but generally does not. Even so, it is almost certainly as effective as the much more expensive SVP programs in other states, which make no pretense of avoiding confinement.

Another viable and probably more cost-effective alternative to SVP laws is that recommended by a recent Connecticut commission charged with recommending whether that state should enact an SVP civil commitment law.[222] The state's Committee to Study Sexually Violent Persons, which researched the issue for 5 months, "consisted of representatives from the Mental Health and Addiction Services, Correction, Children and Families, and Public Safety departments; the offices of Policy and Management, Attorney General, Chief State's Attorney, Chief Public Defender, Probate Court Administrator, and Protection and Advocacy; Judicial Department; Parole Board; and Psychiatric Security Review Board."[223] The committee examined the experiences of states that had implemented SVP laws, those that were considering doing so, and those that had rejected the idea. They also heard testimony from experts on SVP legislation and sex offender treatment, assessment, and recidivism.

As they reported to the Governor in November 2007:

> The committee found three reasons why civil commitment should not be used to protect the public from sexually violent offenders. First, using civil commitment to detain and incapacitate, rather than to treat psychiatric disorders, would collapse the important distinction between criminal punishment and mental health treatment and would have significant effects on both the mental health and criminal justice systems. Second, in order to confine sex offenders within the mental health system through civil commitment, the state would need to create and fund a quasi criminal justice system within the mental health system, including courts, experts, procedures, and facilities. Based on other states' experiences protracted litigation would likely ensue. Third, reformulating the mental health system would be extremely costly and take years to accomplish. Other states reported that mental health dollars were reallocated from providing services to citizens with psychiatric disabilities to the high security warehousing of sex offenders and litigation.
>
> The committee believed that only those offenders whose behavior is related to, or a manifestation of, a mental illness should be candidates for civil commitment.[224]

The committee "also concluded that the state's criminal justice system offered the quickest, most cost-effective means to protect the public from sexually violent people."[225] Focusing on "the need for (1) additional legislation and resources to increase the court's ability to impose appropriate lengths of incarceration, (2) longer periods of post-release supervision, and (3) effective treatment within and outside of institutions," the committee specifically recommended, inter alia: "tougher up-front sentencing"; "expanded and uniform" sex offender assessments; enhanced treatment opportunities for all sex offenders, both in and out of prison; expanded intensive post-release supervision units for sex offenders on parole; and screening of certain sex offenders about to be released from prison to determine whether they meet the criteria for ordinary civil commitment (i.e., whether they currently have psychiatric disabilities and are gravely disabled or dangerous to themselves or others).[226]

Conclusion And Recommendations

SVP civil commitment laws are based on flawed and unproven premises. They appear to have developed out of mistaken but widely held beliefs that sex offenses are increasing and that sex offenders have a high rate of recidivism. They were fueled largely by sensational media accounts of truly horrifying but rare cases in which women and children were sexually victimized and murdered by repeat offenders. They were enacted in many states by well-meaning but ill-informed or uninformed legislatures who gave little thought to their likely efficacy or even their costs, which have proven to be staggering. They are also based on the unproven premise that sex offender recidivism can be further lowered by incarcerating offenders who have served their legally mandated prison sentences and forcing them to undergo lengthy treatment that is largely psychological in nature. Finally, these laws have strained constitutional principles, sullied the professions of psychology and psychiatry, and drained already sparse resources from government programs designed to treat the mentally ill.

States that have not enacted SVP laws should not do so. States that already have these laws on their books should repeal them and replace them with sensible, cost-effective measures aimed at preventing sex offenses. The Connecticut committee report just cited provides a useful framework for reform.

Ideally, prison sentences for convicted violent sex offenders (i.e., rapists and child molesters) should, in many states, be increased to more accurately reflect the gravity of their offenses, in keeping with concern for deterrence, public protection, and rehabilitation. Indeterminate rather than fixed sentences should be used to give correctional and parole authorities the flexibility needed to meet all three of these concerns. Repeat violent sex offenders who appear resistant to rehabilitative efforts and are not deterred by time-limited prison terms should be considered persistent offenders and be subject to possible life sentences.

State-of-the-art sex offender treatment should be made available to all violent sex offenders throughout their prison sentences, not only when they are about to be released. If sex offender treatment works as well as some of its proponents believe, it makes no sense to reserve it for those whose sentences are soon to expire or have already expired. Indeterminate sentence structures should be used as both a carrot and a stick with regard to treatment participation and progress during incarceration.

Post-release supervision should be made part of the criminal sentence for every convicted violent sex offender (with duration and conditions known to the offender at the time of sentencing), and no such offender should be released from prison without a lengthy period of post-release supervision. Such supervision should not be punitive in nature but designed to facilitate offenders' re-entry into the community and assist them in avoiding re-offense.

Parole authorities should have the discretion to petition courts to discontinue, extend, or modify the conditions of post-release supervision. Persistent violation of post-release supervision conditions should be grounds for re-incarceration.

Sex offender treatment should be available to all released violent sex offenders, but participation in such treatment should not be made a condition of release for offenders who have fully cooperated with such treatment while incarcerated.

Violent sex offenders who are seriously mentally ill and either unable to care for themselves or present a danger to self or others should be referred for regular civil commitment and should have the same substantive and procedural due process rights that are now constitutionally guaranteed to civilly committed individuals.

Many states have already adopted reforms similar to or the same as these. These reforms are not inexpensive and they will not eradicate violent sex offender recidivism. They represent, at best, a more cost-effective approach or, at worst, a cost-competitive alternative to SVP civil commitment that are better in every relevant way. Reforms such as these represent an approach to the problem of violent sex offender recidivism that is more honest, more compatible with fundamental constitutional principles, less likely to undermine the professional integrity of psychologists and psychiatrists, and probably more likely to reduce recidivism by violent sex offenders.

2

SEX OFFENDER REGISTRATION, NOTIFICATION, AND RESTRICTION LAWS

Now for the child molesters and rapists who are out of custody and making normal people feel awkward. I think you might want to ask authorities to let you back into prison, because I sense that America is about to make you very uncomfortable. . . Let's make them shake in their boots . . . Let's get the local TV news to run dailies of their faces and the places they inhabit. Let's get the newspapers to have a special sewage section dedicated to showing and keeping tabs on them. Let's put HazMat signs in the front yards where these creeps live. Let's force them out of our communities and get them their own place where all of them can feel at home and not be judged, and where they can do the dirty deeds to each other.

Doug Giles (2005)[1]

In 2009, Charles McGonagle, a 44-year-old New Hampshire man, voluntarily testified before a subcommittee of the U.S. House of Representatives regarding the Adam Walsh Act of 2006, Title 1 of which is the Sex Offender Registration and Notification Act (SORNA). Among other things, SORNA requires states to establish and maintain an online registry of sex offenders, retroactively applicable to all sex offenders regardless of when they committed their offenses, were convicted, or were released.[2] Specifically the hearing was aimed at determining why most states were failing to comply with the mandates of the 2006 law.

McGonagle told the House Subcommittee on Crime, Terrorism, and Homeland Security:

My story began in 1985. I was twenty years old and met a young woman at a party. It never occurred to me to ask her age, as she appeared to be in the same age range as myself and the other partygoers. We fooled around, but never had intercourse. I liked her and gave her my phone number. Her parents found my phone number later and turned it over to the police. I did not know she was actually underage and I was told by the police that it was in my best interest to speak with them and that everything would be alright. I pled guilty, served a couple months in county jail and moved on with my life. A full 10 years after my conviction I was thrown into the nightmare I've been living ever since.

Before being required to register as a sex offender, I had moved on with my life. I got married and had two children. In 1990 I went back to college and got my degree. I was living the American dream of owning my own home. I had a great career as an executive chef and was doing rather well. Then in 1996 I was informed by my state of residence (NH) that I was now considered an offender against children. I was told I must register as a sex offender until I die. I was also informed that there was nothing I could do about this. I had never told my wife about the past situation as it was just that, the past. She did not understand. This along with the fact that the registration had put me into a great depression ended up causing my divorce in 1997. I had lost everything. All marital bills and child support were placed on me by the court because my wife's lawyer made sure she told the court that I was a "sex offender." I ended up having to live in my car so I could afford to pay everyone and support my children. I was angry and rightfully so for the next few years. I got into some minor trouble with the law in the years directly following my initial registration but none that could be considered another sexual crime. Over the years I have rebuilt my life. I have been the executive chef on the seacoast of NH for eight years now. I purchased another home again and my daughter from my first marriage came to live with me in December of 2006.

In 2007, with passing of more retroactive "sex offender" laws, I [was] placed on the public list for the very first time for all to see, labeled an offender against children, more than 20 years after my first and only statutory rape conviction. It took only about a month for my neighbors to find out. One moved telling me I dropped his property value. Most just think I rape children. My daughter is harassed at school and she is not allowed to have friends over to the house as I fear everything. One evening in the dining room at my job a woman stood up and pointed me out as a sex offender in front of about 60 guests. These laws also affect my romantic life and my ability to be intimate with my current wife because the overwhelming stigma makes me feel dirty and worthless. The list of so-called "non-punishing" situations I deal with on a daily basis goes on but I hope you've got a feel for what happens to someone who is labeled a sex offender and treated like a pedophile when he never did such a thing to begin with.

Since completing my sentence all those years ago, I have been subject to the Jacob Wetterling Act, Megan's Law, and now the Adam Walsh Act, and let's not forget any state laws I am required to abide [by] as well. The Adam Walsh Act would in fact allow me to be removed from the duty to register after 25 years, however the state of NH has interpreted the Act as allowing them [to] exceed the 25 years required and will continue with lifetime registration to look "tough on sex crimes." Over two decades ago I made a careless and stupid mistake when fooling around at a party and I can't seem to get past that one night in my life. Today, because of what I feel are retroactive laws, I will go to prison if I fail to follow all of these extraneous rules. It is ironic that I never went to prison for this "crime" in the first place. Worse yet, I am constantly reminded by law makers that I am not being further punished. But if this isn't punishment, what is?

Twenty-five years is a long time to wait for a young man who made a foolish mistake with another teenager, whom he believed to be of age. Circumstance matters and intent should as well. I never intended to harm anyone, never forced this young lady to kiss me back, never harmed her in any way. My only crime was being stupid and careless by not asking her age and I paid for that crime in county jail and with probation over twenty years ago. When will I be done paying for my crime? When will my family not have to live with the shame and stigma of the sex offender label?[3]

Today McGonagle remains on the New Hampshire sex offender registry website, which is directly accessible on the Internet or on the National Sex

Offender Registry, a site maintained by the U.S. Department of Justice.[4] The website contains an updated photograph of McGonagle, his home address, age, date of birth, height, weight, hair color, eye color, the location of his tattoos, and his criminal record, including the offense that landed him on the registry. McGonagle's criminal record is more extensive than he told the Congressional subcommittee but does not include any sexual offense other than the one that got him listed on the registry in the first place. According to the sex offender registry website, that offense was "NH RSA 632-A:3, II Felonious Sexual Assault (Victim 13 or older & under 16 & age diff more than 3 years)." Any viewer of this information astute enough to look up the New Hampshire statute under which McGonagle was convicted would see the following information:

TITLE LXII
CRIMINAL CODE
CHAPTER 632-A
SEXUAL ASSAULT AND RELATED OFFENSES
Section 632-A:3

632-A:3 Felonious Sexual Assault. – A person is guilty of a class B felony if such person:

I. Subjects a person to sexual contact and causes serious personal injury to the victim under any of the circumstances named in RSA 632-A:2; or

II. Engages in sexual penetration with a person, other than his legal spouse, who is 13 years of age or older and under 16 years of age where the age difference between the actor and the other person is 4 years or more; or

III. Engages in sexual contact with a person other than his legal spouse who is under 13 years of age.

IV. Engages in sexual contact with the person when the actor is in a position of authority over the person and uses that authority to coerce the victim to submit under any of the following circumstances:

(a) When the actor has direct supervisory or disciplinary authority over the victim by virtue of the victim being incarcerated in a correctional institution, the secure psychiatric unit, or juvenile detention facility where the actor is employed; or

(b) When the actor is a probation or parole officer or a juvenile probation and parole officer who has direct

> supervisory or disciplinary authority over the victim
> while the victim is on parole or probation or under
> juvenile probation.
> Consent of the victim under any of the circumstances set forth
> in paragraph IV shall not be considered a defense.[5]

Today, Charles McGonagle is one of over 700,000 Americans who are registered sex offenders. They are required by law, both state and federal, to provide law enforcement officials with their names, photographs, addresses, and other identifying information, all or most of which is made readily available to anyone with a computer and access to the Internet. Not only are these registered sex offenders thus identified to the public at large, but they are also often subject to significant legal restrictions on where they can reside or even go. In many states and municipalities, for example, registered sex offenders are not allowed to live within a specified distance of a school, child care facility, school bus stop, and/or any other place where children generally congregate.

Early Reporting Laws

The idea of maintaining a registry of sex offenders is often assumed to be a product of the past two decades. Most of today's sex offender registries and restrictions, like most of the sexually violent predator laws described in the previous chapter, are the result of legislation and court decisions that date to about 1990. However, the notion that the government should keep track of convicted sex offenders dates back to the 1930s, when many cities and towns passed local ordinances requiring convicted criminals to register with the police upon entering the limits of the municipality. Some of the ordinances applied to all crimes, some to felonies, some to crimes of "moral turpitude," and some only to particular enumerated criminal offenses.[6]

Sex offenders were included in some of these early local registration laws, but California enacted the first statewide sex offender registration law in 1947. The California law, which was made retroactive to 1944, required convicted sex offenders (primarily felony convicts but some misdemeanor offenders as well) to register with the local police department within 30 days of arriving in any city or county for temporary or permanent residence. The purpose of the law was to provide "local police authorities with the knowledge of the whereabouts of habitual sex offenders and sex deviates" and ensure that they would be "readily available for police surveillance at all times."[7]

The policy of registering sex offenders on a statewide basis was gradually adopted over the next couple of decades by four other states: Arizona (1951), Nevada (1961), Ohio (1963), and Alabama (1967). These laws remained on the books but "fell into disuse" over time.[8] Lack of enthusiasm for these early reporting laws appears to have been the result of a number of factors. First, "[s]everal informal studies in the 1980s, including one attempt by a sheriff to use the registration data to locate a missing child, found that as many as ninety percent of the entries were inaccurate."[9] Also, "early registration information had limited practical value, merely allowing police to keep tabs on the registrants; because the collected registration data was confidential, the statutes did not require or even permit the police to notify communities about registered offenders."[10] Finally, "as many California police officers learned, the enormity of the collected data, with registration lists filled with nonviolent offenders and outdated information, made the statutes ineffective tools to investigate serious, violent crimes."[11]

The State Of Washington Community Protection Act

The first modern sex offender registration law was enacted in the state of Washington in 1990.[12] The Washington statute was the first in the nation to authorize law enforcement authorities to notify community residents when certain released sex offenders moved into their neighborhoods.[13] Support for the statute arose quickly following a 1989 incident in Tacoma in which Earl Shriner, an ex-convict with a long history of sexually and physically abusing children, kidnapped a 7-year-old boy. Shriner, who had been released from prison just 5 months earlier and was believed by authorities to pose a sexual threat to children, raped and sexually mutilated the boy and left him for dead.[14]

Within months of the assault, the Washington legislature enacted and the governor signed into law the Community Protection Act of 1990. The Act's most publicized and controversial provisions authorized the indefinite civil commitment and confinement of so-called sexual predators following completion of their criminal sentences. But the Act also made Washington the nation's first jurisdiction not only to register sex offenders but also to make details of their registration known to the public.

Under Washington's Community Protection Act, sex offenders would be registered and classified as Level I, II, or III. Registry information regarding Level I offenders, those deemed at low risk of re-offending, was to be shared with law enforcement agencies and, upon request, could be disclosed to any victim or witness to the offense and to any individual community member who lived near where the offender resided, expected to reside, or was regularly found. Registry information about Level II offenders, those believed to present a moderate risk of re-offending, could be disclosed to public and private schools, child care centers, day care providers, businesses and organizations primarily serving children, women, or vulnerable adults, neighbors of the offender, and community groups located near the residence where the offender resided, expected to reside, or was regularly found. Registry information regarding Level III offenders, those determined to be at a high risk of re-offending, was to be disclosed to the public at large.

Over the next 16 years or more, the Washington statute would serve as a model for portions of dozens of state and several federal laws that now control sex offender registration, notification, and restriction.

The Jacob Wetterling Act

At about 9 PM on Sunday, October 22, 1989, 11-year-old sixth-grader Jacob Wetterling was kidnapped at gunpoint by a masked man who emerged from the woods on a rural road in a small Minnesota town. Jacob had been with two other boys who were ordered by the gunman to leave the scene immediately.[15]

Decades have passed since the crime occurred. Jacob has never been found and no one has been arrested. No clear evidence has ever emerged to indicate that Jacob was the victim of a sex crime, but the kidnapping soon played a crucial role in the American legal system's response to sex offenders.

Within months of Jacob's disappearance, his mother, Patty Wetterling, founded the Jacob Wetterling Foundation and began lobbying for, among other reforms, laws requiring the registration of sex offenders.[16] In 1994, Congress passed the Jacob Wetterling Crimes against Children and Sexually Violent Offender Registration Act, which effectively required every state to establish a sex offender registry by 1997.[17] Under the Act, upon release from custody, those convicted of sexual abuse of children or sexually violent crimes against adults were required to register their current addresses with local law enforcement agencies for 10 years. The Act also authorized, but did not require, states to make public information about a registered sex offender if law enforcement officials determined that notice of such an offender's presence in the community was "necessary to protect public safety."[18]

New Jersey's Megan's Law

On July 29, 1994, in the New Jersey suburb of Hamilton Township, 7-year-old Megan Kanka was lured into the home of a neighbor, Jesse Timmendequas, who promised to show her a puppy. Instead, the neighbor raped and strangled the child.[19] Unknown to Megan's parents, Timmendequas, who lived across the street from them, had earlier been convicted for aggravated assault and attempted sexual assault of another child and had been imprisoned for 6 years.[20] Megan's mother said of her daughter's killer, "We knew nothing about him. If we had been aware of his record, my daughter would be alive today."[21]

In the immediate aftermath of Megan Kanka's death, over 400,000 New Jersey residents signed a petition demanding that the state legislature enact a law that would, among other things, require the state to register sex offenders and notify the public of their presence in the community.[22] In less than 90 days, and without holding a single public hearing, the New Jersey legislature responded favorably by enacting the original "Megan's Law."[23] New Jersey's Megan's Law required anyone "convicted, adjudicated delinquent or found not guilty by reason of insanity for commission of a sex offense" to register with local law enforcement upon release from incarceration, upon relocation from another state, or after a conviction without a sentence of incarceration.[24] The statute further required previously convicted sex offenders, who were not then incarcerated or subject to supervision, to register. Moreover, Megan's Law required public notification regarding certain offenders based upon their potential for recidivism, as determined by the prosecutor in the offender's county of residence. Notification regarding low-risk offenders would be made only to law enforcement agencies likely to encounter the offender. Offenders deemed to be at moderate risk for recidivism would have information about them released to educational, religious, and youth organizations as well. Finally, information about high-risk offenders would be disseminated to members of the general public likely to come into contact with the offender. All of the law's provisions were deemed lifetime requirements unless a registrant was offense-free for 15 years after conviction or release from a correctional facility (whichever came later) or persuaded a court that he or she no longer posed a threat to the safety of others.

The constitutionality of these aspects of New Jersey's Megan's Law was challenged almost immediately. In 1995, in *Doe v. Poritz*, the New Jersey Supreme Court held that the registration and notification requirements specified by the Act were constitutional:

> The essence of our decision is that the Constitution does not
> prevent society from attempting to protect itself from convicted sex

offenders, no matter when convicted, so long as the means of protection are reasonably designed for that purpose and only for that purpose, and not designed to punish; that the community notification provided for in these laws, given its remedial purpose, rationality, and limited scope, further assured by our opinion and judicial review, is not constitutionally vulnerable because of its inevitable impact on offenders; that despite the possible severity of that impact, sex offenders' loss of anonymity is no constitutional bar to society's attempt at self-defense. The Registration and Notification Laws are not retributive laws, but laws designed to give people a chance to protect themselves and their children. They do not represent the slightest departure from our State's or our country's fundamental belief that criminals, convicted and punished, have paid their debt to society and are not to be punished further. They represent only the conclusion that society has the right to know of their presence not in order to punish them, but in order to protect itself...

The choice the Legislature made was difficult, for at stake was the continued apparently normal lifestyle of previously-convicted sex offenders, some of whom were doing no harm and very well might never do any harm, as weighed against the potential molestation, rape, or murder by others of women and children because they simply did not know of the presence of such a person and therefore did not take the common-sense steps that might prevent such an occurrence. The Legislature chose to risk unfairness to the previously-convicted offenders rather than unfairness to the children and women who might suffer because of their ignorance, but attempted to restrict the damage that notification of the public might do to the lives of rehabilitated offenders by trying to identify those most likely to reoffend and limiting the extent of notification based on that conclusion.

The legislative choice was undoubtedly influenced by the fact that if the law did not apply to previously-convicted offenders, notification would provide practically no protection now, and relatively little in the near future. The Legislature reached the irresistible conclusion that if community safety was its objective, there was no justification for applying these laws only to those who offend or who are convicted in the future, and not applying them to previously-convicted offenders. Had the Legislature chosen to exempt previously-convicted offenders, the notification provision of the law would have provided absolutely no protection whatsoever on the day it became law, for it would have applied to no one. . . [25]

Federal Megan's Law

Support for a national Megan's Law followed quickly upon enactment of the New Jersey version. In 1996, a federal version of the statute, requiring all states to establish some form of community notification, was proposed and debated only briefly in Congress.[26]

Prior to the bill's passage in the House of Representatives by a vote of 418-0 and in the Senate by unanimous consent, Rep. Jim Ramstad of New Mexico stated that a "study of imprisoned child sex offenders found that 74 percent had a previous conviction for another child sex offense."[27] Within minutes, another congressman stated that sex offenders had a recidivism rate of 74 percent. His statement was followed by that of Rep. Mark Foley of Florida, who told the House that "There is a ninety percent likelihood of recidivism for sexual crimes against children. Ninety percent. That is the standard. That is their record. That is the likelihood. Ninety percent."[28] Meanwhile, in the Senate, Sen. Kay Bailey Hutchinson of Texas informed her colleagues that "[W]e know that more than 40 percent of convicted sex offenders will repeat their crimes."[29]

After signing the bill into law, President Bill Clinton told the nation in one of his weekly radio addresses: "Nothing is more threatening to our families and communities and more destructive of our basic values than sex offenders who victimize children and families. Study after study tells us that they often repeat the same crimes. That's why we have to stop sex offenders before they commit their next crime, to make our children safe and give their parents peace of mind."[30]

The federal version of Megan's Law required community notification, providing that each state "shall release relevant information that is necessary to protect the public."[31] Subsequent federal guidelines, developed under the new law, provided that "Information must be released to members of the public as necessary to protect the public from registered offenders."[32]

Following enactment of the federal Megan's Law, every state that had not already done so enacted some form of public notification regarding sex offenders. By the end of 1996, every state, the District of Columbia, and the federal government had enacted some variation of Megan's Law. Subsequently, the constitutionality of aspects of two of these laws was considered by the U.S. Supreme Court.

In *Connecticut Department of Safety v. Doe*, the court examined a state Megan's Law that requires "all persons convicted of criminal offenses against a minor, violent and nonviolent sexual offenses, and felonies committed for a sexual purpose [to] register with the Connecticut Department of Public Safety (DPS) upon their release into the community."[33] Under the statute, "each must provide personal information (including his name, address, photograph, and DNA sample); notify DPS of any change in residence; and periodically submit an updated photograph."[34] The law specifies that this "registration requirement runs for 10 years in most cases; those convicted of sexually violent offenses must register for life." As the Court further explained:

> The statute requires DPS to compile the information gathered from registrants and publicize it. In particular, the law requires DPS to post a sex offender registry on an Internet Website and to make the registry available to the public in certain state offices. Whether made available in an office or via the Internet, the registry must be accompanied by the following warning: "Any person who uses information in this registry to injure, harass or commit a criminal act against any person included in the registry or any other person is subject to criminal prosecution."
>
> [T]he State's Website enabled citizens to obtain the name, address, photograph, and description of any registered sex offender by entering a zip code or town name. The following disclaimer appeared on the first page of the Website:
>
> "The registry is based on the legislature's decision to facilitate access to publicly-available information about persons convicted of sexual offenses. [DPS] has not considered or assessed the specific risk of reoffense with regard to any individual prior to his or her inclusion within this registry, and has made no determination that any individual included in the registry is currently dangerous. Individuals included within the registry are included solely by virtue of their conviction record and state law. The main purpose of providing this data on the Internet is to make the information more easily available and accessible, not to warn about any specific individual."[35]

Doe, the fictitious name used to identify the sex offender who brought the case on behalf of himself and similarly situated offenders, claimed that the law "deprives him of a liberty interest—his reputation combined with the alteration of his status under state law—without notice or a meaningful opportunity to be heard."[36] The federal trial court agreed, granted summary judgment for Doe, and permanently enjoined the law's public disclosure provisions.[37]

The state appealed and the federal Court of Appeals affirmed, holding that sex offenders were constitutionally entitled to a hearing "to determine whether or not they are particularly likely to be currently dangerous before being labeled as such by their inclusion in a publicly disseminated registry."[38] Since Connecticut had not provided such a hearing, the Court of Appeals enjoined the state from "disclosing or disseminating to the public, either in printed or electronic form (a) the Registry or (b) Registry information concerning [class members]" and from "identifying [them] as being included in the Registry."[39] According to the Court of Appeals, the Connecticut law implicated a "liberty interest" because it stigmatized Doe by implying that he was currently dangerous and that it imposed upon him "extensive and onerous" registration obligations.[40]

The U.S. Supreme Court disagreed with both lower courts, holding that Doe and others in his situation were not entitled to a hearing on their current dangerousness because, under the state law, the requirement that they register as sex offenders and have information about them disseminated did not hinge upon current dangerousness. In the words of the Court:

> [T]he fact that [Doe] seeks to prove—that he is not currently dangerous—is of no consequence under Connecticut's Megan's Law. As the DPS Website explains, the law's requirements turn on an offender's conviction alone—a fact that a convicted offender has already had a procedurally safeguarded opportunity to contest. ("Individuals included within the registry are included *solely* by virtue of their conviction record and state law" (emphasis added [by the Court])). No other fact is relevant to the disclosure of registrants' information. Indeed, the disclaimer on the Website explicitly states that respondent's alleged nondangerousness simply does not matter. ("[DPS] has made no determination that any individual included in the registry is currently dangerous").[41]

In *Smith v. Doe*, the U.S. Supreme Court considered the constitutionality of Alaska's Megan's Law, which required that persons convicted of sex or child-kidnapping offenses register with state or local law enforcement authorities and that portions of the resulting information, including an offender's name, alias, address, photograph, physical description, driver's license number, motor vehicle identification number, place of employment, date of birth, crime, date and place of conviction, and length and conditions of sentence, be published on the Internet.[42] The statute was made applicable retroactively to offenders convicted before its enactment.

Doe, the fictitious name used to identify the two sex offenders who brought the case, argued that, as applied to them, persons who had been convicted of sex offenses prior to its enactment, Alaska's Megan's Law violated the constitutional ban on ex post facto laws. The federal trial court disagreed, finding that the law was not intended to punish offenders but rather only to civilly regulate them, and gave summary judgment to the state.[43] The federal Court of Appeals agreed that the law was not intended to be punitive but held that its effects were punitive despite the legislature's intent and thus violated the Constitution's ex post facto clause.[44]

The Supreme Court reversed the Court of Appeals, concluding that Alaska's Megan's Law was not punitive and thus could not be said to violate the federal constitution's prohibition against ex post facto punishment. As the Court reasoned:

> A conclusion that the legislature intended to punish would satisfy an *ex post facto* challenge without further inquiry into its effects, so considerable deference must be accorded to the intent as the legislature has stated it . . . The courts "must first ask whether the legislature, in establishing the penalizing mechanism, indicated either expressly or impliedly a preference for one label or the other." Here, the Alaska Legislature expressed the objective of the law in the statutory text itself. The legislature found that "sex offenders pose a high risk of reoffending," and identified "protecting the public from sex offenders" as the "primary governmental interest" of the law. The legislature further determined that "release of certain information about sex offenders to public agencies and the general public will assist in protecting the public safety." As we observed in *Hendricks*, where we examined an *ex post facto* challenge to a post-incarceration confinement of sex offenders, an imposition of restrictive measures on sex offenders adjudged to be dangerous is "a legitimate nonpunitive governmental objective and has been historically so regarded." In this case, as in *Hendricks*, "nothing on the face of the statute suggests that the legislature sought to create anything other than a civil . . . scheme designed to protect the public from harm."[45]

In 1996, less than 5 months after the federal version of Megan's Law was signed into law, Congress amended it, passing the Pam Lyncher Sexual Offender Tracking and Identification Act of 1996, which mandated, inter alia, that recidivist sex offenders and those convicted of "aggravated" sexual violence register for life.[46]

The Adam Walsh Act And The Sex Offender Registration And Notification Act (SORNA)

Ten years after enacting the federal Megan's Law, Congress passed the Adam Walsh Child Protection and Safety Act of 2006, named in honor of a 6-year-old boy who was abducted and murdered in Florida.[47] Adam's father, John Walsh, went on to become a victims' rights advocate and host of a popular television program, "America's Most Wanted."[48]

The Adam Walsh Act specifically repealed the Jacob Wetterling Law, Megan's Law, and the Pam Lyncher Law. Title 1 of the Adam Walsh Act is the Sex Offender Registration and Notification Act (SORNA), which created a national sex offender registry, required every state (as well as all U.S. territories, Indian tribes, and Puerto Rico) to establish and maintain an online registry of sex offenders, and mandated that every jurisdiction upload its registry to a federal website accessible to the public by 2009.[49] SORNA also applies retrospectively to all sex offenders regardless of when they committed their offenses, were convicted, or were released; requires all registered offenders to update their required information in person; and expands registry data to include updated photographs, social security numbers, fingerprints, palmprints, DNA samples, and motor vehicle license numbers and descriptions.

SORNA also requires certain juvenile sex offenders to register and creates a three-tiered risk assessment scheme based upon the severity of the offense rather than any individual risk determinations. Under the Act, depending upon the crime(s) for which they were convicted, sex offenders are assigned to one of three levels or tiers. Tier-one offenders, those whose offense(s) are among the least serious, must register for at least 15 years and update their registration annually. Tier-two offenders are required to register for 25 years and verify their registrations semi-annually. Tier-three offenders, whose offense(s) are among the most serious, must register for the duration of their lives and update their registrations every 3 months. The Act provides no means by which a registrant may challenge the required duration of his registration.

The Adam Walsh Act provides that if states, territories, American Indian nations, and the District of Columbia do not fully comply with SORNA, they will lose 10 percent of their federal law enforcement (Byrne Grant) funding. As of 2010 only one of these jurisdictions, the state of Ohio, had fully complied with the requirements of SORNA.[50] However, as a result of the establishment of a national sex offender registry, the existing sex offender registries of Guam, Puerto Rico, the District of Columbia, all 50 states, and five American Indian tribes are now readily accessible from a single online source, the Dru

Sjodin National Sex Offender Public Website, named in honor of a 22-year-old North Dakota college student who was kidnapped, sexually assaulted, and murdered in 2003.[51] Visitors to this website may search for a registered sex offender by name; state, territory, or Indian nation; county; town; and/or zip code. The information available on the website about any given offender depends on the state, but all listings contain offenders' names; aliases if any; photographs; dates of birth; and physical descriptions. All contain some description of the offender's sex crime(s), some of which are nothing more than the name given the offense in the state's penal law or a vague reference such as "sex offense, second degree." Others are a bit more detailed—for instance, "Mr. _____ forcibly raped an adult female who was unknown to him" or "Subject had sexual contact with 15 year old." Most listings contain offenders' addresses and vehicle information, including make, model, color, and license plate number. Some also contain links to an online map pinpointing the exact location of the offender's address. Other data sometimes available include the name and location of any school the offender is attending, current supervision status, employment address, and scars, marks, and tattoos. A few websites even allow visitors to sign up to receive e-mailed updates when there is a change in the offender's reported address or to submit information to law enforcement authorities regarding the whereabouts of an offender.

In 2008, the National Sex Offender Public Website had nearly 5 million visits, and sex offender files were "hit" or viewed more than 772 million times.[52]

Residency, Employment, And Other Restrictions

In addition to requiring sex offenders to register and have their information made readily available to the public, numerous jurisdictions have also imposed residency and travel restrictions. At least 30 states have enacted residency restrictions that prohibit sex offenders from living within a specified distance of schools, day care centers, parks, or other places where children congregate. The required distance a registered sex offender must live from these places ranges from 500 to 2,500 feet. As many as 400 municipalities have passed similar local ordinances. In fact, some cities, towns, and villages have effectively banned registered sex offenders from living anywhere within their limits.

At the state level, for example, in Alabama and Iowa, a sex offender may not reside or work within 2,000 feet of schools or child care facilities; Arkansas has the same rule but limits it to the most serious sex offenders; Oklahoma maintains the same distance requirement but limits it to schools. Other states, including Florida, Kentucky, Indiana, Louisiana, Missouri, Michigan, Tennessee, and West Virginia, have similar laws but impose a distance limit of 1,000 feet; some of these states also include playgrounds, ball fields, school buses and bus stops, or any other places minors congregate. Georgia law provides that a registered sex offender may not reside, work, or loiter within 1,000 feet of any school, child care facility, school bus stop, or place where minors congregate. Still other states, such as Illinois and South Dakota, apply a 500-foot buffer zone.

Some localities have enacted residency restrictions for sex offenders where the state government has declined to do so. One prominent example is New Jersey, which has no statewide law but had over 100 municipal laws governing where registered sex offenders may live. In 2009, these municipal laws were all effectively voided by a decision of the New Jersey Supreme Court. In *G.H. v. Township of Galloway*,[53] that court examined two municipal ordinances, both of which prohibited registered sex offenders from residing within 2,500 feet of a school, park, playground or day care center. The effect of these ordinances was that in one of the towns convicted sex offenders were precluded from residing in virtually the entire township, while the other's ordinance barred such offenders from living in roughly two thirds of the township. In striking down these ordinances, the state Supreme Court adopted the reasoning of a lower appeals court that had refused to consider whether the ordinances were constitutional and determined that they were unlawful because they were pre-empted by the state legislature's decision not to impose such residency restrictions on sex offenders at the statewide level. New Jersey legislators responded by introducing a statewide bill that would bar sex offenders from living within 2,000 feet of schools, parks, playgrounds, or day care centers.[54]

Even in states that have placed statewide residency restrictions on registered sex offenders, those laws have not stopped some municipalities from enacting more stringent restrictions. For example, in Florida, which does have a statewide ban on registered sex offenders living within 1,000 feet of schools, day care centers, parks, and other places that attract children, more than 60 municipalities have their own residency restriction ordinances, which include parks, playgrounds, churches, and libraries, among other places where minors might be expected to congregate. In Miami and Dade County, for example, sex offenders are required by local ordinance to live no less than 2,500 feet from any school, park, day care center, or playground, a ban that has effectively eliminated any eligible housing for sex offenders. The ordinance is being challenged in court but meanwhile has led to a "shantytown" of shacks and tents housing 70 or more sex offenders beneath the Julia Tuttle Causeway.[55]

In Georgia, which prohibits sex offenders from living within 1,000 feet of any school, at least one municipality has banned sex offenders from residing within 2,500 feet of a school.[56] In Texas, where state law directs the Parole Board to decide how close a sex offender can live or even go near to a "child safety zone," several municipalities have enacted laws requiring buffer zones of between 1,000 and 2,000 feet and at least one has criminalized knowingly renting a sex offender a place to live within a restricted zone.[57] And, in California, parts of Sacramento County have restricted registered sex offenders from being within 300 feet of libraries.[58]

Also, even where sex offenders' living arrangements are restricted by public law, they are in some instances being further restricted by private legal agreements. For example, some developers in Texas and Kansas have begun offering new homes in "sex offender-free housing developments."[59] In at least one Texas development, would-be homeowners must first pass a criminal background check and then be rescreened every 90 days.[60] By agreement, a person convicted of a sex crime while living in the development must pay the subdivision $1,500 a day until he or she moves away.[61]

Along with residency restrictions, some states and municipalities have also enacted employment restrictions, under which registered sex offenders are not allowed to work at and/or within a certain physical proximity to a school, day care center, park, or other place where children might be expected to congregate.[62] These laws are generally in addition to others that prohibit convicted sex offenders from being employed in teaching, child care, or other occupations that serve children. Such laws are not limited by the nature of the work or limited to work done at a school, day care center, park, or other place where children may congregate. Thus, for instance, a taxi driver would not be allowed to operate his cab even close to one of these places, a salesperson could not make a call upon a business within the prohibited zone, and a deliveryman could not deliver a package in such an area.

At least nine states have such laws.[63] For example, in Alabama, a convicted sex offender may not work within 2,000 feet of a school or child care center, while a sex offender convicted of a crime against a child is also prohibited from working within 500 feet of a park, athletic field, or any business primarily engaged in educating, entertaining, or caring for minors. These restrictions apply for the natural life of the offender. A handful of municipalities have also enacted ordinances geographically restricting the employment of registered sex offenders. For example, in Ohio, a state that imposes residency restrictions on registered sex offenders (1,000 feet from a school, child care center, or other place children congregate) but does not restrict the workplaces of such offenders, one town, Upper Arlington, recently barred all sex offenders from living or working within 1,000 feet of a school, park, pool, library, or day care center.[64] According to media reports, some Upper Arlington residents are pushing for an ordinance "barring sex offenders from even hanging out within 1,000 feet of those places."[65]

In 2008, California voters overwhelmingly approved a public ballot initiative, Proposition 83. Proposition 83 made a number of changes to the state's sex offender laws, including barring all registered sex offenders from living within 2,000 foot of a school or park and requiring that all paroled felony sex offenders wear a global positioning satellite (GPS) tracking device (a so-called ankle bracelet) for the rest of their lives.[66] With passage of Proposition 83, California became one of at least 24 states that require GPS monitoring of paroled sex offenders.[67]

To date the U.S. Supreme Court has declined to hear any challenges to the constitutionality of the residency and work restrictions placed on sex offenders under statutes and ordinances such as those just described. Numerous lower courts, however, have reviewed such challenges and have found these laws constitutional. For example, the U.S. Court of Appeals for the Eighth Circuit has upheld the constitutionality of two of these laws, one from Iowa and the other from Arkansas.

In *Doe v. Miller*, a class of sex offenders whose areas of residency were limited by Iowa's law brought suit in U.S. District Court seeking to have the statute declared unconstitutional.[68] A number of the plaintiffs and members of their families told the trial court how the state law's 2,000-foot buffer zone around schools and child care facilities negatively affected their ability to find housing:

> Plaintiffs testified that in many cases they had a difficult time
> obtaining housing that was not within 2000 feet of a school or child
> care center. John Doe VII testified that he investigated 40 residences,
> but was unable to find any housing that would not place him in
> violation of [the residency restriction] . . . The mother of John Doe
> IV made efforts to help her son find housing, and she testified
> that she was able to find two potential residences for her son, but
> neither residence had any vacant units. John Doe VI was renting an
> apartment in compliance with [the residency restriction], but had to
> move out when the landlord decided that he did not want to rent to
> a sex offender. Similarly, John Does VIII and XI each found at least

one possible compliant apartment, but their applications were denied because of their criminal records.[69]

In testimony that the trial court found "exceedingly compelling and informative":

> John Doe XIV's wife [testified that before the residency restriction] went into effect, [she] had a good job in the city where she grew up and where her family lived. She lived with her husband and their young daughter, and they had recently purchased their first home. After July 1, 2002, her life was thrust into a depressing turmoil when she learned that her husband would be arrested if he continued to live in the house they had just bought. After a frustrating search, she and her family moved away from her lifelong home to live forty-five miles away in the country. Where she used to do her part to support the family with one job, she now works two and still has difficulties making ends meet. Because there are no child care facilities nearby, she drives an extra thirty miles every day to take her two children to daycare so that she can work two jobs that pay less together than the job she was forced to leave. She testified that she has suffered nervous breakdowns since moving and is often depressed. On many nights, her four-year-old daughter cries and asks when they will be able to go home. Yet she has remained by her husband's side and has honored her marital vows, even though doing so has caused extreme hardship. And she endures this all because three years before she even met him, her then nineteen-year-old husband exposed himself at a party where a thirteen-year-old girl happened to be present.[70]

The court also heard testimony from two psychologists, one testifying for the state and the other for the plaintiffs, as well as from a parole and probation officer with experience treating sex offenders.

The District Court held that the Iowa statute was unconstitutional and enjoined the state from enforcing it. As the court reasoned, in part:

> Both sides agree that the State has a compelling interest in protecting children from sex offenders. The State argues that the law is narrowly tailored to meet this end because the residency restriction creates a buffer zone around schools and child care facilities, thereby reducing the "precursor events" leading to re-offense and eliminating nearby access to potential victims. The Court disagrees.

While restricting the access sex offenders have to children is likely to reduce the opportunity for re-offense, the State has offered no evidence demonstrating that a two thousand foot "buffer zone" around schools and child care facilities actually protects children. Rather, the State's expert witness, Dr. McEchron, testified that the scheme could actually prove detrimental to a sex offender's treatment because the offender may become depressed after deciding that society has given him no chance to rehabilitate. Both Drs. [Luis] Rosell [the plaintiff's expert psychologist] and McEchron, and Dudley Allison testified that they knew of no specific distance that would protect children. Dr. Rosell further explained that the residency restriction would not stop a determined offender from finding another victim.

Defendants produced no research showing the effect a proximity restriction has on sex offender recidivism rates. In the large meta-analyses, a number of variables are considered when reviewing recidivism, but proximity is not one of them. The one study that has reviewed the effect of restricting sex offenders from residing within a certain distance from locations frequented by children reported its findings unequivocally: "there is no evidence . . . that residential proximity to schools or parks affects re-offense." With nothing to suggest that restricting a sex offender from living within two thousand feet of a school or child care facility would actually protect children, the Court finds that [the residency restriction] is not narrowly tailored to achieve a compelling State interest.

The Act also fails to apply the least restrictive means necessary to achieve its goal. As noted, the purpose of [the residency restriction] is to protect children, yet the Act applies to all relevant sex offenders without consideration of whether the individual is actually a danger to the public. Risk assessments produced by the Iowa Department of Corrections show that not all sex offenders are made alike. Defendants' witness Dudley Allison testified that he has no problem with certain offenders living near schools or child care facilities because he does not find those individuals a danger to re-offend in such a situation. With the enormous restriction placed on the offender, the State cannot justify applying the scheme to all Plaintiffs regardless of whether they pose a danger to the community.

The Court finds that [the residency restrictions] cannot survive strict scrutiny. There is no close fit between the restriction and the intended purpose of protecting children. The Act also goes too far in its attempt to meet a compelling State concern by restricting all offenders without regard to the actual danger to the community. The Court, therefore, holds that [the Act] unconstitutionally infringes on Plaintiffs' substantive rights under the Due Process Clause of the Fourteenth Amendment.[71]

The state appealed the District Court's decision, that decision was unanimously reversed by the Court of Appeals for the Eighth Circuit, and the U.S. Supreme Court refused further review. The Court of Appeals concluded that no fundamental right was affected by the residency restrictions, so there was no need for the court to apply strict scrutiny in assessing the constitutionality of the law. Instead, the court held that the law would be sustained if there was a rational basis for it. As the Court explained:

We do not believe that the residency restriction . . . implicates any fundamental right of the Does that would trigger strict scrutiny of the statute. . . [T]he Does' characterization of a fundamental right to "personal choice regarding the family" is so general that it would trigger strict scrutiny of innumerable laws and ordinances that influence "personal choices" made by families on a daily basis . . .

Unlike the precedents cited by the Does, the Iowa statute does not operate directly on the family relationship. Although the law restricts where a residence may be located, nothing in the statute limits who may live with the Does in their residences. . .

While there was evidence that one adult sex offender in Iowa would not reside with his parents as a result of the residency restriction, that another sex offender and his wife moved 45 miles away from their preferred location due to the statute, and that a third sex offender could not reside with his adult child in a restricted zone, the statute does not directly regulate the family relationship or prevent any family member from residing with a sex offender in a residence that is consistent with the statute. We therefore hold that [the residency restriction] does not infringe upon a constitutional liberty interest relating to matters of marriage and family in a fashion that requires heightened scrutiny . . .

The Does also urge that we recognize a fundamental right "to live where you want" . . . Some thirty years ago, our court said "we cannot agree that the right to choose one's place of residence is necessarily a fundamental right," and we see no basis to conclude that the contention has gained strength in the intervening years. . .

Because [the residency restriction] does not implicate a constitutional liberty interest that has been elevated to the status of "fundamental right," we review the statute to determine whether it meets the standard of "rationally advancing some legitimate governmental purpose." The Does acknowledge that the statute was designed to promote the safety of children, and they concede that this is a legitimate state interest. They also allow that perhaps "certain identifiable sex offenders should not live right across the street from a school or perhaps anywhere else where there are children." The Does contend, however, that the statute is irrational because there is no scientific study that supports the legislature's conclusion that excluding sex offenders from residing within 2000 feet of a school or child care facility is likely to enhance the safety of children.

We reject this contention because we think it understates the authority of a state legislature to make judgments about the best means to protect the health and welfare of its citizens in an area where precise statistical data is unavailable and human behavior is necessarily unpredictable...

The record does not support a conclusion that the Iowa General Assembly and the Governor acted based merely on negative attitudes toward, fear of, or a bare desire to harm a politically unpopular group. Sex offenders have a high rate of recidivism, and the parties presented expert testimony that reducing opportunity and temptation is important to minimizing the risk of reoffense...[72]

A year later, the same court reviewed a challenge to the constitutionality of the Arkansas residency restriction statute. *Weems v. Little Rock Police Department* was brought by two level-three sex offenders.[73] Under the Arkansas statute, sex offenders designated by the state screening process as level three ("high risk") or level four ("sexual predator") are not permitted to reside within 2,000 feet of the property on which any public or private elementary or secondary school or day care facility is located unless the offender owned and occupied the residence prior to the opening of the school or day care center or prior to the effective date of the law. The Arkansas Registration Act for sex offenders defines "residency" to include "place of employment, training, or education."[74]

Donald Weems had been found guilty of indecent exposure in 2000 and served a 1-year prison sentence. Upon release he was classified as a level-three offender and moved back to Little Rock, where he was informed that he was in violation of the 2,000-foot rule and ordered to relocate. His co-plaintiff, Michael Briggs, was convicted of first-degree rape in 1986 and served 15 years in prison. Also classified as a level-three offender, he moved into his mother's home when he was released from prison. Three years later he was informed that living in his mother's home was a violation of the residency restriction law and he, too, was directed to relocate.

The U.S. District Court dismissed the lawsuit for failure to state a claim, rejecting plaintiffs' arguments that the restriction requirements were constitutionally invalid because they did not have rights to counsel and to confront witnesses in the risk assessment process, that the Registration Act was unconstitutionally vague, that the residency restriction violated the equal protection rights of non-property-owning level-three and -four sex offenders, that the residency restriction violated sex offenders' substantive due process rights, and that the residency restriction violated the ex post facto clause.[75]

The Eighth Circuit Court of Appeals, relying in part on its earlier decision in *Doe v. Miller,* affirmed the District Court's dismissal:

> Our holding in *Miller* controls the level of scrutiny applicable to
> the Arkansas residency restriction. Because the residency
> restriction does not infringe upon a "fundamental right," we
> consider only whether the statute rationally advances some
> legitimate government purpose. The Arkansas legislature
> undoubtedly has a legitimate interest in protecting children from
> the most dangerous sex offenders, and we believe that a residency
> restriction designed to reduce proximity between the most
> dangerous offenders and locations frequented by children is within
> the range of rational policy options available to a state legislature
> charged with protecting the health and welfare of its citizens.[76]

As for the plaintiffs' claims that the Arkansas registration statute defines "residency" to include "place of employment, training, or education," the Court felt no need to address its constitutionality:

> The [law] does not define the term "reside," and we do not assume
> that the General Assembly and the Governor necessarily intended to
> apply the broad definition of "residency" when crafting a restriction
> on where a sex offender may "reside" . . . We thus employ the
> normal rule that terms are given "their ordinary and usually
> accepted meaning," and we construe "reside" to mean "to dwell
> permanently or continuously." On this understanding, the residency
> restriction in Arkansas is no broader than the restriction at issue in

Miller, and for the same reasons discussed there, we conclude that the Arkansas law does not infringe on a constitutional right . . . [77]

The U.S. Supreme Court refused to hear an appeal of the Eighth Circuit's decision upholding the Arkansas statute. While at least one federal court has found a state residency requirement for registered sex offenders to violate the ex post facto clause of the U.S. Constitution,[78] most federal courts that have been confronted with constitutional challenges to state residence and/or employment restrictions for these offenders have found the laws in question to be constitutional.

"Common Sense" Versus Data

> Common sense appears to be only another name for the thoughtlessness of the unthinking. It is made of the prejudices of childhood, the idiosyncrasies of individual character and the opinion of the newspapers.
>
> W. Somerset Maugham (1949)[79]

It is clear from their legislative histories and the court decisions affirming their constitutionality that sex offender registration and notification laws and their accompanying restrictions on residency and employment were intended to enhance public safety by reducing the likelihood that a previously convicted sex offender will re-offend. While the courts have acknowledged the heavy burden these laws place on convicted offenders who already have been appropriately punished for their crimes, they have almost unanimously upheld these laws in large measure because they believe that reducing sex offense recidivism is a salutary goal and that "common sense" dictates that these laws are helping, or at least will help, achieve that goal. For example, as the New Jersey Supreme Court said in upholding the original Megan's Law, if people in a community are made aware of the sex offenders among them, they can take "common-sense steps" to protect themselves and their children.[80] And, as the U.S. Court of Appeals for the Eighth Circuit concluded in upholding Iowa's residency restriction law: "One expert in the district court opined that it is just 'common sense' that limiting the frequency of contact between sex offenders and areas where children are located is likely to reduce the risk of an offense. The policymakers of Iowa are entitled to employ such 'common sense'..."[81]

It is hard to argue with "common sense," but whether these laws have the effect (or even the potential) the legislatures and courts believe or hope they do is, of course, an empirical question. To put that question most bluntly: Do these registration, notification, and residency/employment laws reduce recidivism among previously convicted sex offenders?

To date no research has directly answered that question, but a number of studies, using various methods, have at least provided data that may be more useful than mere reliance upon "common sense."

Over the past two decades, at least 18 published and unpublished studies have attempted to assess the effectiveness of sex offender registration and notification laws in reducing recidivism among convicted sex offenders (specific deterrence) or the commission of sex offenses more generally (general deterrence). In 2009, a team of researchers at the Washington State Institute for Public Policy conducted a meta-analysis of some of these studies with the goal of answering the question: "Does sex offender registration and notification affect measured crime outcomes?"[82] After examining the methodologies and results of 18 studies, the Washington team "located nine evaluations of sex offender registration/notification laws with sufficiently rigorous research to be included in [their] analysis."[83] Data used in these studies were gathered from 16 states: California, Delaware, Florida, Illinois, Maryland, Michigan, Minnesota, New Jersey, New York, North Carolina, Ohio, Oregon, South Carolina, Texas, Virginia, and Washington.

The two studies directed at the general deterrence effect of registration and notification laws were insufficient for a meta-analysis but provided interesting results. The first, reported by Prescott and Rockoff in 2008, used data from the National Incident Based Reporting System (NIBRS),[84] "an incident-based reporting system for crimes known to the police. For each crime incident coming to the attention of law enforcement, a variety of data are collected about the incident. These data include the nature and types of specific offenses in the incident, characteristics of the victim(s) and offender(s), types and value of property stolen and recovered, and characteristics of persons arrested in connection with a crime incident."[85] Prescott and Rockoff examined the effects of sex offender registration and notification laws in 15 states and were the first and only researchers to date to separately examine the effects of registration and notification. Their data suggest that while the average registration law results in a statistically significant 10 percent reduction in overall sex offense rates, that positive effect is more than overcome by the negative effects of notification laws. As they explain:

> We find evidence that registration reduces the frequency of sex
> offenses by providing law enforcement with information on local
> sex offenders. . . We also find evidence that community notification

deters crime, but in a way unanticipated by legislators. Our results correspond with a model in which community notification deters first-time sex offenses, but increases recidivism by registered offenders due to a change in the relative utility of legal and illegal behavior. This finding is consistent with work by criminologists suggesting that notification may increase recidivism by imposing social and financial costs on registered sex offenders and making non-criminal activity relatively less attractive. We regard this latter finding as potentially important, given that the purpose of community notification is to reduce recidivism.[86]

The second study related to general deterrence (and not included in the Washington meta-analysis) was conducted by Shao and Li and reported in 2006.[87] Shao and Li used FBI Uniform Crime Reports data from all states from 1970 to 2002 to explore the effect of registration laws on reported rapes.[87] They found a statistically significant 2 percent reduction in reported rapes associated with sex offender registration laws.

Reviewing these two studies before describing the results of their broader meta-analysis of studies dealing with specific deterrence, the Washington researchers suggested that while these studies do provide "some indication" that sex offender registration laws may lower the rates of certain sex crimes, efforts to generalize should be undertaken with caution, given the extremely limited number of studies.[88]

The Washington meta-analysis of seven studies dealing with the possible deterrent effects of sex offender registration and notification laws provides a more robust finding. The individual results of these studies showed no clear pattern. One study found increased rates of recidivism, two found decreases in recidivism, and four found no statistically significant differences in recidivism.

For example, in 2008, Agan reported the results of a study of the impact of registration/notification laws in 14 states (California, Delaware, Florida, Illinois, Maryland, Michigan, Minnesota, New Jersey, New York, North Carolina, Ohio, Oregon, Texas, and Virginia).[89] Agan compared recidivism rates of sex offenders in each of two groups—registered and unregistered— using three definitions of recidivism: subsequent arrest for rape, subsequent arrest for a sex offense other than rape, and subsequent conviction for a sex offense. Multivariate regression analysis was used to control for differences between the two groups and for differences across states. Differences between those who were registered and those who were not were small and not statistically significant across the three definitions of recidivism, but did show that "offenders who had to register were more likely to be arrested for an offense other than a sex offense than those who did not."[90]

In 2009, Freeman reported the results of a New York study that compared the recidivism of registered sex offenders who were subject to community notification with that of similar offenders who were released into the community during the same time period, but were not (as the result of a court injunction) subject to notification laws because their offenses were committed before enactment of the state's notification law.[91] Utilizing a 5-year survival analysis, and examining re-arrests for both nonsexual offenses and "registerable sexual offenses... including but not limited to rape, incest, sodomy, sexual misconduct, sexual abuse, and promoting sexual performance by a child," Freeman found that offenders who were subject to community notification offended much more quickly than did those offenders who were not subject to such notification requirements.[92] With regard to nonsexual offenses, Freeman found that after 1 year, 13.4 percent of those in the notification group and 10.7 percent of those in the non-notification group had re-offended. After 3 years, the rate of nonsexual re-offending was 28.8 percent and 26.0 percent for the two groups respectively. After 5 years, the rate of nonsexual re-offending was 36.6 percent and 36.1 percent for the two groups respectively. The mean number of years to re-offense for nonsexual crimes was 1.7 for the notification group and 3.1 for the non-notification group. As regards "registerable sexual offenses," Freeman found that after 1 year, 1.6 percent of those in the notification group and 1.1 percent of those in the non-notification group had re-offended. After 3 years, the rate of sexual re-offending was 3.8 percent and 2.7 percent for the two groups respectively. After 5 years, the rate of sexual re-offending was 5.2 percent and 4.4 percent for the two groups respectively. The mean number of years to re-offense for "registerable" sex crimes was 2.3 for the notification group and 4.4 for the non-notification group.

Summing up these results, Freeman reported: "[T]he study proposed the general question of whether there was a relationship between community notification and sex offenders' nonsexual and sexual rearrests. Results of the study indicate that those sex offenders who are subject to community notification requirements are rearrested twice as quickly for subsequent sexual offenses and 47% more quickly for nonsexual offenses than sex offenders who are not subject to the same notification requirements. These results remain even after controlling for several risk factors, as well as time at risk in the community."[93]

At the other end of the spectrum, a study in Washington reported by Barnoski in 2005 compared the recidivism of sex offenders released from prison before and after passage of the state's registration/notification law and used multivariate regression analysis to control for differences between the groups.[94] Utilizing a 5-year follow-up, Barnoski looked at reconvictions for felonies, violent felonies, and sex offenses. He found a sharp and statistically significant decrease in felony sex convictions and violent felony convictions for offenders subject to the state's registration and notification laws. Barnoski notes but appropriately qualifies these results: "Violent and sexual felony recidivism by sex offenders in Washington has decreased since passage of the 1997 statute. The causal link to notification laws is not proven by this research. Other conditions may be contributing to this reduction, such as the national and state drop in crime rates and the state's increased incarceration (incapacitation) of sex offenders. However, the drop in recidivism rates by sex offenders is clear, and the influence of community notification laws cannot be ruled out."[95]

When the data from these three studies (Agan, Freeman, and Barnowski) were combined with those gathered in four other studies and subjected to a meta-analysis by the Washington research team in 2009, the results were clear: "For this group of studies, we performed a meta-analysis and found no statistically significant difference in recidivism rates for either sex offenses or total offenses."[96]

It should also be noted that even those studies that were not included in the Washington meta-analysis because they lacked sufficient methodological rigor yielded results that were predominantly consistent with the finding of the meta-analysis.

For example, in a study of the original Megan's Law in New Jersey reported by Zgoba, Witt, Dalessandro, and Veysey in December 2008, researchers compared the re-arrest rates of registered sex offenders with those of sex offenders not required to register prior to implementation of Megan's Law.[97] In this study, conducted under the auspices of the Research & Evaluation Unit of the Office of Policy and Planning in the New Jersey Department of Corrections and sponsored by the National Institute of Justice, researchers utilized a 6-year follow-up and conducted a time-series analysis. This study was excluded from the Washington meta-analysis because offenders in the registration group had fewer prior sex offenses than those in the non-registration group and the research team did not use multivariate analysis to control for between-group differences. Still, the study's results and conclusions are noteworthy if not striking:

Megan's Law has no effect on community tenure (i.e., time to first re-arrest).

Megan's Law showed no demonstrable effect in reducing sexual re-offenses.

Megan's Law has no effect on the type of sexual re-offense or first time sexual offense (still largely child molestation/incest).

Megan's Law has no effect on reducing the number of victims involved in sexual offenses.

Sentences received prior to Megan's Law were nearly twice as long as those received after Megan's Law was passed, but time served was approximately the same.

Significantly fewer sexual offenders have been paroled after the implementation of Megan's Law than before (this is largely due to changes in sentencing).

Costs associated with the initial implementation as well as ongoing expenditures continue to grow over time. Start-up costs totaled $555,565 and current costs (in 2007) totaled approximately 3.9 million dollars for the responding counties.

Given the lack of demonstrated effect of Megan's Law on sexual offenses, the growing costs may not be justifiable.[98]

In 2006, Yessine and Bonta reported the results of their study of Canada's National Flagging System, a program similar to sex offender registration in the United States.[99] While these researchers did not include an appropriate comparison group, leading the Washington team to exclude this study from their meta-analysis, Yessine and Bonta did compare (among other things) the recidivism rate of "flagged" offenders with that of offenders in general. They reported that "Using a comparable methodology, the overall rate of recidivism of the flagged offenders was similar to the one reported among the general federal male offender population [but] the new offences committed by the flagged offenders were more serious."[100] They also reported that after a 2-year follow-up, "base rates for both violent and sexual reconvictions were much higher among the [flagged offenders] (22.2% and 7.6%) than among typical federal male offenders (13% and less than 2%).[101] In summarizing these comparisons, Yessine and Bonta also reported that "After five years the reconviction rate for sexual crimes among the flagged offenders was 13.3 percent, which is comparable to the 14 percent sexual offence recidivism rate typically reported among sexual offenders."[102]

In attempting to explain these disappointing findings, Yessine and Bonta wrote, "Finally, it is worth mentioning that this study was conducted over the first four years of implementation of the National Flagging System, when the system was getting off the ground and operational steps were being developed. Had the study been conducted in the most recent years, better results might have been obtained."[103]

In a study reported in 2000, Adkins, Huff, and Stageberg, researchers with the Iowa Department of Human Rights Division of Criminal and Juvenile Justice Planning and Statistical Analysis Center, compared the recidivism of two groups of sex offenders in Iowa: a "registry" sample of 233 individuals who were placed on the state's Sex Offender Registry in its first year and a "pre-registry" sample of 201 sex offenders who would have been required to register had the registration law been in effect at the time of their convictions.[104] While the "registry" group appears to have been less risky than the "pre-registry" group (based upon criminal history and risk assessment data), thus leading to exclusion of this research from the Washington meta-analysis, the study's results are consistent with other studies. Using an average follow-up period of 4.3 years, these researchers found that the recidivism rate was some-what lower for those in the "registry" group but that there were no statistically significant differences in recidivism between the two groups.

In summarizing these findings, Adkins et al. concluded: "The results found in this study suggest that the registry had mixed effects on recidivism, but the findings were not statistically significant and could have occurred by chance."[105]

In 2008, Sandler, Freeman, and Socia reported on their evaluation of New York State's sex offender registration act (SORA).[106] These researchers used 252 months of arrest data and univariate time-series analyses to answer "the general question of whether there are differences in sexual offense arrest rates before and after the enactment of SORA, as well as the two specific questions of: (a) whether registration and notification laws are decreasing re-arrest rates for convicted sex offenders, or (b) whether registration and notification laws are deterring nonregistered offenders from committing registerable sexual offenses."[107] The results: "According to the analyses, all three of these questions are answered negatively. That is, results of the analyses indicate that the 1996 enactment of SORA (and thus the beginning of the registry) had no significant impact on rates of total sexual offending, rape, or child molestation, whether viewed as a whole or in terms of offenses committed by first-time sex offenders or those committed by previously convicted sex offenders (i.e., repeat offenders)."[108] As Sandler et al. concluded, "[These] results provide no support for the effectiveness of registration and commu-nity notification laws in reducing sexual offending by: (a) rapists, (b) child molesters, (c) sexual recidivists, or (d) first-time sex offenders. Analyses also showed that over 95% of all sexual offense arrests were committed by first-time sex offenders, casting doubt on the ability of laws that target repeat offenders to meaningfully reduce sexual offending."[109]

Other research has examined whether residency restrictions placed upon sex offenders reduce recidivism by such offenders. For example, in a 2004 study for the Judiciary Committees of both houses of the Colorado legislature, conducted by the state's Division of Criminal Justice Sex Offender Management Board, government researchers attempted to answer this question: "Do the location of sex offender residences, specifically in proximity to schools and childcare centers, have an impact on community safety?"[110] The Colorado researchers reviewed state probation files on "both a random sample of sex offenders under probation supervision in the Denver metropolitan area and an all-inclusive sample of sex offenders under probation supervision in the Denver metropolitan area living in a Shared Living Arrangement (n = 130 for the combined sample)."[111] Most of the offenders in the sample (54 percent) had been assessed as "high risk" by the Probation Department; 34 percent were considered to present a medium risk; and 9 percent were seen as being at low risk for re-offense. Maximum-risk offenders had two face-to-face contacts with probation officers per month and regular home visits. Medium-risk offenders had one face-to-face contact a month and one verification of residence every 60 days. Minimum-risk offenders received one face-to-face contact every 60 days and no verifications of residency.

All offenders in the sample were subjected to a 15-month follow-up of recidivism. During the follow-up period a total of 15 new sexual offenses were known to have been committed by 13 of the 130 offenders in the sample. Not a single one of these offenses involved direct contact with the victim; all were classified as "'hands off' offenses—peeping, voyeurism, or exposure."[112] Additionally, 52 nonsexual criminal violations were reported for the entire sample.

The Colorado researchers were unable to make exact measurements of the proximity of the offenders' residences to schools and child care centers but did utilize mapping software to plot the proximity of schools and child care facilities to the residences of offenders who had had at least one criminal offense during the 15-month follow-up. According to the researchers, "These maps illustrated that these offenders seemed to be randomly located, and were, in fact, not usually within 1000 feet of a school or childcare center. In addition, the maps illustrated... that in a densely populated area it is nearly impossible for anyone to find a residence that is not relatively close to a school or childcare center."[113]

Among the conclusions the Colorado research team reported to the state legislature was: "Placing restrictions on the location of correctionally supervised sex offender residences may not deter the sex offender from re-offending and should not be considered as a method to control sexual offending recidivism."[114]

More recently, in 2008, Duwe, Donnay, and Tewksbury analyzed the offenses committed between 1990 and 2002 by 224 sex offenders released from prison in Minnesota, none of whom were subject to a residency restriction law.[115] These offenders were drawn from a larger class of sex offenders (N = 3,166) who were released from the state's eight prisons during that time period. Of that number, 374 were rearrested for sex crimes between 1990 and 2005. Among that cohort, 70 were not convicted and 80 were convicted but not reincarcerated, thus leaving the 224 offenders who were studied. As the authors suggest, this sample of 224 offenders represents what are likely the most serious cases of sexual recidivism that occurred in Minnesota between 1990 and 2005.

Upon examination of numerous state records and reports regarding these 224 offenders and their crimes, Duwe et al. found that only 21 percent victimized someone they did not know; 28 percent of these "stranger-on-stranger" offenses were committed in the offender's own residence; and 49 percent of "stranger-on-stranger" offenses were committed more than a mile from the offender's residence. These researchers also found that only 35 percent of the offenders "directly established contact with the victim"—for instance, "by approaching them on the street, meeting them in a bar, or breaking into the victim's home."[116] Among the remaining 65 percent of offenses, "the offenders were biologically related to their victims (14%), or they gained access to their victims through a form of collateral contact such as a girlfriend, wife, coworker, friend, or acquaintance (51%)."[117] Looking solely at the 61 "direct contact" cases for which address information was available, the researchers found that 31 offenses occurred more than a mile from the offender's residence and 30 took place less than a mile from the offender's home. Two of those 30 offenses occurred in a correctional facility or halfway house where residency restrictions would not apply. Of the remaining 28 offenses, "21 would qualify for less than a 2,500-foot (less than 0.5 miles) zone, whereas this number would drop to 16 for a 1,000-foot (less than 0.2 miles) zone."[118] Finally, among the entire cohort of 224 cases, there were only 3 "in which the offender established contact with the victim at a possible prohibited area where children are known to be present."[119] In two offenses, initial contact was made in a park; the other involved an initial contact made at a school. As Duwe et al. observe, however, in two of these cases the offender lived more than 10 miles away from the initial contact location; in the other case, the victim was an adult. In their words: "Therefore, none of the 224 incidents of sex offender recidivism fit the criteria of a known offender making contact with a child victim at a location within any of the distances typically covered by residential restriction laws."[120]

Summarizing and discussing the implications of these data, Duwe et al. concluded that:

> Residency restriction laws would likely offer, at best, a marginal impact on the incidence of sexual recidivism. . . This is not to say that housing restrictions would never prevent a sex offender from reoffending sexually. Based on the results presented here, however, the chances that it would have a deterrent effect are slim. Indeed, during the past 16 years, not one sex offender released from a MCF has been reincarcerated for a sex offense in which he made contact with a juvenile victim at or near a school, park, or daycare center close to his home. In short, it is unlikely that residency restrictions would have a deterrent effect because the types of offenses that such laws are designed to prevent are exceptionally rare and, in the case of Minnesota, virtually nonexistent in the past 16 years.[121]

Finally, some researchers have examined what might be called the unintended consequences of sex offender registration and notification laws, the sorts of burdens addressed by Justice Thomas in his concurring opinion in *Smith v. Doe*.

For example, Levenson and Cotter reported in 2005 on an "exploratory study" of a non-random sample of 135 sex offenders from two outpatient sex offender counseling centers in Fort Lauderdale, Florida.[122] All subjects in this study were on probation for sex offenses, all were in sex offender treatment, and all volunteered to complete a survey developed by Levenson and Cotter. Ninety-seven percent of these subjects identified themselves as child molesters.

At the time of this study, Florida prohibited sex offenders from living within 1,000 feet of a school, park, playground, day care center, or other place where children regularly congregate. In response to questions about the effects of these residency restrictions, 22 percent of the offenders reported having had to move out of a home they owned; 28 percent said they had to move from an apartment they had rented; 25 percent indicated that they had been unable to return to their homes when released from prison; 44 percent stated that they were unable to live with supportive family members; 57 percent reported having trouble finding housing; 48 percent said they had suffered financially; and 60 percent indicated that they had suffered emotionally. A majority of these offenders reported that the residency restrictions would have no impact on their future offending behavior. Many reported feeling that if they wanted to re-offend, the residency restriction would not stop them; many also reported that they "have always been careful not to reoffend in close proximity to their homes, so geographical restrictions provided little deterrence."[123]

The effects of sex offender residency restrictions have been examined by a number of other recent studies as well. For example, in a study reported in 2009, Chajewski and Mercado tried to determine the effects that various sex offender residency restrictions (1,000 feet vs. 2,500 feet from schools) would have in three New Jersey settings: a rural town, a suburban county, and a city.[124] Using the addresses of registered sex offenders and a geographical information system (GIS), they found that if a 1,000-foot residency restriction were enacted in a rural town with a population of approximately 17,402, 31.25 percent of the sex offenders living there would have to relocate, and that a 2,500-foot residency restriction would require all sex offenders to move out of the town. They also found that in a large, mostly suburban county with a population of approximately 982,561, a 1,000-foot residency restriction would require 37.50 percent of the county's registered sex offenders to find alternative housing, and that a 2,500-foot restriction would require 91.07% of registered sex offenders to relocate. Finally, these researchers found that enactment of a 1,000-foot restriction in a city with a population of about 273,546 would put almost two thirds (64.80 percent) of registered sex offenders in violation, and that with a 2,500-foot restriction almost all (98.47 percent) such offenders would be in violation of the residency restriction.

Significantly, Chajewski and Mercado also found that "nearly all sex offenders and community members lived within 2,500 feet of the schools, suggesting that these are not deterministic choices made uniquely by sex offenders to live in these locations, but rather are dependent upon urban planning."[125] They cautioned that their study "examined the distances around registered schools and daycare centers with school components only, and did not consider parks, playgrounds, shopping centers, bus stops, or other areas where children gather that have been included in some statutes and local ordinances."[126] As a result, they observed that "this analysis should be considered exceptionally conservative in that these findings would likely be amplified were the analyses to have included these additional areas."[127]

Earlier, in a 2006 report, Zandbergen and Hart described using GIS methodology to quantify the impact of residency restrictions on registered sex offenders in Orange County, Florida.[128] These researchers found that housing options for registered sex offenders, who were prohibited from living within 1,000 feet of places where children congregate (schools, parks, day care sites, parks, and bus stops), "were limited to only 5 percent of potentially available parcels... mostly in low-density rural areas."[129] They also found that "[i]ncreasing the buffer zone from 1,000 to 2,500 feet had only a minor impact on housing options."[130] Zandbergen and Hart concluded that "These findings support the argument that residency restrictions for sex offenders contribute significantly to their social and economic isolation [and to the risk of] larger numbers of sex offenders being homeless and transient."[131]

The Costs Of "Common Sense"

America's sex offender registration, notification, and restriction mandates have been established and maintained at an extremely high personal and economic cost.

For the registered sex offender, the costs of registration and notification are both direct and indirect. As Justice David Souter wrote, though concurring with the Supreme Court's judgment in *Smith v. Doe* upholding the constitutionality of Alaska's registration and notification act:

> Widespread dissemination of offenders' names, photographs, addresses, and criminal history serves not only to inform the public but also to humiliate and ostracize the convicts. It thus bears some resemblance to shaming punishments that were used earlier in our history to disable offenders from living normally in the community. While the [majority] accepts the State's explanation that the Act simply makes public information available in a new way, the scheme does much more. Its point, after all, is to send a message that probably would not otherwise be heard, by selecting some conviction information out of its corpus of penal records and broadcasting it with a warning. Selection makes a statement, one that affects common reputation and sometimes carries harsher consequences, such as exclusion from jobs or housing, harassment, and physical harm.[132]

And as one federal appeals court found, in examining whether New Jersey's Megan's Law was punitive:

> The direct effects of Megan's Law clearly do not rise to the level of extremely onerous burdens that sting so severely as to compel a conclusion of punishment. All Megan's Law mandates is registration and notification. Under Megan's Law, New Jersey has not deprived appellants of their freedom or their citizenship. The state has imposed no restrictions on a registrant's ability to live

and work in a community, to move from place to place, to obtain a professional license or to secure governmental benefits.

What concerns registrants, however, are the indirect effects: Actions that members of the community may take as a result of learning of the registrant's past, his potential danger, and his presence in the community. People interact with others based on the information they have about them. Knowing that someone is a convicted sex offender and has been evaluated as a continuing risk is likely to affect how most people treat that person.

There can be no doubt that the indirect effects of Tier 2 and Tier 3 notification on the registrants involved and their families are harsh. The record documents that registrants and their families have experienced profound humiliation and isolation as a result of the reaction of those notified. Employment and employment opportunities have been jeopardized or lost. Housing and housing opportunities have suffered a similar fate. Family and other personal relationships have been destroyed or severely strained. Retribution has been visited by private, unlawful violence and threats and, while such incidents of "vigilante justice" are not common, they happen with sufficient frequency and publicity that registrants justifiably live in fear of them. It also must be noted that these indirect effects are not short-lived . . . [133]

The instances of "vigilante justice" of which the court spoke were well illustrated in more than 100 affidavits gathered and presented to the court by New Jersey public defenders representing the class of registrants challenging the law.[134] Many of these convicted sex offenders had been victims of vigilante violence after their addresses were made public, either on the Internet or by other means of community notification. According to a report issued recently by Human Rights Watch:

Registrants [spoke] of having glass bottles thrown through their windows; being "jumped from behind" and physically assaulted while the assailants yelled "You like little children, right?"; having garbage thrown on the lawn; people repeatedly ringing the doorbell and pounding on the sides of the house late at night; being struck from behind by a crowbar after being yelled at by the assailant that "People like you who are under Megan's Law should be kept in jail. They should never let you out. People like you should die. When you leave tonight, I am gonna kill you" . . . [135]

According to the Human Rights Watch report in 2007, in the two preceding years at least four registered sex offenders had been killed by vigilantes who located their victims using online sex offender registries.[136] However, one advocacy group reported that during 2008, 36 registered sex offenders were killed outside of jails, prisons, and civil commitment facilities, including 5 in Florida, 3 in Pennsylvania, 3 in Texas, 2 in California, 2 in Maryland, 2 in Massachusetts, 2 in North Carolina, 2 in Tennessee, and 1 each in Arizona, Colorado, Delaware, Georgia, Illinois, Indiana, Iowa, Kansas, Kentucky, Maine, Missouri, New Mexico, New York, Utah, and Washington. Of these registered sex offenders, 15 were reportedly "murdered," 6 were killed after being accused of a sex offense, 8 were "killed in domestic situations," and 1 was an "innocent bystander."[137]

Lawmakers have apparently realized the possibility if not the likelihood that sex offender registration and notification laws may lead to vigilantism. Fourteen states and the District of Columbia have passed laws prohibiting the use of sex offender registry information for purposes of harassing, discriminating against, or assaulting sex offenders. Several states have also given sex offender registrants a civil cause of action against persons who misuse registry information.

The direct and indirect economic costs of sex offender registration, notification, and restriction laws are also immense. For example, although Congress allocated $47 million to cover the initial costs of setting up the federal sex offender registry under the Adam Walsh Act, the costs of implementing the SORNA mandates are otherwise left almost completely to the states.[138] The estimated startup costs for SORNA implementation for each state as well as the District of Columbia are listed in Table 2.1. As can be seen in that table, the overall first-year cost of implementing the new federal sex offender registration and notification mandates is estimated to be nearly half a billion dollars ($488,945,150).

These are first-year costs only and do not reflect the ongoing annual costs of continued compliance with SORNA. Nor do these figures include the costs to Guam, Puerto Rico, or American Indian tribes required to comply with the Act.

As noted earlier in this chapter, states that fail to comply with the Act face a loss of 10 percent of their federal law enforcement (Byrne Grant) funding. Indeed, it is only by threatening to withhold portions of federal anticrime funding to states that do not comply with SORNA that the federal government has the legal leverage to enforce the Act's requirements. However, as also noted earlier, only one state (Ohio) had complied with SORNA by the 2009 deadline for full implementation.[140] It is likely that cost is a major factor

TABLE 2.1. Estimated First-Year State Expenditures to Implement the Sex Offender Registration and Notification Act (SORNA)

ALABAMA	$7,506,185
ALASKA	$1,108,573
ARIZONA	$10,281,201
ARKANSAS	$4,597,925
CALIFORNIA	$59,287,816
COLORADO	$7,885,178
CONNECTICUT	$5,680,602
DELAWARE	$1,402,612
DISTRICT OF COLUMBIA	$954,186
FLORIDA	$29,602,768
GEORGIA	$15,481,193
HAWAII	$2,081,603
IDAHO	$2,431,969
ILLINOIS	$20,846,306
INDIANA	$10,291,799
IOWA	$4,846,488
KANSAS	$4,502,553
KENTUCKY	$6,879,497
LOUISIANA	$6,963,401
MAINE	$2,136,456
MARYLAND	$9,112,724
MASSACHUSETTS	$10,461,238
MICHIGAN	$16,336,082
MINNESOTA	$8,430,328
MISSISSIPPI	$4,734,150
MISSOURI	$9,534,548
MONTANA	$1,553,611
NEBRASKA	$2,878,281
NEVADA	$4,160,944
NEW HAMPSHIRE	$2,134,219
NEW JERSEY	$14,088,206
NEW MEXICO	$3,195,121
NEW YORK	$31,300,125
NORTH CAROLINA	$14,696,622
NORTH DAKOTA	$1,037,592
OHIO	$18,598,869
OKLAHOMA	$5,867,138
OREGON	$6,078,218
PENNSYLVANIA	$20,165,479
RHODE ISLAND	$1,715,760
SOUTH CAROLINA	$7,149,123
SOUTH DAKOTA	$1,291,426
TENNESSEE	$9,985,946
TEXAS	$38,771,924
UTAH	$4,290,617
VERMONT	$1,007,649
VIRGINIA	$12,508,695

TABLE 2.1. *(continued)*

WASHINGTON	$10,491,519
WEST VIRGINIA	$2,939,046
WISCONSIN	$9,085,630
WYOMING	$848,009
TOTAL	$488,945,150

Source of Data: Justice Policy Institute[139]

for this unanticipated and unprecedented degree of noncompliance with a federal mandate imposed under the threat of a loss of federal funding. In not a single state were the estimated startup costs for SORNA, to be borne fully by the state, even close to the money the federal government threatened to withhold for noncompliance.[141] For example, in California, where the first-year implementation costs were projected to be $59,287,816, the amount of federal money the state stood to lose by failing to fully implement SORNA was just $2,187,682.[142] Similarly, for example, it would cost Florida, New York, and Texas over $29 million, $31 million, and $38 million respectively in the first year to implement SORNA, but failure to comply with the Act would cost each state less than $1.5 million in federal law enforcement grant funds.[143] Even Wyoming, which would have to spend less than $1 million to implement SORNA in the first year, would be hit with a loss of only $58,404 in federal crime-fighting funds for failing to comply with the new federal sex offender registration and notification mandates.[144]

Whether states will eventually absorb the staggering costs of financing SORNA, it is clear that they are already spending huge sums of money financing their own sex offender registries as well as other sex offender restrictions. For example, the estimated cost of maintaining Megan's Law in New Jersey for one recent year was $5.1 million.[145] And California, which has in recent years teetered on the edge of bankruptcy, will be spending much more than that each year to comply with the many sex offender restrictions mandated by the recently passed voter initiative, Proposition 83. As noted earlier in this chapter, under Proposition 83, California became one of at least 23 states that require the use of GPS technology to supervise paroled sex offenders. Prior to passage of Proposition 83, the California Department of Corrections and Rehabilitation developed cost estimates for the mandatory GPS program. At the request of the California Assembly's Public Safety Committee, researchers at the Hastings Law School Public Law Research Institute estimated that "it would cost the state approximately $88.4 million per year to monitor and supervise sex offenders using GPS."[146] That estimate was calculated on the basis of 9,560 sex offenders who were on parole at the time of the report, 2006.[147]

By early 2009, as required by the ballot initiative, all 6,622 paroled California sex offenders were being monitored by GPS technology.[148] If the earlier cost estimates remain correct (and they are by now likely an underestimate), California will likely spend at least $61 million a year on the GPS monitoring and supervision program alone.

In addition to direct economic costs, sex offender registration and notification laws also exact indirect economic costs. Most notably, economic research indicates that these laws have a negative effect on the value of real property located near the residence of a registered sex offender. For example, in 2003, Larsen, Lowrey, and Coleman, a research team from Wright State University, examined approximately 3,200 home transactions in Montgomery County, Ohio, for the year 2000.[149] These researchers found that, on average, houses located within one tenth of a mile of a sexual offender sold for 17.4 percent less than similar houses located farther away; houses located between one and two tenths of a mile from an offender sold for 10.2 percent less; and houses located between two and three tenths of a mile from an offender sold for 9.3 percent less. As Larsen et al. explained, speaking of public notification of the presence of a registered sex offender, "Once that information is made available to the public, we have found that it has an effect on the price of houses. If you have a person who committed a sex offense next door to you, or even a block away, or two-tenths of a mile away, you pay a price."[150]

More recently, Columbia University researchers Linden and Rockoff reported in 2006 their multiyear study of home assessments and sales in Mecklenburg County, North Carolina, which contains the city of Charlotte.[151] In total, they "examine[d] 9,086 sales that occurred within a 0.3 mile radius of 174 registered offenders and took place within two years of the offenders' arrivals; 1,344 of these 9,086 sales occurred within 0.1 miles of an offender location."[152] Linden and Rockoff found "extremely localized" but "economically and statistically significant negative effects" of the location of sex offenders' residences on the value of nearby real estate: "Houses within a one-tenth mile area around the home of a sex offender fall by 4 percent on average (about $5,500)... [But] the effect varies with distance... [H]ouses next to an offender sell for about 12 percent less while those a tenth of a mile away or more show no decline."[153]

Beyond "Common Sense"

It appears from the research to date that sex offender registration, notification, and restriction laws, which cost untold millions if not billions of dollars to enforce each year, have not reduced the number of sex offenses in the United States or even that among previously convicted sex offenders who have been the direct targets of these laws. It appears that the actual effects of these laws are (1) creating the impression that government is doing something to reduce the number of sex offenses; (2) giving the public a greater sense of safety and security in the face of what is erroneously perceived as a growing threat of sexual victimization; and (3) adding another layer of punishment to the criminal justice system's response to sex offenders. There is nothing inherently wrong with these effects. Sometimes, in order to maintain the respect and support of its citizens, government needs to appear more powerful and capable than it really is. Sometimes people need to be made to feel safer and more secure than they actually are in order to reduce their anxieties and improve the quality of their lives. And sometimes extraordinary punishments are warranted by the demands of deterrence, incapacitation, and/or retribution. But at what cost?

The major problem with America's current sex offender registration, notification, and restriction laws is that, by virtue of their punitive nature, they not only fail to reduce recidivism among convicted sex offenders but may, in some instances, actually increase the likelihood that convicted sex offenders will recidivate. As a recent report by Human Rights Watch explained:

> Current registration, community notification, and residency restriction laws may be counterproductive, impeding rather than promoting public safety. For example, the proliferation of people required to register even though their crimes were not serious makes it harder for law enforcement to determine which sex offenders warrant careful monitoring. Unfettered online access to registry information facilitates—if not encourages—neighbors, employers, colleagues, and others to shun and ostracize former offenders—diminishing the likelihood of their successful reintegration into communities. Residency restrictions push former offenders away from the supervision, treatment, stability, and supportive networks they may need to build and maintain successful, law abiding lives.[154]

A second, perhaps equally significant problem with sex offender registration, notification, and restriction laws is that the sense of added safety and security they convey to the public, while often misleading if not altogether false, may lead some citizens, especially parents and other caretakers of children, to become less mindful of the dangers of sexual victimization. For example, the citizen who logs onto the Dru Sjodin National Sex Offender

Public Website (or directly onto his or her own state's registry website) may be relieved to find that that there are no registered sex offenders in his or her zip code or, if there are, that their names, photographs, addresses, and other identifying information are immediately visible. Even those who never peruse a registry website may take false comfort in the belief that although they are not aware of the names, addresses, and other identifying features of nearby convicted sex offenders, the existence of the registry and website means that some people are aware, and their awareness makes all of us at least somewhat safer. "Common sense" may suggest that notification helps citizens protect themselves, their children, or others from sex offenders. Unfortunately, the data indicate otherwise. Similarly, armed with the knowledge that convicted sex offenders are not allowed to live within 2,500, 1,000, or even 500 feet of a school, day care center, playground, park, or other place where children regularly congregate, parents and other caretakers may conclude that their children are thus safer and less in need of care and supervision when they are in these "protected" places. Sadly, the facts do not bear out any such conclusion.

Some commentators have suggested that the ills of the current sex offender registration, notification, and restriction laws could be cured by relatively minor changes. For instance, many have complained that SORNA requires registration and notification for juveniles who have committed sex crimes, thereby undermining the rehabilitative efforts that have long been the hallmark of the juvenile justice system. Others worry that by making these laws retroactive and greatly extending the class of sex offenders who are covered by registration and notification requirements, SORNA will overburden law enforcement and decrease the resources available to deal with serious offenders; too many relatively harmless offenders, they say, will be included in the registries and the public may not be able or willing to distinguish them from truly dangerous offenders. Some decry the one-size-fits-all approach of SORNA to classifying sex offenders by their offenses and without any individualized form of risk assessment. Still others are troubled by the duration of registration requirements, some of which include a registered offender's entire lifetime.

Critics of sex offender registration and notifications laws have also complained that there is little or no due process afforded those who are mandated to register. They would like to see more procedural safeguards built into a process that holds such grave potential for negatively affecting an offender's life.

These are all certainly valid concerns, but they are all predicated on the assumption that sex offender registration and notification laws are necessary and useful tools if administered properly. But is that so? If these laws were "fixed" as their critics suggest, would they be any more likely to reduce sexual offending than they are now? The answer to that question, it seems, is "no."

To see why, consider the uses to which sex offender registration data can reasonably be put by law enforcement and members of the general public. A registry that was available to law enforcement officials might have some marginal effect on their ability to locate suspects and make arrests in some cases of rape, sexual assault, or other sex crimes. The effect is likely to be only marginal, however, because most such crimes are committed by family members and/or perpetrators known to the victim. In those rare (but often highly publicized) cases in which a sex crime is committed by an unknown perpetrator, sex offender registries would enable the police to literally or at least figuratively "round up the usual suspects," those registered offenders known to have committed similar crimes in the past. It is impossible to calculate the extent to which closed sex offender registries would assist law enforcement in solving such crimes, but the possibility that these registries might sometimes be helpful in that regard certainly cannot be ruled out. Of course, the use of sex offender registration information in the investigation of unsolved sex crimes might also be expected, in at least some cases, to lead to abuses. But even with that caveat in mind, it is difficult to reject out of hand the notion that closed sex offender registries are a potentially useful law enforcement tool.

But how useful, if at all, are sex offender registries open to the general public, whose protection has purportedly led to their development and proliferation? To answer that question, consider what the average or even highly conscientious citizen or parent would be able to do with the information contained on the registries now or that which would be contained on these registries if and when the states comply with the requirements of SORNA.

The amount of information made available to the public regarding registered sex offenders, either on websites or by other means, is limited. Even SORNA exempts from disclosure "the identity of any victim of a sex offense, the social security number of the sex offender, and any reference to arrests of the sex offender not resulting in conviction."[155] To get an idea of what information is readily available to the public, or at least to those who seek it out on state sex offender registry websites, consider that which is made available on the Kansas website (one of the most, if not the most, detailed), which can be accessed directly online or through the Dru Sjodin Nation Sex Offender Website.[156] Below is a summary (with changes made to obscure the registrant's actual identity) of what is listed on the Kansas website (in addition to a recent color headshot photograph and eight other similar photographs of the offender) about a randomly selected man who appears to be a typical registrant:

Name: Doe, John Henry
DOB: 09-11-1978
Registered Since: 09-22-2003
Height: 5-10
Weight: 190
Eye Color: Brown
Hair Color: Brown
Race: White
Gender: Male
Scars, Marks & Tattoos: None on file for this offender
Alias Names: None on file for this offender
Alias Dates of Birth: None on file for this offender
Address Date: 09-29-2009
Street: 1235 Any Avenue
City: Topeka
State: KS
ZIP: 12345
County: SN
Length of Registration: Lifetime
Most Recent Offense: Sexual Assault Second Degree
City: Smallville
County: MO
State: WY
Date: 8-01-1996
Conviction: 06-23-1997
Age: 10
Sex: F
Employer's Address
Street: MAIN STREET
City: Topeka
State: KS
ZIP: [NONE GIVEN]
County: SN
Motor Vehicle(s)
Year: [NONE]
Make: [NONE]

Model: [NONE]
Style: [NONE]
Plate: [NONE]
State: [NONE]

Absent an active form of notification (such as mailing or other direct dissemination of information to the public) as opposed to the passive form utilized by the state and federal websites, only those who bothered to look at these websites would likely have any information about Mr. Doe's offending. But assuming that the average parent or citizen either received directly or looked for and found this information on the Internet, what could or would he or she do with it? If they know Mr. Doe, if they live near him or the street where he works, or if they or their children have reason to go near his residence or the street on which he is employed, they might take certain steps to avoid contact with him and/or keep their children away from him. However, even the most conscientious efforts to do that would not be foolproof. Moreover, even if a relatively small number of people (and/or their children) manage to avoid Doe altogether, their efforts are not likely to have much if any effect on Doe's recidivism for several reasons.

First, as the data consistently show, the recidivism rates for sex offenders is quite low, especially as compared to that for other offenses; also, most sex offenses are committed by first-time offenders rather than those who have already committed such offenses. Second, as the data also consistently demonstrate, most sex offenses are committed by relatives and/or persons known to the victim. Thus, if notification is helpful to anyone, it is most likely to be those who already know Mr. Doe but may not know that he is a convicted sex offender. In all likelihood this will be a tiny fraction of those thought to be at risk for future victimization by Doe. Third, if Doe wishes to recidivate, he may well do so outside of the areas immediately surrounding his residence and workplace, in places where even those "in the know" are unlikely to be on the lookout for him and where he will be less readily identifiable. Thus, the people who are most likely to be interested in knowing about Doe's status as a convicted sex offender (i.e., those living in closest proximity to his residence) may not be the people to whom he poses the most, if any, risk.

For related reasons, sex offender residency restrictions are also inherently unlikely to do much if anything to reduce the number of sex crimes in any given geographical location. To begin with, it should be obvious that most of these laws do not restrict convicted sex offenders from living near children, only from living near schools, day care centers, parks, playgrounds, and other places where children congregate. Thus, for example, a child sex offender might be barred from living within 2,500 feet of one of these "protected" areas but still be allowed to live in a large apartment complex brimming with children. Moreover, in some instances, sex offender residency restrictions may heighten the risk of sexual victimization for some individuals—that is, those living in or near areas where convicted sex offenders cluster because they are effectively shut out of housing elsewhere.

Even aggressive, active notification processes coupled with residency restrictions are unlikely to significantly reduce sex offending because sex offenders recognize the burdens and purposes of these laws and easily can, and often do, seek victims in areas where they are unknown and not likely to be recognized.

In failing to comply for more than 3 years with the dictates of the Sex Offender Registration and Notification Act of 2006 (Title 1 of the Adam Walsh Act) at a time when both public antipathy toward sex offenders and political support for harsh treatment of such offenders may be at an all-time high, legislators and officials in 49 of the 50 states may be implicitly recognizing the inherent problems in these laws that make it unlikely that they will ever succeed in reducing the number of sex crimes, no matter how many taxpayer dollars are spent to support them. Confronted with chronic budget deficits, competing demands from other highly desired goals (such as ending the threat of terrorism, offering universal health care, and rebuilding an aging and crumbling transportation infrastructure), and an unyielding public appetite for lower taxes and a stronger economy, state and federal lawmakers and officials may, for the first time, be forced to conduct honest and realistic cost–benefit analyses in deciding whether sex offender registration, notification, and restriction laws are worth the hundreds of millions if not billions of dollars they cost taxpayers each year. If they do, and if they can withstand the political pressures they will undoubtedly face—admittedly a very big "if"—these laws seem destined to be scaled back rather than expanded as Congress wanted when it passed the Adam Walsh Act in 2006.

Conclusion And Recommendations

Like the SVP civil commitment statutes detailed in the previous chapter, sex offender registration, notification, and community restriction laws arose out of an understandable visceral response to a small number of outrageous sex crimes, coupled with false beliefs that sex offenses were increasing and that sex offenders have a high rate of recidivism. Also, like the SVP statutes, these laws have often, if not usually, been passed with no concern for either cost or the likelihood that they will, in fact, reduce either sex offender recidivism or the number of sex offenses in general. Indeed, some of these laws have been passed with no public input and little if any debate. Finally, these laws have been upheld by courts willing to stretch or contract fundamental legal and constitutional principles on an ad hoc basis because they deferred to the "common sense" conclusions of legislatures that these laws would actually reduce the number of sex crimes.

From the research, however, it appears that the emperor has no (or very few) clothes. The consensus of empirical research is that these sex offender registration and notification laws have no statistically significant effect on sex offender recidivism and thus fail to provide the protection upon which they are premised and which they promise the public. Related laws that restrict the residences, workplaces, and movements of sex offenders also appear to do little if anything to reduce recidivism and may have the unintended negative consequence of making sex offender recidivism more likely because they engender hopelessness and homelessness in some offenders, impede their contact with social support networks in the community, and create disincentives for pro-social behavior. Moreover, these laws may make citizens (especially children) less rather than more safe because they engender a false sense of security.

Finally, economic data indicate that the direct costs of these laws is in the hundreds of millions, most likely billions, of dollars annually. These are dollars that might be spent more productively on personnel and programs that stand a better chance—and it appears that almost any chance would be better—of reducing sex offender recidivism. For example, taxpayer dollars diverted from these largely ineffective, cosmetic, and possibly dangerous programs could be used to develop and implement more effective sex offender treatment regimens, post-release supervision programs, education and prevention strategies, and law enforcement responses to sex crimes.

Given the possibility that knowing the recent whereabouts of convicted sex offenders and their offense histories may be of some investigative assistance to law enforcement officials in even a small number of cases, a very limited form of mandated sex offender registration may provide a useful and not terribly expensive tool. Thus, absent proof to the contrary, the basic registration aspects of Megan's Laws should be retained. However, since the classification and public notification aspects of these laws are extremely costly, have not proven to be effective in reducing recidivism, and may even increase recidivism, these aspects of Megan's Laws and their progeny should be repealed. Finally, since residency, workplace, and travel restrictions have not been shown to have any appreciable positive impact on the incidence of sexual recidivism, but do have a profoundly negative and sometimes punitive impact on sex offenders (which may paradoxically increase the likelihood of such recidivism), these state laws and local ordinances should also be repealed.

3

POSSESSION
OF CHILD
PORNOGRAPHY

In 2006, in *State v. Berger*, the Arizona Supreme Court confronted an appeal by a first-time offender convicted under that state's child pornography law.[1] In Arizona, an individual commits "sexual exploitation of a minor" by "knowingly distributing, transporting, exhibiting, receiving, selling, purchasing, electronically transmitting, possessing or exchanging any visual depiction in which a minor is engaged in exploitive exhibition or other sexual conduct."[2] Under this law, "visual depiction... includes each visual image that is contained in an undeveloped film, videotape or photograph or data stored in any form and that is capable of conversion into a visual image"[3]; the possession of each image of child pornography is a separate offense; consecutive sentences are required for each conviction involving children under 15; each sentence carries a minimum term of 10 years, a presumptive term of 17 years, and a maximum term of 24 years; and there is no possibility of probation, early release, or even gubernatorial pardon.

Morton Berger, a 52-year-old Phoenix high school teacher, with no other criminal record, collected thousands of child pornography images via the Internet over a period of 6 years. He was indicted on 35 counts of sexual exploitation of a minor based on possession of photographs, computer photo images, and computer video files depicting children engaged in sexual acts. Bail was set at $700,000, which Berger was unable to pay, so he remained jailed pending trial.

In response to a motion from the prosecution, the trial court dismissed 15 counts and the case ultimately went to trial on the remaining 20 counts. Evidence at trial showed that among the various photographic and video images Berger possessed were some of children less than 10 years old engaged in sexual acts with adults, children, and animals. A jury convicted Berger of

20 counts of sexual exploitation of a minor and found that each count included a child under the age of 15. The trial judge rejected the prosecution's demand for a sentence of 17 years on each of the 20 counts and instead sentenced Berger to the minimum period of incarceration for each count: a 10-year sentence. Thus, because by law the judge had to impose such sentences consecutively, Berger avoided the 340-year sentence demanded by the prosecution and was sentenced instead to 200 years in prison without hope of parole or even pardon.

Berger appealed, claiming that the sentence violated the cruel and unusual punishment clause of the Eighth Amendment to the U.S. Constitution. The Arizona Court of Appeals and the state's Supreme Court both affirmed the sentence, finding no violation of the Eighth Amendment, and the U.S. Supreme Court refused to hear the case.[4] As the Arizona Supreme Court saw it, Berger's punishment was not disproportionate to his crimes:

> . . . Berger received a statutorily mandated minimum sentence for each of his separate, serious offenses. The ten-year sentence imposed for each offense is consistent with the State's penological goal of deterring the production and possession of child pornography.
>
> The evidence showed that Berger knowingly gathered, preserved, and collected multiple images of child pornography. When confronted by the police, he acknowledged that he had "downloaded some things that he was not proud of, and was not sure if he should have downloaded them or not." Additionally, in response to police questions, Berger admitted he had downloaded images of people under eighteen and that he believed these people were involved in sexual conduct. He also possessed a news article describing a recent arrest of another person in Arizona for possession of child pornography.
>
> The images for which Berger was convicted, graphically depicting sordid and perverse sexual conduct with pre-pubescent minors, were well within the statutory definition of contraband. Nor did Berger come into possession of these images fleetingly or inadvertently. Berger had obtained at least two images in 1996, some six years before his arrest. The websites Berger flagged as "favorites" included graphic titles indicating that they provide underage, and illegal, pornographic depictions. His computer contained "cookie" files and text fragments indicating he had searched for or visited websites providing contraband material.

Berger also had recordable CDs indicating he had specifically set up a "kiddy porn" directory, which included other subfolders with titles indicating a collection of contraband images.

Taken together, this evidence indicates that . . . Berger's sentences are "amply supported" by evidence indicating his "long, serious" pursuit of illegal depictions and are "justified by the State's public-safety interest" in deterring the production and possession of child pornography.[5]

Over the last two to three decades, American legislatures and courts, like those in Arizona, have created a new type of sex offender: the possessor of child pornography.

Child pornography, of course, existed long before the law's determination that simple possession of it should be a criminal offense. Some authorities have traced the history of this phenomenon as far back as the paintings of the ancient Greeks and have noted that "[b]y the late 1800s child pornography was widely available in Victorian England."[6] It was not, however, until the 1960s and 1970s that the production and distribution of child pornography became an international commercial industry, leading to the relatively wide-spread availability of magazines, films, and photographs of children depicted in a sexual manner.

By the late 1970s, for example, Congress was informed that child pornography and child prostitution had become "highly organized, multimillion dollar industries," operating "nationwide."[7] By 1977, the existence of more than 260 child pornography magazines had been documented—publications said to "depict children, some as young as three to five years of age [engaged] in activities [that] ranged from lewd poses to intercourse, fellatio, cunnilingus, masturbation, rape, incest and sado-masochism."[8]

In response to the growing availability of these materials, in the late 1970s and early 1980s, Congress and many state legislatures enacted laws prohibiting and criminally punishing the production and dissemination—but not the mere possession—of child pornography. By 1982, 15 states had crimi-nalized dissemination of child pornography, but only if such material was determined to be legally obscene; 20 other states prohibited and punished dissemination of child pornography regardless of its obscenity; and 12 states prohibited and punished only the use of minors in the production of child pornography. Today both the federal government and every state have laws that criminalize not only the manufacture and distribution but also the simple possession of child pornography. These laws provide for criminal punishments ranging from probation to life in prison.

The Legal Path To Modern Child Pornography Law

In 1982, the U.S. Supreme Court began paving the way for modern American child pornography laws by upholding a conviction under a New York statute that prohibited "promoting a sexual performance by a child."[9] Paul Ferber, the operator of a Manhattan sexually oriented bookstore, sold two films to an undercover police officer. The films depicted young boys masturbating. Ferber was convicted under the New York statute, which defined the term "promote" to include "procure, manufacture, issue, sell, give, provide, lend, mail, deliver, transfer, transmute, publish, distribute, circulate, disseminate, present, exhibit or advertise, or to offer or agree to do the same" but did not require proof that the material in question was obscene.[10]

Ferber appealed his conviction, arguing that the materials he "promoted" were protected by the First Amendment because they had not been proven to be obscene. While the lower state appellate court rejected his claim, the state's highest court agreed that the conviction was barred because the statute under which Ferber had been convicted "would... prohibit the promotion of materials which are traditionally entitled to constitutional protection from government interference under the First Amendment."[11] The statute, the court held, "was underinclusive because it discriminated against visual portrayals of children engaged in sexual activity by not also prohibiting the distribution of films of other dangerous activity"[12] and "overbroad because it prohibited the distribution of materials produced outside the State, as well as materials, such as medical books and educational sources, which 'deal with adolescent sex in a realistic but nonobscene manner.'"[13]

In 1982, in *New York v. Ferber*, the U.S. Supreme Court reversed the decision of the New York Court of Appeals.[14] The Supreme Court held that criminalizing the knowing promotion of child pornography, such as that offered for sale by Ferber, did not violate the First Amendment, even if the material in question was not obscene by then-prevailing legal standards.

In exempting child pornography from the constitutional protections previously accorded material that was not legally obscene, the court relied primarily upon two rationales: (1) The state has a compelling interest in protecting the physical and emotional well-being of children and (2) Child pornography causes direct harm to children that can be effectively prevented only by curtailing the market for it.

Observing that "[t]he prevention of sexual exploitation and abuse of children constitutes a government objective of surpassing importance,"[15] the

Court pointed to articles and studies published in various psychiatric journals. In the words of the Court,

> It has been found that sexually exploited children are unable to develop healthy affectionate relationships in later life, have sexual dysfunctions, and have a tendency to become sexual abusers as adults. Sexual molestation by adults is often involved in the production of child sexual performances. When such performances are recorded and distributed, the child's privacy interests are also invaded.[16]

As the Court further observed:

> [T]he materials produced are a permanent record of the children's participation and the harm to the child is exacerbated by their circulation. [T]he distribution network for child pornography must be closed if the production of material which requires the sexual exploitation of children is to be effectively controlled. Indeed, there is no serious contention that the legislature was unjustified in believing that it is difficult, if not impossible, to halt the exploitation of children by pursuing only those who produce the photographs and movies. While the production of pornographic materials is a low-profile, clandestine industry, the need to market the resulting products requires a visible apparatus of distribution. The most expeditious if not the only practical method of law enforcement may be to dry up the market for this material by imposing severe criminal penalties on persons selling, advertising, or otherwise promoting the product.[17]

Although the *Ferber* decision upheld the constitutionality of punishing the distribution of child pornography, it did not reach the question of criminalizing the possession or viewing of such materials. The Supreme Court would not reach that issue until 1990.

In 1969, 13 years prior to its decision in *Ferber*, the Supreme Court had struck down a Georgia law that criminalized private possession of obscene material.

In *Stanley v. Georgia*, Robert Stanley's home was searched as part of a bookmaking investigation.[18] Authorities found little evidence of bookmaking but did come across several reels of 8millimeter films depicting men and women engaged in sexual intercourse and sodomy. Stanley was charged and convicted, under Georgia law, of knowingly possessing obscene matter.

Ultimately, the U.S. Supreme Court struck down the statute under which Stanley had been convicted. In the words of the Court:

> [Stanley] is asserting the right to read or observe what he pleases—the right to satisfy his intellectual and emotional needs in the privacy of his own home. He is asserting the right to be free from state inquiry into the contents of his library. Georgia contends that [he] does not have these rights, that there are certain types of materials that the individual may not read or even possess. Georgia justifies this assertion by arguing that the films in the present case are obscene. But we think that mere categorization of these films as "obscene" is insufficient justification for such a drastic invasion of personal liberties guaranteed by the First and Fourteenth Amendments. Whatever may be the justifications for other statutes regulating obscenity, we do not think they reach into the privacy of one's own home. If the First Amendment means anything, it means that a State has no business telling a man, sitting alone in his own house, what books he may read or what films he may watch. Our whole constitutional heritage rebels at the thought of giving government the power to control men's minds.[19]

In 1990, the doctrines of *Stanley* and *Ferber* clashed in *Osborne v. Ohio*, a case in which police found nude photographs of an adolescent boy or boys posed sexually: "Three photographs depict the same boy in different positions: sitting with his legs over his head and his anus exposed; lying down with an erect penis and with an electrical object in his hand; and lying down with a plastic object which appears to be inserted in his anus. The fourth photograph depicts a nude standing boy; it is unclear whether this subject is the same boy photographed in the other pictures because the photograph only depicts the boy's torso."[20]

Osborne was charged and convicted under an Ohio statute criminalizing "possess[ing] or view[ing] any material or performance that shows a minor who is not the person's child or ward in a state of nudity."[21] On appeal, Osborne argued, inter alia, that criminalizing his possession of the photographs was unconstitutional under *Stanley*. Affirming his conviction, the U.S. Supreme Court disagreed and distinguished *Stanley*:

> *Stanley* should not be read too broadly. We have previously noted that *Stanley* was a narrow holding . . . and, since the decision in that case, the value of permitting child pornography has been characterized [in *Ferber*] as "exceedingly modest, if not

de minimis." But assuming, for the sake of argument, that Osborne has a First Amendment interest in viewing and possessing child pornography, we nonetheless find this case distinct from *Stanley* because the interests underlying child pornography prohibitions far exceed the interests justifying the Georgia law at issue in *Stanley...*

In *Stanley*, Georgia primarily sought to proscribe the private possession of obscenity because it was concerned that obscenity would poison the minds of its viewers... The difference here is obvious: [T]he State does not rely on a paternalistic interest in regulating Osborne's mind. Rather, Ohio has enacted [the current law] in order to protect the victims of child pornography; it hopes to destroy a market for the exploitative use of children...

[As stated in *Ferber*:] "It is evident beyond the need for elaboration that a State's interest in 'safeguarding the physical and psychological well-being of a minor' is 'compelling.' ... The legislative judgment, as well as the judgment found in relevant literature, is that the use of children as subjects of pornographic materials is harmful to the physiological, emotional, and mental health of the child. That judgment, we think, easily passes muster under the First Amendment." It is also surely reasonable for the State to conclude that it will decrease the production of child pornography if it penalizes those who possess and view the product, thereby decreasing demand... [22]

Although the Supreme Court was willing to countenance laws criminalizing simple, private possession of pornographic images of actual children, the Court later struck down a law criminalizing the possession of so-called virtual child pornography—sexually explicit images that appear to but, in fact, do not depict actual children. Such images include computer-generated images as well as images of persons 18 or older who appear to be minors.

In the Child Pornography Prevention Act of 1996 (CPPA), Congress amended the criminal definition of child pornography to include "any visual depiction, including any photograph, film, video, picture, or computer or computer-generated image or picture" that "is, or appears to be, of a minor engaging in sexually explicit conduct."[23] In 2002, in *Ashcroft v. Free Speech Coalition*, the Supreme Court held that this definition was unconstitutional.[24]

Pointing to depictions of teenage sexuality in works of art, ranging from Shakespeare's "Romeo and Juliet" to award-winning contemporary films such as "Traffic" and "American Beauty," the Court noted that "The CPPA prohibits speech despite its serious literary, artistic, political, or scientific value."[25]

Distinguishing the images made contraband by CPPA from those criminalized under the law upheld in *Ferber*, the Court concluded:

> In contrast to the speech in *Ferber*, speech that itself is the record of sexual abuse, the CPPA prohibits speech that records no crime and creates no victims by its production. Virtual child pornography is not "intrinsically related" to the sexual abuse of children, as were the materials in *Ferber*. While the Government asserts that the images can lead to actual instances of child abuse, the causal link is contingent and indirect. The harm does not necessarily follow from the speech, but depends upon some unquantified potential for subsequent criminal acts.[26]

The Court also distinguished the rationale for the CPPA from that relied upon in *Osborne*:

> Later, in *Osborne v. Ohio*, the Court . . . justified a ban on the possession of pornography produced by using children. "Given the importance of the State's interest in protecting the victims of child pornography," the State was justified in "attempting to stamp out this vice at all levels in the distribution chain." *Osborne* also noted the State's interest in preventing child pornography from being used as an aid in the solicitation of minors. The Court, however, anchored its holding in the concern for the participants, those whom it called the "victims of child pornography." It did not suggest that, absent this concern, other governmental interests would suffice.[27]

Current Child Pornography Law: An Overview

Two decades after the *Osborne* decision, it has long been a federal crime to knowingly possess, manufacture, distribute, or access with intent to view child pornography. Possession of child pornography was made a federal crime in 1991. Moreover, all 50 states and the District of Columbia have now enacted laws criminalizing the possession, manufacture, and distribution of child pornography. As a result, a person who knowingly possesses child pornography may be subject to federal and/or state charges and lengthy incarceration.

While state laws vary in scope, most share aspects of the more commonly used federal law against possessing child pornography. The federal law is applicable in nearly every case because it applies to images that in any way affect interstate or foreign commerce or have been transported (by whatever means) across state lines. Given that virtually all child pornographic images are today sent and received via the Internet or were created and/or stored at some point on media that traveled in interstate or foreign commerce, the federal law reaches virtually all child pornography offenders. As the U.S. Department of Justice (USDOJ) has noted, "Even in cases where the image itself has not traveled in interstate or foreign commerce, federal law may still be violated if the materials used to create the image—such as the CD-ROM on which the child pornography was stored, or the film with which child pornography was created—traveled in interstate or foreign commerce."[28]

Both federal and state laws are expansive in the scope of images, possession of which they forbid. As the USDOJ recently made clear:

> Child pornography is defined by law as the visual depiction of a person under the age of 18 engaged in sexually explicit conduct. This means that any image of a child engaged in sexually explicit conduct is illegal contraband. Notably, the legal definition of sexually explicit conduct does not require that an image depict a child engaging in sexual activity. A picture of a naked child may constitute illegal child pornography if it is sufficiently sexually suggestive. In addition, for purposes of the child pornography statutes, federal law considers a person under the age of 18 to be a child. It is irrelevant that the age of consent for sexual activity in a given state might be lower than 18. A visual depiction for purposes of the federal child pornography laws includes a photograph or videotape, including undeveloped film or videotape, as well as data stored electronically which can be converted into a visual image. For example, images of children engaged in sexually explicit conduct stored on a computer disk are considered visual depictions.[29]

And, as the USDOJ has also warned, "[P]eople possessing, receiving, distributing or producing child pornography can be prosecuted under state laws in addition to, or instead of, federal law. Congress recently significantly increased the maximum prison sentences for child pornography crimes and in some instances created new mandatory minimum sentences. These prison terms can be substantial, and where there have been prior convictions for child sexual exploitation, can result in a life sentence."[30]

Prosecuting a defendant in a child pornography case in both state and federal courts for the same images is unusual but far from unheard of. For example, in 2006, a Connecticut man, Edward J. Burke III, pleaded guilty in state court to two counts of first-degree possession of child pornography and was granted a suspended sentence of 10 years and placed on probation for 5 years. In the wake of media coverage of the case, including one account headlined "Connecticut Judge Lets Child Porn Defendant Walk, No Jail Time,"[31] Burke was prosecuted in federal court, again pleaded guilty, and was sentenced to more than 3 years in federal prison.[32]

Criminal Punishment For Possession Of Child Pornography

The criminalization of the possession of child pornography in the United States is expansive not only in terms of its definitional aspects and reach of jurisdiction, but even more so in the nature of the criminal sentences imposed under these state and federal laws. Individuals convicted of possessing child pornography, especially those prosecuted in the federal courts, face almost certain lengthy prison sentences. By statute, one convicted of knowingly possessing (or attempting or conspiring to possess) child pornography or knowingly accessing child pornography with intent to view it (or attempting or conspiring to do so) shall be fined, imprisoned not more than 10 years, or both.[33] However, if one so convicted has a prior conviction for "aggravated sexual abuse, sexual abuse, or abusive sexual conduct involving a minor or ward, or the production, possession, receipt, mailing, sale, distribution, shipment, or transportation of child pornography," he shall be fined and imprisoned for no less than 10 years and no more than 20 years.[34]

Federal law also prescribes a minimum sentence of 5 years and a maximum of 20 years of imprisonment for any person who "through the mails, or using any means or facility of interstate or foreign commerce or in or affecting interstate or foreign commerce by any means, including by computer" knowingly receives, mails, transports, ships, distributes, reproduces for distribution, advertises, promotes, presents, distributes, or solicits, sells, or possesses (with the intent to sell) any child pornography.[35] The penalties are the same for attempting or conspiring to commit any of these acts. However, if one so convicted has a prior conviction for "aggravated sexual abuse, sexual abuse, or abusive sexual conduct involving a minor or ward, or the production, possession, receipt, mailing, sale, distribution, shipment, or transportation of child pornography," he shall be fined and imprisoned for no less than 15 years and no more than 40 years.[36] It should be noted that among these acts prohibited by federal law, and carrying a minimum sentence of 5 years in prison, is the *receipt* of child pornography. There has been some legal confusion over the difference between receipt of child pornography and possession of child pornography, which has no minimum sentence. Those found in possession of child pornography have sometimes been charged with possession, sometimes with receipt, and sometimes with both offenses for the same images. It has been argued by some defendants that they cannot be charged with both offenses for the same images because "as a practical matter, for anyone to knowingly possess something, he or she must necessarily have received it."[37]

At least one federal trial court recently rejected this argument and distinguished the two offenses, relying upon precedent from both the U.S. Supreme Court and the U.S. Court of Appeals for the Seventh Circuit. As the federal district court held in 2007 in *United States v. Skotzke*:

> The Supreme Court has held that the prohibition on receipt of child pornography . . . includes a scienter requirement, and therefore encompasses only situations in which the defendant knows that the material he is receiving depicts minors engaged in sexually explicit conduct. Accordingly, a person who seeks out only adult pornography, but without his knowledge is sent a mix of adult and child pornography, will not have violated that statutory provision. That same person, however, could be in violation of the possession provision . . . if he or she decides to retain that material, thereby knowingly possessing it. . . It is certainly not irrational to punish more severely the person who knowingly receives such material, because it is that person who is creating and/or perpetuating the market for such material. As numerous courts have recognized, increasing the punishment when the conduct involves receiving such materials, trafficking in such materials, or producing such materials, serves the purpose of the statute to end the abuse of children because those actions are more directly tied to the market for such products. Because possession and receipt are not the same conduct and threaten distinct harms, the imposition of different base offense levels is not irrational and therefore [defendant's] challenge must fail.
>
> [The Seventh Circuit's decision] makes clear that the offense of receipt targets those who intentionally seek out child pornography because such behavior contributes to the demand and the survival of the child pornography industry. The harm created by the receipt occurs regardless of whether the offender is an "end-user" or distributer (which logically would cause even greater harm). The harm created by the receipt also occurs regardless of whether the offender "possesses" such materials by keeping or retaining them

(although it is reasonable to conclude that possession of such material is also harmful). Accordingly, a consumer who purchases child pornography for his own use may be charged with receipt, and this is not mutiplicitous of a charge of possession.[38]

Under this definition and reasoning, since most offenders who "possess" child pornography have also "received" such contraband, they may be charged with either or both crimes. Thus, by charging "receipt" in addition to or instead of "possession," a prosecutor is able to virtually ensure that one found in possession of child pornography will be subject to a minimum sentence of 5 years in prison. As one U.S. Attorney candidly testified before the U.S. Sentencing Commission in 2009, "[I]nstead of charging a child pornographer with only possession, which carries no mandatory minimum, we encourage AUSAs [Assistant United States Attorneys] to work with their investigative agents to establish grounds for a charge of "receipt" too because that offense has a mandatory minimum."[39]

Additionally, federal law prescribes minimum and maximum sentences of 5 to 20 years in prison for a first offender and 15 to 40 years for a repeat offender who "knowingly distributes, offers, sends, or provides to a minor any visual depiction, including any photograph, film, video, picture, or computer-generated image or picture, whether made or produced by electronic, mechanical, or other means, where such visual depiction is, or appears to be, of a minor engaging in sexually explicit conduct."[40]

Finally, federal law prescribes a fine and sentence of no more than 15 years for anyone who knowingly produces with intent to distribute or does distribute "child pornography that is an adapted or modified depiction of an identifiable minor."[41]

Actual sentences handed down in federal child pornography prosecutions depend not only on the nature of the conviction and the defendant's prior convictions, if any, for child pornography or other child-related sex crimes, but on the presence of so-called enhancements specified under the U.S. Sentencing Guidelines, a point system driven by factors such as the number of child pornography images possessed, the age(s) of the children depicted, whether or not a computer was used to obtain or store the depictions, and whether the material portrays sadism, masochism, or other violence.[42] Since 2005, under the U.S. Supreme Court decision in *United States v. Booker*, federal judges are no longer required to strictly adhere to the Sentencing Guidelines.[43] Instead, "the starting point in determining a proper sentence in federal court is to first calculate the advisory guideline range under the United States Sentencing Guidelines."[44] The court then must consider the factors required in the general federal sentencing statute to determine a "fair and just sentence."[45] That statute provides, in pertinent part:

(a) Factors To Be Considered in Imposing a Sentence. The court shall impose a sentence sufficient, but not greater than necessary, to comply with the purposes set forth in paragraph (2) of this subsection. The court, in determining the particular sentence to be imposed, shall consider:

    (1) the nature and circumstances of the offense and the history and characteristics of the defendant;

    (2) the need for the sentence imposed

        (A) to reflect the seriousness of the offense, to promote respect for the law, and to provide just punishment for the offense;

        (B) to afford adequate deterrence to criminal conduct;

        (C) to protect the public from further crimes of the defendant; and

        (D) to provide the defendant with needed educational or vocational training, medical care, or other correctional treatment in the most effective manner;

    (3) the kinds of sentences available;

    (4) the kinds of sentence and the sentencing range established for ... the applicable category of offense as set forth in the U.S. Sentencing [G]uidelines ...;

    (5) any pertinent policy statement ... issued by the Sentencing Commission ...

    (6) the need to avoid unwarranted sentence disparities among defendants with similar records who have been found guilty of similar conduct; and

    (7) the need to provide restitution to any victims of the offense.[46]

Since the mid-1990s, the number of persons in the United States convicted of child pornography offenses as well as the sentences meted out to these offenders has increased dramatically. As Troy Stabenow, a federal public defender, has pointed out recently, relying upon publicly available data:

In 1997, child pornography offenders received a mean sentence of 20.59 months confinement. In 2007, defendants sentenced for the same conduct received a mean sentence of 91.30 months confinement. This represents a 443% increase in the mean imposed sentence for this class of offenders.[47]

Several recent cases illustrate the continued impact of the federal sentencing guidelines on convictions for the possession of child pornography and help explain why child pornography offenders are receiving such lengthy sentences.

For instance, in 2009, in *United States v. Moore*, Jeremy Moore—who had downloaded more than 600 child pornographic images from an Internet peer-to-peer file-sharing network known as Limewire and made these images available to others via the same medium—pleaded guilty to a single count of interstate transportation of child pornography and was sentenced to 210 months in federal prison.[48]

Moore did not contest that, under federal sentencing guidelines, his basic offense level called for a sentence of between 41 and 51 months. However, as the court explained, Moore's sentence was adjusted under the guidelines as follows:

> [A] two-level increase [was assessed] because the material
> involved a prepubescent minor or a minor who had not reached
> the age of twelve; a four-level increase because the material
> involved portrayed sadistic or masosadistic [sic] conduct or other
> depictions of violence; a two-level increase because the offense
> involved the use of a computer; and a five-level increase because
> the offense involved 600 or more images. Over Moore's objection,
> the district court also assessed a five-level increase because the
> offense involved distribution for the receipt or expectation of
> receipt of a thing of value but not for pecuniary gain. Accordingly,
> Moore's adjusted offense level was 40. The district court
> granted a two-level reduction in offense level for acceptance of
> responsibility, and granted a reduction of one additional level
> upon motion of the United States for the timely acceptance of
> responsibility. Accordingly, the adjusted offense level was 37.
> [T]his yielded an advisory Guidelines range of 210 to 240
> months (which is the statutory maximum for the offense of
> conviction).[49]

Thus, because some of the 600-plus images Moore downloaded for free using a computer were of prepubescent children, some involved violent or sadomasochistic conduct, and some were made available to others without charge via Limewire, his prison sentence was more than tripled and he was ultimately sentenced to serve 17.5 years in a federal penitentiary.

The sentencing adjustments applied in Moore's case are typical and are drawn from a federal sentencing guideline that provides for increases and decreases as follows:

Specific Offense Characteristics

(1) If . . . the defendant's conduct was limited to the receipt or solicitation of material involving the sexual exploitation of a minor . . . and . . . the defendant did not intend to traffic in, or distribute, such material, decrease by 2 levels.

(2) If the material involved a prepubescent minor or a minor who had not attained the age of 12 years, increase by 2 levels.

(3) (Apply the greatest) If the offense involved:

(A) Distribution for pecuniary gain, increase by the number of levels . . . corresponding to the retail value of the material, but by not less than 5 levels.

(B) Distribution for the receipt, or expectation of receipt, of a thing of value, but not for pecuniary gain, increase by 5 levels.

(C) Distribution to a minor, increase by 5 levels.

(D) Distribution to a minor that was intended to persuade, induce, entice, or coerce the minor to engage in any illegal activity, other than illegal activity covered under subdivision (E), increase by 6 levels.

(E) Distribution to a minor that was intended to persuade, induce, entice, coerce, or facilitate the travel of, the minor to engage in prohibited sexual conduct, increase by 7 levels.

(F) Distribution other than distribution described in subdivisions (A) through (E), increase by 2 levels.

(4) If the offense involved material that portrays sadistic or masochistic conduct or other depictions of violence, increase by 4 levels.

(5) If the defendant engaged in a pattern of activity involving the sexual abuse or exploitation of a minor, increase by 5 levels.

(6) If the offense involved the use of a computer or an interactive computer service for the possession, transmission, receipt, or distribution of the material, increase by 2 levels.

(7) If the offense involved—

(A) at least 10 images, but fewer than 150, increase by 2 levels;

(B) at least 150 images, but fewer than 300, increase by
3 levels;

(C) at least 300 images, but fewer than 600, increase by
4 levels; and

(D) 600 or more images, increase by 5 levels.[50]

Determining the number of images, whether any images have been distributed for pecuniary gain or anything of value, and whether any images are sadomasochistic or otherwise violent has proven controversial.

In most cases, the number of child pornography images possessed by a defendant may be determined by simply counting them. But under an "application note" to the federal sentencing guidelines, the counting process is not always simple.[51] For instance, "[e]ach photograph, picture, computer or computer-generated image, or any similar visual depiction shall be considered to be one image" but "[i]f the number of images substantially underrepresents the number of minors depicted, an upward departure [i.e., increasing the estimated number of images] may be warranted."[52] Furthermore, under the application note, "Each video, video-clip, movie, or similar recording shall be considered to have 75 images. If the length of the recording is substantially more than 5 minutes, an upward departure may be warranted."[53]

The question of whether possessed images have been distributed for pecuniary gain or anything of value is, as the *Moore* case illustrates, not as easily answered as one might expect.[54] Moore admittedly possessed child pornography obtained through use of a popular peer-to-peer file-sharing network, often used to trade music, videos, pictures, etc. This network allows users to search the computers of others who are logged into the network and to locate and download files from those computers. In affirming the sentencing enhancement for distribution for gain in Moore's case, the appellate court pointed to another federal appellate court's 2007 decision in *United States v. Griffin*.[55]

James Griffin had pleaded guilty to possessing and to receiving child pornography. In explaining why a sentencing enhancement for distribution for gain was warranted in his case, the court noted that Griffin "'distributed' child pornography when he used the network to share child pornography files with others, and his expectation, that they would swap such materials with other network users, constituted an expectation that he would receive a 'thing of value.'"[56] As the court went on to explain:

Griffin admitted that he downloaded child pornography from
Kazaa—an internet peer-to-peer file-sharing network—but
maintains that he only downloaded the images and videos for his

personal use, not for distribution to others. However, Griffin also admitted that he knew Kazaa was a file-sharing program and knew that, by using Kazaa, other Kazaa users could also download files from his computer. The government asserted that Griffin's use of Kazaa with knowledge of its capabilities constituted distribution. By using the file-sharing site, Griffin enabled other Kazaa users to download files from Griffin's shared folder, including any child pornography files stored there. . . By introducing these admissions into evidence, the government met its burden of establishing that Griffin expected to receive a thing of value—child pornography— when he used the file-sharing network to distribute and access child pornography files. "By placing child pornography in his shared folder and by running [the file-sharing network], Defendant intended to barter his images of child pornography in the expectation that he would receive other [network] users' images of child pornography."[57]

Perhaps the most subjective call to be made by the courts in sentencing possessors and distributors of child pornography relates to whether any of the images in question portray sadistic, masochistic, or otherwise violent conduct. Two cases decided in 2009, *United States v. Freeman* and *United States v. Lee*, illustrate the problem.

In *Freeman*, a New York man was charged with receiving child pornography after authorities found over 200 images of child pornography on his home computer.[58] He was sentenced to 78 months in prison by a federal judge who applied a sentencing enhancement for possession of materials portraying sadistic or masochistic conduct. As the judge explained in an unusually graphic description of some of the photographs found on the defendant's computer:

One depicts an obviously prepubescent [girl] engaging in intercourse with an adult male. The second photograph . . . depicts . . ., again, a prepubescent girl, I judge, to be 7 or 8 with a penis inserted in her vagina; . . . [another] is a picture of an obviously prepubescent girl with a penis in her mouth and an adult penis in her vagina at the same time; . . . [another] picture [is] of an obviously prepubescent child with her legs spread open, an adult male holding his penis in close proximity to her vagina and there appears to be a sock stuck in her mouth; . . . [another picture showed] obviously, prepubescent children with their hands—with one's hands tied to the other's legs.[59]

In *Lee* (2009), a North Carolina man with between 275 and 295 child pornography images on his computer was convicted of transmitting child pornography over the Internet.[60] Like Freeman, his sentence of 420 months in prison included an enhancement for possessing child pornography portraying sadistic, masochistic, or other violent conduct. As the Court of Appeals explained in affirming his 35-year prison sentence:

> The district court found that one of the images possessed by
> defendant depicted a minor, was sexually explicit, and was sadistic,
> masochistic, or otherwise violent. Defendant conceded that the
> image was sexually explicit and depicted a minor. Defendant
> disputed the district court's factual finding that the image portrayed
> sadistic or masochistic conduct or other depictions of violence. The
> image depicted a boy wearing a leather strap around his torso and
> holding his hands behind his back. The court found that both the
> leather strap and the placement of the boy's hands behind his back
> gave rise to an inference that the boy's hands were bound. Thus, the
> district court did not clearly err in finding the image sadistic,
> masochistic, or violent. [The guideline dealing with masochistic,
> sadistic or other violent content] clearly applied to the image. The
> district court therefore calculated the advisory guidelines range
> correctly. Thus, there was no procedural error in defendant's
> sentencing.[61]

While these cases and the harsh sentences imposed on these defendants may seem unusual, they are not. As Stabenow recently noted, the "enhancements" that lead to 20-year sentences in child pornography prosecutions have become the norm rather than the exception:

> The flaw with U.S. S[entencing] G[uidelines] today is that the
> average defendant charts at the statutory maximum, regardless
> of Acceptance of Responsibility and Criminal History. As noted
> by the Guidelines Commission, there are "several specific offense
> characteristics which are expected to apply in almost every case
> (e.g., use of a computer, material involving children under 12 years
> of age, number of images)." The internet provides the typical means
> of obtaining child pornography, resulting in a two-level
> enhancement. Furthermore, as a result of internet swapping,
> defendants readily obtain 600 images with minimal effort, resulting
> in a five-level increase. . . Undoubtedly, as the Commission
> recognized, some of these images will contain material involving

a prepubescent minor and/or material involving depictions of violence (which may not include "violence" *per se*, but simply consist of the prepubescent minor engaged in a sex act), thereby requiring an additional six-level increase. Finally, because defendants generally distribute pornography in order to receive pornography in return, most defendants receive a five-level enhancement for distribution of a thing of value. Thus, an individual who swapped a single picture, and who was only engaged in viewing and receiving child pornography for a few hours, can quickly obtain an offense level of 40. Even after Acceptance of Responsibility, an individual with no prior criminal history can quickly reach a Guideline Range of 210–262 months, where the statutory maximum caps the sentence at 240 months.[62]

In addition to federal child pornography laws, each state has its own sentencing structure for possession of child pornography. Forty-nine states criminally punish simple possession of child pornography; the sole exception is Nebraska, which criminalizes only possession of child pornography with intent to distribute. Most states prescribe criminal penalties much less severe than those meted out in federal court. As the *Berger* case (mentioned at the beginning of this chapter) indicates, however, that is not always the case.

While Arizona's law, under which Berger was charged and sentenced, is one of the harshest in the nation, other states also prescribe severe punishments for those who possess child pornography. Twenty-two of the 49 states that punish simple possession of child pornography prescribe mandatory minimum sentences.

Mandatory minimum terms of incarceration range from 6 months in Indiana and Ohio to 100 years in Montana. The median mandatory minimum sentence in state courts is 2 years. In Massachusetts, for instance, conviction for purchase or possession of child pornography carries a minimum 5-year prison sentence and a minimum of 10 years for a second offense.

In Connecticut, conviction for possession of child pornography carries a minimum prison sentence of 1 to 5 years, depending upon the number of images possessed. In Idaho, one convicted of possessing child pornography for other than commercial purposes faces a sentence of up to 10 years in prison. In Louisiana a convicted possessor of child pornography faces a prison term of from 2 to 10 years, to be followed by a lifetime of electronic monitoring.

In Maryland, a person convicted of using a computer to possess child pornography faces up to 10 years in prison and a $25,000 fine for a first offense and up to 20 years in prison and a $50,000 fine for a subsequent offense.

Under Michigan law, a person who knowingly possesses child pornography is guilty of a felony punishable by imprisonment for not more than 4 years or a fine of not more than $10,000. In Minnesota, one convicted of possessing child pornography may be sentenced to imprisonment for not more than 5 years and a fine of not more than $5,000 for a first offense and for not more than 10 years and a fine of not more than $10,000 for a second or subsequent offense.

In Nevada, a person convicted of possessing child pornography may be sentenced to imprisonment for 1 to 6 years and a fine of $5,000 for a first offense and for 1 year to life and a fine of $5,000 for any subsequent offense. In Oklahoma, conviction for possession of computerized child pornography is punished by the imposition of a fine of not less than $500 nor more than $20,000, or by imprisonment for not less than 30 days nor more than 10 years, or by both such a fine and imprisonment. In South Carolina, one convicted of possessing child pornography must be imprisoned not more than 10 years.

Convicted possessors of child pornography face not only lengthy prison terms but also the possibility of indefinite—even lifetime—civil confinement to prison-like institutions under laws such as those described in the first chapter of this volume. For example, in 2006, Graydon Comstock had served all but 6 days of his 37-month federal sentence for possession of child pornography when, acting under the newly minted federal law allowing indefinite civil commitment for sex offenders, the U.S. Attorney General certified him as "sexually dangerous."[63] Although Comstock fought that designation in court and won in both the federal district court and the federal court of appeals, he was detained in federal prison for more than 3 years after his sentence expired, while the government's appeal made its way to the U.S. Supreme Court. The Supreme Court reversed the decisions of the lower courts and held that the federal government has constitutional authority to impose indefinite civil commitment on sex offenders convicted in federal court.[64]

Child pornography offenders, of course, are also subject to sex offender registration laws of the sort discussed in the second chapter of this volume. But, when convicted in federal court, they also face the possibility of a lifetime term of supervised release once they complete their prison sentences. In addition to ordering that convicted child pornography offenders be released only on supervision (essentially a form of parole), federal courts may also impose special conditions of supervised release. For example, they may ban offenders from using computers and/or the Internet, prohibit them from having access to a computer without first obtaining prior approval from a probation officer, or require them to allow probation officers to search their computers and monitor their computer usage. As the federal courts have held:

> "District courts have broad latitude to impose conditions on supervised release." The court may impose any condition it deems appropriate, so long as it is "reasonably related" to: "the nature and circumstances of the offense and the history and characteristics of the defendant;" the need "to afford adequate deterrence to criminal conduct;" the need "to protect the public from further crimes of the defendant;" and the need "to provide the defendant with needed educational or vocational training, medical care, or other correctional treatment in the most effective manner." The condition must not cause a "greater deprivation of liberty than is reasonably necessary" to achieve the above goals and must be consistent with Sentencing Commission policy statements.[65]

One convicted of possessing child pornography also may, under existing federal law, be required to make restitution to all of his victims—in other words, every child victimized in the making of each child pornography image he possessed. Federal law provides that district courts are required to order restitution in the "full amount of a victim's losses"[66] stemming from any offense involving "sexual exploitation and other abuse of children,"[67] which includes possession of child pornography. Under this law, "the term "victim" means the individual harmed as a result of a commission of a crime."[68] The "full amount of the victim's losses" includes "any costs incurred by the victim for: (A) medical services relating to physical, psychiatric, or psychological care; (B) physical and occupational therapy or rehabilitation; (C) necessary transportation, temporary housing, and child care expenses; (D) lost income; (E) attorneys' fees, as well as other costs incurred; and (F) any other losses suffered by the victim as a proximate result of the offense."[69] Moreover, the law explicitly provides that an order of restitution is mandatory for these offenses and that "[a] court may not decline to issue an order under this section because of: (i) the economic circumstances of the defendant; or (ii) the fact that a victim has, or is entitled to, receive compensation for his or her injuries from the proceeds of insurance or any other source."[70]

Finally, federal law also provides that one convicted of possession of child pornography "shall forfeit [to the government] any interest" in:

> (1) any visual depiction . . . or any book, magazine, periodical, film, videotape, or other matter which contains any such visual

> depiction, which was produced, transported, mailed, shipped or
> received in violation of [the law];
>
> (2) any property, real or personal, constituting or traceable to gross
> profits or other proceeds obtained from such offense; and
>
> (3) any property, real or personal, used or intended to be used to
> commit or to promote the commission of such offense.[71]

Generally this law results in the forfeiture of computers, printers, CDs, and related items, but in numerous recent cases defendants convicted of possessing child pornography have been ordered to turn their homes over to the federal government. For example, a Kentucky man, convicted in federal court of possessing more than 30,000 images of child pornography on approximately 100 CDs and three computers found in his home, was sentenced to 188 months in prison and required to forfeit his home "because of the high volume of images and the length of time [he] used his home to download and view child pornography."[72] Earlier, a Texas man, who admitted to downloading more than 600 child pornography images and storing them on floppy disks and a computer at his residence, was sentenced to 10 years in prison, 20 years of post-release supervision, and the forfeiture of his home. In a press release issued by the federal government following this man's sentencing, the U.S. Attorney said, "We're taking the war on child exploitation very seriously and we're making it very personal. None of your property is safe if you use it to exploit children—you can even lose your home."[73] To which a federal law enforcement officer added, "These significant sentences and forfeitures must send a loud and clear warning signal to anyone who considers using child pornography. [We] will not tolerate anyone who sexually exploits innocent children."[74]

Computers, Child Pornography, And The Law

Today, most if not all child pornography is transferred via the Internet in digital form and stored by its possessors on computer hard drives and/or other media such CDs, DVDs, and flash drives. The digitization of child pornography images has led to serious legal questions about what it means to "possess" these images.

Images viewed on the Internet or received via e-mail or instant messaging or through any other form of electronic transmission find their way onto the hard drive of the computer being used by the viewer in one or both of two ways.

The viewer may affirmatively download the images or they may be automatically stored electronically by the computer in temporary cache files. In some cases, these cache files may be deleted by the viewer, but almost invariably even deleted images will remain on the computer's hard drive. While they will no longer be accessible to the viewer once they are deleted, especially once they are deleted from the computer's recycle bin, viewed images (or even some images that have been received but not actually viewed) will remain on the computer's hard drive in a form that is accessible by law enforcement authorities using sophisticated recovery software.

As the attorney for one child pornography defendant who was convicted and sentenced to federal prison for possessing child pornography images he had deleted from his computer, said recently, "Unfortunately, the only way to get rid of what you have on your computer is to smash it with a baseball bat or burn it."[75] The sentencing judge considered the fact that the defendant had made a good-faith effort to delete the illicit materials from his computer and sentenced him to the statutory minimum of 5 years in prison instead of a sentence in the guidelines range of 97 to 120 months in prison. In the words of the court:

> The seriousness of the offense thus clearly calls for prison as Congress has mandated. The question presented here is whether a sentence in excess of the mandatory five years is warranted.
>
> In concluding that it is not, I have considered the fact that the defendant had deleted the material from his computer and attempted to extricate himself from involvement in the offense before the attention of law enforcement was focused on him. It is typical to see a defendant change his behavior after he is caught or has reason to believe he is under investigation. That is not what occurred here. [This defendant] had no reason to suspect he was under investigation when he deleted the child pornography from his computer in an attempt [as he testified] to "get away from that type of life." This behavior suggests that he is sincere in his remorse and poses less of a risk of re-offending.[76]

In this case one might have expected the defendant to argue that he was not guilty because he had deleted all child pornography from his computer before the authorities seized the machine, analyzed it, and recovered only illicit images that had been deleted and were "waiting to be overwritten."[77] As a matter of law, however, that argument had already been foreclosed by a number of court decisions determining that even a defendant who deletes child pornography from his computer remains in possession of that contraband. As one federal judge explained recently:

> Once a computer receives an illicit image by any method, whether spam email, intentional downloading, loading of a CD-ROM, file sharing, etc., the computer user possesses "matter" containing child pornography, even before viewing the electronic screen. The images are in the computer and available for viewing. When he or she intentionally or unintentionally sees the child pornography pictures, the user "knowingly possesses" them—even if the images were unsolicited, unwanted, or a complete surprise. The possession charged is purely passive...
>
> Knowing receipt can be as passive as knowing possession in the computer context. For example, if a person is emailed an unsolicited prohibited visual depiction, when he logs on and opens his email, he "receives." If the person is already logged on to his email and his computer opens his email automatically, he "receives" without taking any action. As soon as he sees the child pornography, he knows he has received it and that he now possesses it. If a defendant did not solicit the material and its appearance on his screen surprised him, he would have, by the act of turning on his computer, both "received" and "possessed" it. Scholars have posited a variety of ways that a technologically-challenged web user could unknowingly or accidentally receive proscribed material...
>
> [Federal law] does provide in part for an affirmative defense or "safe harbor" for some accidental or unintentional situations:
>
> "It shall be an affirmative defense ... that the defendant—
>
> (1) possessed less than three matters containing any visual depiction proscribed by that paragraph; and
>
> (2) promptly and in good faith, and without retaining or allowing any person, other than a law enforcement agency, to access any visual depiction or copy thereof—
>
>   (A) took reasonable steps to destroy each such visual depiction; or
>
>   (B) reported the matter to a law enforcement agency and afforded that agency access to each such visual depiction."
>
> But this affirmative defense is applicable only to a charge of possession of child pornography ... It is no defense at all to receipt of child pornography ... Putting aside the lack of an effective

factual or legal defense against receipt, what if you open, without knowing in advance its contents or having sought it, a digital file which includes three thumbnail-sized images advertising a child pornography website? You now knowingly possess more than two illegal images that you never wanted—and [the law's] safe harbor offers no protection, even if you try to destroy the pictures or want to report them to the police. Or suppose you are conducting an automatically recorded video-teleconference or viewing a live internet broadcast. The person at the other end, unrequested, flashes a series of pornographic pictures of children. Have you committed a crime by receiving? Do you commit a crime of possession by keeping the videotape or not throwing out your computer? Destroying such tapes, pictures, or files after the event will not avoid guilt—since the crime has arguably already been committed by receipt and possession. Smashing the computer in outrage at the images would support an obstruction of justice charge for destroying evidence. As one FBI agent put it, "One click, you're guilty. A federal offense is that easy."[78]

This "one click and you're guilty" observation might appear to be hyperbole, but it is not. The digital nature of most child pornography images has also led to the use of controversial law enforcement measures such as so-called child pornography sting operations. In these stings, law enforcement officers post on various Internet sites, including message boards, bogus hyperlinks offering what appears to be child pornography. Anyone who clicks on these hyperlinks receives an encrypted file full of meaningless data. Law enforcement officers then obtain the Internet protocol (IP) address of the computer from which the hyperlinks were clicked, obtain subpoenas to get from Internet service providers the names of the customers associated with those IP addresses, raid their homes, and arrest them for attempting to possess child pornography.

One such sting netted "several hundred" suspects during a single 24-hour period.[79] An undercover FBI agent in San Francisco discovered an Internet site located in Japan. The site was a message board on which Internet visitors were able to post and download links, images, videos, and other files related to or including child pornography. The site also included instructions regarding exchanging, encrypting, and removing identifying information from files.

The undercover agent posted two files to the website, accompanied by a purported description of their contents. The text of the agent's post, which included five hyperlinks (one marked "Preview" and the others "Full 25 MB") read: "Here is one of my favs—4yo hc with dad (toddler, some oral, som[e] anal)—supercute! Haven't seen her on the board before—if anyone has anymore, PLEASE POST."[80] Although each link led to an actual file, none of the files contained child pornography.

When several hundred visitors to the website clicked on any one or more of these hyperlinks, thereby opening the government-planted files, an FBI computer in California captured their IP addresses, which enabled the authorities, working through Internet service providers around the country, to locate and prosecute them for attempted possession of child pornography.[81]

One of those who clicked on the FBI agent's hyperlinks was Roderick Vosburgh, a 45-year-old Pennsylvania man, who was a doctoral student, part-time history professor, and former police dispatcher.[82] When FBI agents arrived at his home with a search warrant for his computer, he did not answer their knock. They waited nearly half an hour before Vosburgh opened the door. Upon entry to the apartment, where he lived alone, they found his computer hard drive and several thumb drives smashed to pieces. On an external hard drive, however, they found hundreds of adult pornography images and two images of naked prepubescent girls.

In a rare trial of a child pornography case (most defendants plead guilty), a jury convicted Vosburgh of one count of possession of child pornography for the two images found on his external drive and one count of attempted possession of child pornography for clicking on the bogus government-planted hyperlink.[83] While Vosburgh was also charged with destroying evidence for allegedly smashing his hard drive and thumb drives while the agents stood outside his door, he was acquitted of that charge. He was sentenced to serve 15 months in federal prison, to be followed by 3 years of post-release supervision.[84]

The Nature Of Child Pornography And Those Who Possess It

Child pornography is almost universally regarded as a phenomenon of major proportions. Given the vast, uncharted, global reach of the Internet, which has clearly become the prime medium for the transmission of child pornography, it is fair to say that no one knows precisely (or perhaps even approximately) how much child pornography exists today. Interpol, the international police agency, has cataloged over 550,000 child pornographic images that have been used to identify 870 child victims throughout the world.[85] Perhaps less reliable, but at least indicative of how widespread child pornography is believed to be, are estimates from various other sources. For example, the National

Society for the Prevention of Cruelty to Children has estimated that 20,000 new images of child pornography are made available on the Internet every week.[86] Criminologists Wortley and Smallbone report that "At any one time there are estimated to be more than one million pornographic images of children on the Internet, with 200 new images posted daily. One offender in the UK possessed 450,000 child pornography images. It has been reported that a single child pornography site received a million hits a month..."[87]

The problem of counting or even estimating the number of unique child pornography images available on the Internet at any given time is explained well but succinctly by Wortley and Smallbone:

> These images may be stored on servers located almost anywhere in the world. Distribution may involve sophisticated pedophile rings or organized crime groups that operate for profit, but in many cases, is carried out by individual amateurs who seek no financial reward. Child pornography may be uploaded to the Internet on websites or exchanged via e-mail, instant messages, newsgroups, bulletin boards, chat rooms, and peer-to-peer (P2P) networks. . . Child pornography websites are often shut down as soon as they are discovered, and openly trading in pornography via e-mail or chat rooms is risky because of the possibility of becoming ensnared in a police sting operation . . . Increasingly those distributing child pornography are employing more sophisticated security measures to elude detection and are being driven to hidden levels of the Internet.[88]

If assessing the magnitude of this phenomenon is difficult, determining the general nature of child pornographic images and those who view them is even more problematic because all that can be relied upon are known images and viewers—essentially those coming to the attention of legal authorities. Be that as it may, and subject to obvious limitations, it is possible to at least sketch the nature of these contraband images and that of the individuals who have been arrested for possessing them.

Nature of the Images

Relying upon data from the National Juvenile Online Victimization study, Wolak, Finkelhor, and Mitchell reported on the nature of child pornography images produced and possessed by arrested offenders. In a sample of 122 child pornography producers (individuals who took pornographic pictures of minors), these researchers found that 72 percent "took images that focused on a child's genitals or showed explicitly sexual activity"; 43 percent "took images that portrayed sexual conduct between a child and an adult, defined as an adult touching the child's genitals (or breasts) or vice versa"; 30 percent "created pictures of adults sexually penetrating children"; 15 percent "took photographs that showed other sexual penetration of children [such as] sex between minors, penetration with objects or masturbation"; and 6 percent "took pictures that showed children enduring sexual violence, including sadism, bondage, and beatings."[89] Ten percent of the minors victimized by these child pornography producers were 5 years old or younger, 43 percent were 5 to 12 years old, and 47 percent were teenagers, 13 to 17 years old. Eighty percent were girls, 20 percent boys.

Relying upon data from the same national study, these researchers also detailed the nature of the images in the cases of a sample of 429 arrested child pornography possessors. They reported that 92 percent of these offenders "had images focused on genitals or showing explicit sexual activity"; 80 percent "had pictures showing the sexual penetration of a child, including oral sex"; 71 percent "had images showing sexual contact between adults and minors"; and 21 percent "had images showing sexual violence committed against minors."[90] Nineteen percent of these offenders possessed pornographic images of children younger than 3; 39 percent possessed images of children 3 to 5; 83 percent possessed images of children 6 to 12; and 75 percent possessed images of teenagers. Sixty-two percent of these child pornography offenders possessed images of mostly girls, 14 percent possessed images of mostly boys, and 15 percent possessed images of boys and girls in roughly equal numbers.

Characteristics of the Offenders

Several studies have examined the characteristics of individuals who have been criminally charged with possessing child pornography.

In the study of 429 arrested child pornography possessors just mentioned, Wolak et al. found that virtually all (more than 99 percent) were men; 91 percent were white; 86 percent were 26 or older, 45 percent were 40 or older; 41 percent were married; only 5 percent were not high school graduates, 38 percent had only a high school education, 21 percent had post-high school education, 16 percent were college graduates, and 4 percent had graduate degrees; 22 percent had a prior arrest for a nonsexual offense and 11 percent had a prior arrest for a sexual offense against a minor; and only 5 percent had been diagnosed with any mental illness.

Wolak et al. also detailed some of the characteristics of their sample of 122 child pornography producers. They reported that 98 percent were men;

93 percent were white; 89 percent were 26 or older while 44 percent were 40 or older; 37 percent were married or cohabiting, 27 percent were divorced, separated, or widowed, and 36 percent had never married; 81 percent were employed full-time; 26 percent had prior arrests for nonsexual offending but only 12 percent had previously been arrested for sexually offending against minors; and 1 percent were mentally ill.

Webb, Craissati, and Keen reviewed the characteristics of a convenience sample of 90 British child pornography possessors.[91] They reported that the average age of these offenders was 38 and that all were male; 91 percent were white; 38 percent were married or cohabiting, 56 percent were single, and 6 percent were divorced or separated; 92 percent had no previous sexual convictions; 4 percent had prior convictions for sexual offending against a child; and 41 percent had prior contact with mental health services.

O'Brien and Webster reviewed a convenience sample of 123 adult males convicted of Internet child pornography offenses, who were either incarcerated or on probation in Great Britain.[92] Their mean age was 40.1 years; 95 percent were white; more than half (52 percent) were single and nearly a third (32 percent) were married or living with a partner; and more than half (51.2 percent) had some college, were college graduates, or had post-graduate degrees.

More recently, Endrass et al. surveyed a Swiss sample of 231 men charged with possession of child pornography during a special police Internet operation.[93] They reported the average age of these men was 36 years with a range of 18 to 65; 94 percent were Swiss nationals; 58 percent were single, 33 percent were married, 8 percent were divorced and one percent were widowed; 45 percent worked in positions that required a university level diploma, 50 percent in jobs requiring formal vocational training and only five percent in unskilled positions; and 32 percent worked in computer science or engineering-oriented professions, 26 percent had blue collar jobs, and 33 percent were employed in the service industry.

An obvious question regarding possessors of child pornography is whether they are or will become "hands-on" child sex offenders.

Seto and Eke identified 205 child pornography offenders through a search of the Ontario Sex Offender database and followed their subsequent criminal histories for approximately 3 years (April 2001–April 2004).[94] Four of these offenders were dropped from further analysis, one because she was the only woman in the group and three others because they remained incarcerated throughout the entire follow-up period. One hundred twelve of these offenders had been charged with a criminal offense prior to their child pornography convictions: 45 percent had committed prior nonviolent offenses, 30 percent had prior violent offenses, 24 percent had prior contact sexual offenses, and 15 percent had prior child pornography offenses.

Thirty-four (17 percent) of these offenders re-offended during the follow-up period—30 in the community and 4 while still incarcerated. Of those who re-offended while incarcerated, two were charged with new child pornography offenses, one with a nonsexual violent offense, and one with a contact sexual offense against a fellow inmate. Of the remaining re-offenders, 11 (6 percent of the follow-up sample) committed a violent offense; 9 (4 percent of the sample) committed sexual contact offenses; and 11 (6 percent of the sample) were again charged with a child pornography offense.

Seto and Eke found that among these 201 child pornography offenders, those "with a prior criminal history were significantly more likely to fail probation or parole and significantly more likely to offend again in some way."[95] Moreover, they found that those "child pornography offenders who had ever committed a contact sexual offense were the most likely to reoffend, either generally or sexually"[96] and that "only one of the offenders with only child pornography offenses committed a contact sexual offense in the follow-up period."[97]

Seto and Eke concluded that "More of this group of offenders might subsequently commit a sexual offense as the duration of the follow-up period increases, but our finding does contradict the assumption that all child pornography offenders are at a very high risk to commit contact sexual offenses involving children."[98]

Interestingly, however, a year after publishing these results, Seto and two other colleagues, Cantor and Blanchard, reported another study, titled "Child Pornography Offenses Are a Valid Diagnostic Indicator of Pedophilia."[99] Seto et al. compared the "phallometrically assessed sexual arousal" (i.e., penile blood volume) of several groups of men in response to slides of nude models of varying age and gender, accompanied in each instance by a narrative describing sexual conduct with the individual depicted.[100] They reported:

> Child pornography offenders were significantly more likely to show a pedophilic pattern of sexual arousal during phallometric testing than were comparison groups of offenders against adults or general sexology patients. In fact, child pornography offenders, regardless of whether they had a history of sexual offenses against child victims, were more likely to show a pedophilic pattern of sexual arousal than were a combined group of offenders against children.[101]

Bourke and Hernandez reported the results of a study which they conclude "challenges the often-repeated assertion that child pornography offenders are 'only' involved with 'pictures.'"[102] These researchers, affiliated with the U.S. Marshall's Service and the U.S. Bureau of Prisons respectively, examined the "Victims Lists" prepared by 155 men who had been convicted of possessing child pornography. The men prepared these lists as part of their sex offender treatment in a federal prison, the Butner Federal Correctional Complex in North Carolina. None of these men had been convicted of producing child pornography, and all of them had voluntarily participated in treatment for at least 6 months at the time of their victim disclosures.

Among these 155 men, at the time of sentencing, 115 had no documented history of "hands-on" sex abuse of children (defined to include "any fondling of the genitals or breasts over clothing, as well as skin-to-skin contact including hand to genital, genital to genital, mouth to genital, and genital to anus") while 40 did have such a history. Among the latter group, the average number of known victims was 1.88 per offender.[103]

By the end of their treatment, 131 offenders (85 percent) admitted to having sexually abused one or more children; 24 (15 percent) denied that they had committed any "hands-on" child sexual abuse. Nine of the 24 offenders who denied any "hands-on" offending were polygraphed and only two were found to be truthful. Offenders who were known to have committed "hands-on" offenses when they were sentenced (an average of 1.8 victims per offender) disclosed during treatment that they had sexually abused many more children: an average of 19.4 victims per offender. Offenders not known to have committed any "hands-on" offenses prior to sentencing acknowledged in treatment an average of 8.7 child sexual abuse victims.

Bourke and Hernandez conclude that from the "dramatic increase (2,369%) in the number of contact offenses acknowledged by the treatment participants... [i]t appears that these offenders are far from being innocent, sexually 'curious' men who, through dumb luck, became entangled in the World Wide Web... [L]ess than 2% of subjects who entered treatment without known 'hands-on' offenses were verified to be 'just pictures' cases. It is noteworthy that both of these offenders remarked that while they had not molested a child prior to their arrest for the instant offense [possession of child pornography], with access and opportunity they would have been at risk for engaging in hands-on molestation."[104]

In the study of British child pornography possessors noted earlier, Webb et al. compared their convenience sample of 90 such men with 120 men who had sexually abused children under the age of 16. Twenty (22 percent) of child pornography offenders had previous convictions: 15 for "general offenses,"

7 for "sexual offenses" (mostly possession or production of child pornography), and 3 for "violent offenses."[105] Contact child sexual abuse offenders in this sample had no prior child pornography convictions.

Webb et al. collected follow-up data for an average of 18 months on 190 of these subjects, all of whom were on probation in the community: 117 child sexual abuse offenders and 73 child pornography offenders. They considered "failure" to include being charged with or convicted of a sexual offense, being convicted of a general criminal offense, being returned to court or custody for "inappropriate behavior," engaging in "high-risk behaviors (for example, increased internet usage, or heavy drinking which was previously associated with internet sexual offending)"; and being the subject of "child protection investigations in relation to new allegations or concerns regardless of the outcome."[106] During the follow-up period, child sexual abuse offenders had significantly more failures (29 percent) than did child pornography offenders (4 percent). Only one child pornography offender was convicted for a general offense and just two were convicted for further Internet sexual offenses. None of the child pornography offenders otherwise breached the conditions of their presence in the community or were recalled to court. Also none of them missed a supervision or treatment session. Among child sexual abuse offenders, 3 percent were charged with or convicted of further violent offenses, and 2 percent were charged with or convicted of further contact sexual offenses. The breach and recall rate for the child sexual abuse offenders, however, was significantly higher at 17 percent.

In the Swiss study mentioned earlier, Endrass et al. examined the subsequent criminal charges over a 6-year period of 231 men charged with possession of child pornography during a special police Internet operation.[107] Among this sample, 11 (4.8 percent) had a prior conviction for a sexual and/or violent offense, 2 (1 percent) for a "hands-on" child sex offense, 8 (3.3 percent) for a "hands-off" sex offense, and 1 for a nonsexual violent offense. "[A]pplying a broad definition of recidivism, which included ongoing investigations, charges and convictions," these researchers found that seven men (3 percent) "recidivated with a violent and/or sex offense," nine (3.9 percent) "with a hands-off sex offense" and just two (0.8 percent) "with a hands-on sex offense."[108]

Based upon these data, Endrass et al. concluded that "Consuming child pornography alone is not a risk factor for committing hands-on sex offenses—at least not for those subjects who had never committed a hands-on sex offense. The majority of the investigated consumers had no previous convictions for hands-on sex offenses. For those offenders, the prognosis for hands-on sex offenses, as well as for recidivism with child pornography, is favorable."[109]

Riegel took another approach to the question of whether possessors of child pornography are or will become "hands-on" child sex offenders."[110] Focusing on a particular subtype of child pornography possessors, he asked: "Does viewing erotic pictures of boys exacerbate the tendency for pedosexually inclined males to seek out boys for sexual purposes?"[111] To gather data, he developed a 101-item Internet survey that drew anonymous responses from 290 men (ages 18 to 60) who identified themselves as "Boy-Attracted Pedosexual Males."[112] More than 90 percent of those who responded were white. The majority were from North America, but many others were residents of the United Kingdom, Europe, Australia, and New Zealand. More than 77 percent reported attending college, more than 39 percent had earned an undergraduate degree, and over 14 percent had an advanced degree. Among this cohort, 228 (78.6 percent) reported no involvement with law enforcement with regard to accusations of sexual contact with boys, but 18 (6.2 percent) reported they had been incarcerated for such conduct. None of the respondents were incarcerated at the time of the survey.

Among this cohort, 33.5 percent reported viewing child pornography on the Internet "quite regularly," 25.5 "frequently," 17.9 percent "occasionally," 10.7 percent "sporadically," 7.2 percent "rarely," and 5.2 percent "never."[113] Overall the "boy erotica" reportedly viewed by these men included images of nudity, disrobing, subjugation, masturbation, fellatio, and/or anal intercourse. Some images reportedly involved boys alone, others boy with boys, and yet others boys with men. The reported mean length of use of such images was over 3 years.

Asked if viewing of these images "was useful as a substitute for actual sexual contact with boys, in that their urges and drives were redirected and given an outlet that affected no other person," 83.8 percent said "frequently" to "invariably."[114] Asked whether the use of such images "increased their tendency to seek out boys for the sole purpose of sexual activity," 84.5 percent said "rarely" or "never."[115] Asked if they used child pornographic images "as an aid to masturbation," 63.9 percent said they did "frequently," 25.0 percent "occasionally," 6.1 percent "rarely," and 5.0 percent "never."[116] Finally, asked if they had shared "boy erotica" with a boy, 76.6 percent said "never," 7.2 percent "once," 10 percent "rarely," and 6.2 percent "occasional[ly]."[117]

Based upon these data, and subject to numerous limitations, Riegel concluded that "There sometimes is a correlation between males who are in possession of sexually explicit materials and those who also run afoul of the law because of accusations of sexual activities with boys. But correlation must not be confused with causation, and there is very little support within these data for the societal perception that the viewing of boy erotica is a substantive causative factor in actual or potential sexual contacts and activities between [Boy-Attracted Pedosexual Males] and minor males."[118]

More recently, two related groups of researchers have conduct separate meta-analyses of existing data (including some from studies that are mentioned above) regarding online sex offenders and their offenses. These meta-analyses examined data dealing with a combination of child pornography offenders and offenders who had used the Internet to solicit sex from minors (so-called luring offenders, whose offenses are described at length in the next chapter of this volume).

Comparing online offenders to offline offenders, Babchishin et al. (2009) relied upon data from 27 studies reported from 2000 to 2009.[119] They reported that online offenders were more likely to be Caucasian and slightly younger than offline offenders.[120] They also found that online offenders showed more victim empathy, more sexual deviancy, fewer cognitive distortions, slightly less emotional identification with children, and less of a tendency to engage in "impression management"—that is, present themselves in an unduly positive light.[121]

Babchishin et al. also reported that while the data in their meta-analysis were insufficient to compare the two groups of offenders in terms of prior criminal involvement, such involvement was "low among the online sexual offenders."[122] "[O]nly 12% of the online offenders" in the studies analyzed had prior records of non-sexual crimes.[123] Moreover, "[e]ven if the rates of prior sexual offenses [were] included (10%), the rate of prior criminal involvement is substantially less than in samples of child molesters."[124] As Babchishin et al. point out, "For example, 59% of U.S. offenders who victimized children had previously served sentences and one in four had a history of violence…"[125]

In conclusion, Babchishin et al. observe that that while research in this field is "too new to conclude whether online offenders are truly distinct from offline offenders,"[126] "[m]any of the observed differences can be explained by assuming that online offenders, compared to offline offenders, have greater self-control and more psychological barriers to acting on their deviant interests."[127]

The other recent meta-analysis, conducted by Seto, Hanson, and Babchishin and reported in 2010, included 24 studies involving 4,697 online offenders.[128] Studies relying upon official records indicated that 12.3 percent of these offenders had prior sexual offenses, mostly against children. Studies relying upon self-report data (including the Butner study by Bourke and Hernandez, described above) indicated that 55.1 percent of offenders "disclosed prior sexual contacts with children."[129] According to Seto et al., the Butner study was "identified as an outlier in the self-report data," but even when "outliers" were excluded from the analysis, "approximately half of the online offenders admitted to prior contact offenses."[130]

Significantly, however, the Seto et al. meta-analysis also examined the rate of sexual recidivism for online offenders. Follow-up periods in the studies analyzed ranged from 1.5 to 6 years (with most under 4 years) and recidivism included a high of 10.3 percent in one study, 8.0 percent in another, under 6.0 percent in five other studies, and zero in two studies. Based upon their meta-analysis, Seto et al. report that "The fixed effect estimate for sexual recidivism was 3.9% and the random effects estimate was 2.8%. The observed rates for other types of recidivism were similarly low (0.7% to 3.4%)."[131]

Seto et al. caution that since the vast majority of online sex offenders are charged with child pornography offenses as opposed to luring offenses, these results appear more specifically applicable to the former rather than the latter offenders. In conclusion, however, they note that "Although there is considerable overlap between online and offline offending, our results suggest there is a distinct group of online offenders whose only sexual crimes involve illegal (most often child) pornography or, less frequently, illegal solicitation of minors using the internet."[132]

"Judging" Child Pornography Law

There is almost universal support for criminalizing and punishing the manufacture and even the simple possession of child pornography. Until recently, only a handful of academics—if that many—have seriously questioned the wisdom and legitimacy of America's child pornography laws. To understand this void in critical commentary, even among normally outspoken academics, one need look no further than to Harris Mirkin, a tenured political science professor at the University of Missouri.

In 1999, Mirkin published a scholarly article, "The Pattern of Sexual Politics: Feminism, Homosexuality, and Pedophilia," in which he asserted that society's contemporary response to pedophiles might be analogized to its earlier response to homosexuals and women before public attitudes were changed by the gay rights and women's rights movements.[133]

The Missouri House of Representatives and the state Senate both responded by voting to cut $100,000 (approximately the amount of Mirkin's salary) from the university's annual budget.[134] Some members of the public responded by denouncing Mirkin as a pervert and threatening to kill him. What mattered most, however, was the reaction of his academic colleagues and administrators. The university's chancellor, the president of the state university system, the faculty senate, the American Council on Education (ACE), and the American Association of University Professors all rallied behind Mirkin. As the general counsel for ACE put it, "The appropriate place to debate the legitimacy of a professor's thought is in the marketplace of ideas... Today's heresy often becomes tomorrow's orthodoxy."[135] Mirkin himself responded to all the attention he had generated by saying: "The article is meant to be subversive; the article is meant to make people think. Because they have tried to stifle discussion, there has been a discussion, which is one of the healthy things about the United States."[136]

With that experience behind him, in 2008, Mirkin, who was still a tenured faculty member, indeed chairman of his department, published another controversial scholarly article, "The Social, Political, and Legal Construction of the Concept of Child Pornography."[137] In this essay, Mirkin challenged the assumptions that underlie modern American child pornography law:

> The ostensible reason for denying even the minimum right to possess non-commercially distributed child pornography is that the production of the pornography harms the children portrayed, but this article has attempted to demonstrate that the argument does not hold up to analysis. In addition to the lack of evidence that the models are hurt, there is not a proximate connection between the production of images and anonymous possession of pictures downloaded for free from the Internet. Neither the private viewing nor the noncommercial distribution of child pornography encourages its commercial production, just as pirated images, texts, software, and music do not encourage their commercial production. At best the claim for the link is a convenience argument, since it might be difficult to establish that privately possessed child pornography was acquired noncommercially, but this type of argument has never been accepted by the [U.S. Supreme] Court in the speech area and is specifically rejected in *Ashcroft* (2002).[138]

In what may be the only other serious general scholarly attack on child pornography laws, Amy Adler, a law professor, wrote "The Perverse Law of Child Pornography."[139] Adler begins by asking, "What, if any, is the relationship between these two concurrent phenomena—the expansion of child pornography law and the growing problem of child sexual abuse, including child pornography? Does their correlative temporal connection allow us to draw any conclusions about a possible causal relationship?"[140] She then proceeds to answer that question, suggesting, inter alia, that child pornography laws may contribute to the problem of child sexual abuse:

> There is a standard, conventional explanation for this correlation. This account casts law in a reactive stance: As the sexual exploitation of children, or at least our awareness of the problem, has risen, legislatures and courts have responded by passing and upholding tougher child pornography laws. . .
>
> I am sure that is at least part of what is going on. But . . . I propose two alternative readings—readings that do not exclude the conventional account described above, but supplement it. In the first reading, I explore the possibility that certain sexual prohibitions invite their own violation by increasing the sexual allure of what they forbid. I suggest that child pornography law and the eroticization of children exist in a dialectic of transgression and taboo: The dramatic expansion of child pornography law may have unwittingly heightened pedophilic desire.
>
> . . . In the second reading, I view law and the culture it regulates not as dialectical opposites, but as intermingled. Child pornography law may represent only another symptom of and not a solution to the problem of child abuse or the cultural fascination with sexual children. The cross purposes of law and culture that I describe above (law as prohibition, which both halts and incites desire) may mask a deeper harmony between them: The legal discourse on prohibiting child pornography may represent yet another way in which our culture drenches itself in sexualized children.[141]

Aside from occasional academic polemics such as those of Mirkin and Adler, which may have been intended to be more provocative than persuasive, there has been only one other major source of public complaints about contemporary child pornography laws: federal judges. While child pornography prosecutions account for only about 2 percent of the entire criminal docket of the federal courts, they represent what is perhaps the most rapidly growing portion of the caseload in these courts. Since the late 1990s, when federal courts handled a "few dozen" such cases annually, their number has grown to well over 2,200 each year. In fact, in one recent 5-year stretch, the number of child pornography prosecutions brought before federal courts doubled.[142]

Despite these numbers, however, it is not the increased workload that is the focus of complaints from the federal judiciary, but rather the fundamental unfairness of child pornography laws and the extremely long, ever-increasing, mandatory prison sentences they seem to require in virtually every such case.

Some federal judges have openly rebelled against the federal sentencing structure for convicted possessors of child pornography and have explained their views in the context of published judicial opinions.

For example, in *United States v. Paul*, a 65-year-old, disabled former minister was convicted of four counts of knowing possession of child pornography and sentenced to 210 months in prison, the bottom of the sentencing guideline range for his offense level.[143] While the U.S. Court of Appeals for the Sixth Circuit affirmed his sentence in 2009, one judge on that panel, Gilbert Merritt dissented, writing that "[O]ur federal legal system has lost its bearings on the subject of computer-based child pornography. Our 'social revulsion' against these 'misfits' downloading these images is perhaps somewhat more rational than the thousands of witchcraft trials and burnings conducted in Europe and here from the Thirteenth to the Eighteenth Centuries, but it borders on the same thing."[144]

In 2008, in *United States v. Johnson*, an Iowa medical student with no criminal record used Limewire, the peer-to-peer file-sharing program, to download and store more than 600 images of minors engaged in sexually explicit conduct.[145] Between the time he was arrested and the time he pleaded guilty to a single count of knowingly receiving visual depictions of minors engaging in sexually explicit conduct, while on conditional release pending trial, the defendant completed medical school and the first year of his medical residency. As Chief Federal District Court Judge Robert W. Pratt explained in his sentencing memorandum:

> Under the guidelines in effect in 2004, Defendant's base offense level under the advisory sentencing guidelines is 17. Because the material involves a minor under the age of twelve, two levels are added. Five levels are added because the offense involved distribution for the receipt, or expectation of receipt, of a thing of value, though not pecuniary gain. Four levels are added because the material portrays sadistic, masochistic conduct or other depictions of violence. Two levels are added because the offense involved the use of a computer for the possession, transmission, receipt, or distribution of the material. Finally, five levels are added because the offense involved at least 600 images. The Court finds that a two-level reduction for acceptance of responsibility is warranted in light of Defendant's timely guilty plea, and the Government has also moved for application of an additional, one-level reduction for acceptance of responsibility. Defendant's total offense level is, therefore, 32. Defendant has no prior criminal history points,

resulting in a criminal history category of I. The resulting advisory sentencing range of imprisonment is 121 to 151 months.[146]

In imposing a sentence of 84 months (7 years) in prison rather than the 121 to 151 months called for by the sentencing guidelines, Chief Judge Pratt took aim not only at the guidelines but at the "Butner study" (described earlier in this chapter), which the prosecution had tried to use to support the highest sentence possible.

With regard to the guidelines, Judge Pratt wrote:

Child pornography offenses are very serious. Many child victims will never live a normal life. As the Government notes in its sentencing memorandum, the market for such images helps foster conduct that is punishable by life in prison in many states for the crimes that are inflicted on children to create the images. Thus, strict punishments are generally necessary to reflect this seriousness, as well as to promote respect for the law, to provide just punishment, and to adequately deter criminal conduct.

However, as [federal sentencing law] makes clear, the Court must also consider factors unique to a particular defendant. For example, the Court must consider the history and characteristics of the defendant. Likewise, the Court must consider what punishment is sufficient to protect the public from further crimes of the particular defendant present before it. . .

The Government urges the Court to give only limited consideration to the factors unique to Defendant. Instead, they argue that the Court should give substantial deference to the relevant sentencing guidelines, arguing that they reflect the will of the people, as expressed through Congress. . .

At the urging of Congress, the Sentencing Commission has amended the guidelines . . . on several occasions over the past two decades, recommending more severe penalties. As far as this Court can tell, these modifications do not appear to be based on any sort of empirical data, and the Court has been unable to locate any particular rationale for them beyond the general revulsion that is associated with child exploitation-related offenses. . .

Congress has created a fifteen-year window, between the statutory minimum (5 years) and maximum (20 years) sentences, within which this Court can penalize a convicted child pornographer. However, on account of Congress' tinkering with the guidelines, the Commission now recommends that nearly all defendants be incarcerated near the twenty-year statutory maximum. Thus, strict adherence to the sentencing guidelines effective at the time of Defendant's arrest, and even more so to those effective today, would make it difficult for the Court to consider the individualized factors that [federal sentencing law] requires. . .

[T]he Court is charged with establishing a punishment that is sufficient, but not greater than necessary, for this defendant, and the Court cannot give too much weight to the sentencing guidelines, given their lack of empirical support. In consideration of Defendant, as an individual, the Court carefully evaluates Defendant's past history and characteristics and the need to protect the public in light of these characteristics. The Court views Defendant's behavior during the three-year period between the seizure of his computer and his indictment as a good indication of what society can expect from . . .[147]

Judge Pratt also excoriated the prosecution for arguing that "[The Butner Study] shows that the Defendant is statistically more likely than not to have actually committed an act of child sexual abuse" even though there was no evidence that he had ever committed "a hands-on child sex offense."[148] In so doing, the judge vehemently rejected the study, its methods, and its results and even went so far as to question the motives of those who conducted it:

The Government offers the Butner Study to demonstrate that Defendant is a threat to the public. However, the Government also offers the Study to show that "defendant is statistically more likely than not to have actually committed [a past] act of ['hands-on'] child abuse." The inference that the Government asks the Court to draw is distasteful and prohibited by law. Uncharged criminal conduct may generally only be considered in sentencing if proved by a preponderance of the evidence. Moreover, the Government bears the burden of proof. The Butner Study, even if credible, falls far short of this standard because it fails to demonstrate whether Defendant has, personally, previously assaulted a child sexually. At most, the Study reveals that a majority of other individuals with a similar criminal history committed crimes against children, but the Court cannot see how evidence of those individuals' crimes establishes by a preponderance of the evidence that Defendant committed a prior sexual crime. This conclusion is only bolstered by the fact that the Government failed to present any physical evidence that Defendant sexually assaulted anyone, let alone a child.

The Government produced no witnesses, no victims, no forensic evidence, no confession, and no other sign that any previous improper sexual activity occurred. Indeed, the Government agreed with the [Presentencing Report's] calculation of Defendant's criminal history, which does not include any references to prior sexual crimes. Therefore, this Court will not accept the implicit invitation to use the Butner Study to hold Defendant accountable for a phantom crime unsupported by any evidence.

The Court also rejects the Government's attempt to use the Butner Study to demonstrate that Defendant is a danger to the community. The Government argues that Defendant is dangerous because the Study indicates other individuals charged with similar crimes have committed "hands-on" sexual abuse of children. The Court rejects this proposition because the Butner Study is not credible. The Butner Study's sample population consisted of incarcerated individuals participating in a sexual offender treatment program at a federal correctional institution. As [a psychologist called by the defendant] testified, the program is "highly coercive." Unless offenders continue to admit to further sexual crimes, whether or not they actually committed those crimes, the offenders are discharged from the program. Consequently, the subjects in this Study had an incentive to lie, despite the fact that participation in the program would not shorten their sentences. [Defendant's psychological expert] testified that the Study's "whole approach" is rejected by the treatment and scientific community. Complicating this bias is the fact that the Butner Study did not report on the nearly 23% (46/201) of individuals in the treatment program who left due to "voluntary withdrawal, expulsion, or death." As a result, the offender population and the Study's results were almost certainly skewed.

The Butner Study also suffers from additional methodological flaws. First, the subjects of the Study were not randomly selected from those who only collect child pornography, which indicates that even setting aside the incentive to lie, the sample population may not be representative of the larger population that collects child pornography. Second, the Study employed an unpublished questionnaire. This prevents other independent researchers from verifying whether the questionnaire is reliable and capable of producing results that are accurate and meaningful. Third, the Study relies, in part, on the results from polygraph examinations, which is highly problematic given the unreliability of such tests, especially since "no standard for training polygraph experts" exists. Fourth, the Study is not peer reviewed, which is the norm in science. According to [defendant's psychological expert], the peer review process would likely be "pretty uncomfortable" for the researchers because the data and statistics in the Study do not fit the researchers' conclusions. Finally, the Study also appears to suffer from flaws relating to its control group and independent variable, or lack thereof.

The Government also tacitly encouraged the Court to look beyond any flaws in the Study because it was "exploratory," a "first step" that the authors believe to be the "tip of the iceberg." [T]he Court will not look past the shortcomings of this Study merely because the Study is unique or new. Indeed, the fact that the Study is revolutionary in nature gives this Court great pause for concern, especially since it produced the sensational result that somewhere between 85% and 98% of child pornography collectors have personally molested children.

The Court finds these results highly questionable given the extraordinarily high percentages, as well as the fact that the researchers saw a 2,369% increase "in the number of contact sexual offenses acknowledged by the treatment participants" during the course of the Study. These astronomical figures lead the Court to question whether this unvetted prison Study, conducted by the former chief of the federal sexual offender treatment program and distributed by the Department of Justice to prosecutors, is, in actuality, a product of the tremendous "political pressure applied" to researchers in this research field.[149]

In another recent child pornography possession case, *United States v. Ontiveros*, U.S. District Judge William C. Griesbach rejected the sentencing guidelines range, which called for imprisonment between 97 and 212 months, and instead sentenced the convicted defendant to 60 months in prison, the minimum sentence allowed by federal law.[150] In so doing, the judge relied upon his belief that the ready availability of child pornography on the Internet has made it easy for people with no criminal record, no criminal intentions, and little if any likelihood of recidivism to obtain these contraband images and to rationalize viewing them. As Judge Griesbach wrote in 2008:

Ontiveros, like many who have accessed child pornography via their computer, seems not to have initially appreciated the magnitude of the offense he was committing or the risk that he would be caught. The manner in which computer technology and high speed internet access have made such material readily available in the presumed privacy of the home has removed several substantial impediments to seeking out such material that previously existed. No longer must a person travel to the seedy side of town, walk into a dirty book store, make a request for the sordid material to another person from whom one's identity could not be readily concealed, and pay for it. The easy availability of the material at no cost with the click of a mouse, while at the same time preserving one's anonymity, leaves little but one's natural aversion to depictions of the abuse and degradation of children to stand in the way of obtaining it. And as the popular culture has become more and more saturated with a debased concept of human sexuality, this natural aversion in many people seems to have grown weaker.

A further factor seems to be the lack of appreciation of the harm that simply viewing such material does to children. In some respects, the internet seems analogous to a huge file cabinet containing an almost limitless number of documents and other forms of information. Under this view, accessing child pornography can be rationalized as simply pulling out a drawer and simply looking at photos that someone else took in the past. As long as the individual who accesses the pornography is not himself abusing children to produce it, selling it in order to profit from it, or paying for it so as to stimulate demand for it, he can tell himself that he has done no harm to the children depicted. This line of reasoning, of course, is directly contrary to Congress' finding . . . that "[e]very instance of viewing images of child pornography represents a renewed violation of the privacy of the victims and a repetition of their abuse." And it also ignores the fact that further demand for such material is fueled by those who seek it out and share it with others. But these harms are indirect and abstract, and thus often unappreciated or easily ignored. This is apparently why people who express shock at the idea that they would ever intentionally harm a child can engage in such behavior.

While these changes in technology and the culture, and the lack of appreciation of the harm done to children do not excuse the behavior, they do suggest an explanation for why people such as Ontiveros with no previous history of criminal or abusive conduct seem to be committing such crimes with increasing frequency.

They also suggest that with the realization that such conduct is not anonymous, that it carries substantial penalties, and that even simply viewing it does substantial harm to children, first-time offenders such as Ontiveros are unlikely to repeat. Treatment directed to increasing such awareness can be provided within the sentence structure I have ordered.[151]

Judge Griesbach added that:

[T]he fact that a person was stimulated by digital depictions of child pornography does not mean that he has or will in the future seek to assault a child. Ontiveros, like all human beings, has free will, and neither a psychologist, nor a judge, can predict what a person will choose to do in the future. A court should exercise caution to avoid imposing a sentence for a crime some fear a defendant could commit in the future, instead of for the crime he actually committed and for which he is before the court.[152]

Finally, in *United States v. Goldberg*, a federal district court judge recently openly aired her concerns about sentencing child pornography offenders and continued to do so even after a lenient sentence she imposed was rejected by the U.S. Court of Appeals for the Seventh Circuit.[153] Twenty-year-old Jeremy Goldberg was convicted of possessing child pornography and faced a maximum sentence of 10 years in prison. Since he was convicted of only possession, there was no mandatory minimum sentence. Federal sentencing guidelines suggested a sentence in the range of 63 to 78 months in prison. U.S. District Judge Joan Gottschall imposed a sentence of 1 day in prison to be followed by a 10-year period of supervised release. She imposed the 1-day sentence, rather than no prison sentence at all, because without any sentence of incarceration there can be no supervised release. In imposing this lenient sentence, Judge Gottschall said in open court:

[T]he way I look at this case, . . . I think that if I sent Mr. Goldberg away for 63 months or anything close to it with the hope that he gets sex offender treatment in prison, we're pretty much guaranteeing his life will be ruined. And I think there's some possibility here that his life can go in a different way, and I'd like to try that, but I'm very worried, because what's gone on here is very, very difficult for me to deal with. I mean, these pictures, I can't even bear to look at them they're so horrible. . .

. . . I'm going to . . . deviate from the guidelines . . . and I'm going to impose . . . a ten-year period of supervised release.

It's more supervised release than I have ever imposed before, but I really think that given the psychiatric reports and given what transpired here, that the period of supervision has to be long enough to ensure that if Mr. Goldberg turns his life in a different direction he does it for a long time. . .

I think I better now talk about why . . . I deviated from the guidelines. My reason in this case is . . . this: It's considering the history and characteristics of the defendant I think that there's a substantial likelihood . . . and also considering the psychiatric reports, that this offense was committed out of boredom and stupidity and not because Mr. Goldberg has a real problem with the kind of deviance that these cases usually suggest. I believe that if that is correct, and if he is sent to prison for a lengthy period, anything of any consequence at all, I think it's going to ruin his life in many ways.

I think that sex offender treatment within the Bureau of Prisons is going to expose him to people who are dangerous to him. I think any substantial period of incarceration is going to ensure that he's not able to take advantage of his education and get a good job, and I think all of this will reinforce whatever negative things he's done in the past rather than pushing him in a positive direction.

I recognize that the viewing of child pornography over the Internet destroys the lives of young children, but I also recognize that the life that I'm concerned with here, the life that I can affect, is Mr. Goldberg's life, and I don't want to destroy his life in the hope that maybe in some very indirect way it's going to help somebody else's life. I don't think it is. . .

The reason for the long period of supervision and the close supervision that I believe I've required is to make sure that if he indeed represents a threat, and if I'm wrong in my assessment of what went on here, that we are able to catch it before any damage is done. . .[154]

The prosecution appealed this sentence and the Seventh Circuit reversed the sentencing judgment and remanded the case for resentencing. The appeals court began its opinion by emphasizing the nature of the defendant and his crime:

The defendant, who is now 23 years old, is the son of a prosperous couple in the wealthy Chicago suburb of Highland Park. He downloaded file-sharing software that gave him access to a web site called "# 100% PreTeenGirlPics." Over a period of some 18 months, he downloaded hundreds of pornographic photographic images, some depicting children as young as 2 or 3 being vaginally penetrated by adult males. He offered these images to other subscribers to the web site to induce them to send similar images in return. He masturbated while viewing the pornographic images. He has a history of drug abuse. His lawyers describe him as a "normal young adult."[155]

The court then gave reasons, both general and specific to this case, why this sentence could not be allowed to stand:

A prison sentence of one day for a crime that Congress and the American public consider grave, in circumstances that enhance the gravity (we refer to the character of some of the images), committed by a convicted drug offender, does not give due weight to the "nature and circumstances of the offense" and the "history and characteristics of the defendant." It does not "reflect the seriousness of the offense," "promote respect for the law," or "provide just punishment for the offense." It does not "afford adequate deterrence to criminal conduct." And it creates an unwarranted sentence disparity, since similarly situated defendants are punished with substantial prison sentences.

***

The district judge was influenced by the erroneous belief that a sentence affects only the life of the criminal and not the lives of his victims. Young children were raped in order to enable the production of the pornography that the defendant both downloaded and uploaded—both consumed himself and disseminated to others. The greater the customer demand for child pornography, the more that will be produced. Sentences influence behavior, or so at least Congress thought when . . . it made deterrence a statutory sentencing factor. The logic of deterrence suggests that the lighter the punishment for downloading and uploading child pornography, the greater the customer demand for it and so the more will be produced.

Why the fact that the defendant committed the offense out of "boredom and stupidity," if it were a fact, should be thought a mitigating factor escapes us and was not explained by the judge. Anyway it is not a fact; the defendant obtained sexual gratification from the pornographic images that he so sedulously collected.

It is also inconsistent with the 10-year term of supervised release that the judge imposed, which includes conditions that require the defendant's participation in programs for the psychological treatment of sex offenders.

The judge's suggestion that the defendant does not have "a real problem" could be interpreted to mean that she disparages Congress's decision to criminalize the consumption and distribution of child pornography, perhaps because she thinks that only people who actually molest children, rather than watching them being molested, have "a real problem." This interpretation is reinforced by her statement elsewhere in the transcript of the sentencing hearing that the defendant's crime was just "a kind of mischief" . . .

The district judge's assertion "that sex offender treatment within the Bureau of Prisons is going to expose [the defendant] to people who are dangerous to him" is ill informed. Sex-offender treatment in federal prisons is voluntary. And "the vast majority" of sex offenders in the program are individuals convicted of "Possession, Receipt, Distribution, and Transportation of Child Pornography," like the defendant. The judge gave no explanation for why she thought a prison sentence would be more ruinous for the defendant than for any other imprisoned criminal other than her mistaken belief that he would be thrown in with violent sexual offenders.[156]

On remand, Judge Gottschall resentenced Goldberg to 4 years imprisonment to be followed by 10 years of post-release supervision. But in so doing, the judge did not back away from the reasoning that led her to the original sentence. She also challenged the reasoning of the appellate judges who overruled her original sentence:

The explanation given for that sentence was the best that this court could do, and, in this court's understanding, a fair reading of that explanation is not consistent with the Seventh Circuit's assessment of it. Regardless, the court believes that the court of appeals opinion quarrels not only with the way the sentence was justified, but quarrels with the sentence itself. . .

The Seventh Circuit stated that this case, involving "hundreds of images," should perhaps be treated differently from a case involving a "handful of images" not as aggravated as these. Thus, the number of images and the nature of those images were issues that the court of appeals considered important. Furthermore, whereas many reported cases see child predators as different from people who view child pornography but are not child predators, the court of appeals seems to view this as a distinction without a difference. It evidently views looking at child pornography as serious a crime as its actual production. . . [157]

Judge Gottschall also responded to the appellate court's concern that her original sentence "create[d] an unwarranted sentence disparity, since similarly situated defendants are punished with substantial prison sentences"[158] by cataloging the stark disparities already found among sentences in child pornography cases:

The court has also considered the sentences imposed in comparable cases in its sister courts. The court recognizes, of course, that no two cases are identical and reported cases may not describe all salient facts. However, it is struck by the inconsistency in the way apparently similar cases are charged and sentenced. . . For example, in the District of Utah, a 120-month sentence was given for an offence with a calculated guideline range of 135–168 months (5,129 images). The District of Nebraska gave a 24-month sentence in a 3000-image case with a guideline range of 63–78 months; in that case, the defendant indicated that he possessed the images but did not intend to share them. In another District of Nebraska case, involving 800 images, with an advisory guideline range of 46–57 months, a sentence of 24 months was also given. In the Eastern District of Tennessee, 135 months was given to a defendant who had knowingly received child pornography via computer (guideline range of 135 to 168 months). Finally, in a 200-image case in which the defendant was charged with both possession and distribution, Judge Manning of this district gave an 84-month sentence; the guideline range was 168 to 210 months with a statutory minimum of 60 months. . .

In cases that went to the courts of appeal, a similar disparity is seen. A sentence of 57 months was affirmed by the Fifth Circuit in a case in which thousands of images were found stored on 4000 compact discs. In a 2007 Sixth Circuit case, where there were 992 images involved and the psychological profile indicated that the defendant was not a pedophile or sexual predator, a sentence of 180 months was affirmed; the guideline range was 210–262 months. . . In US v. Grinbergs, a sentence of 12 months and a day was reversed by the Eighth Circuit. The Eighth Circuit's decision in that case, which featured a number of images similar to this one, and in which

the guidelines were 46–57 months, was vacated by the Supreme Court . . . and remanded to the district court for resentencing. In another Eighth Circuit case, in which the defendant operated a child pornography file server (as in the instant case),
and in which the defendant was found to possess 45–50 images, some sadomasochistic, together with psychiatric testimony that defendant was not a pedophile, a sentence of 151 months, at the low end of the guideline range, was affirmed. A sentence of 180 months (the statutory mandatory minimum) was affirmed by the Ninth Circuit in a multi-count case involving 10,000–12,000 (including some sadomasochistic) images. A sentence of 84 months (guideline range of 151–188 months) was affirmed by the Eleventh Circuit in a 981-image case where the defendant had been previously convicted of lewd acts on a child and diagnosed as a pedophile.

***

With specific reference to cases in the Seventh Circuit, the court discovered that the court of appeals affirmed sentences of 144 months in a 6500-image case and 330 months in a case with advisory guidelines of 292 to 365 months. In a case involving 300 images and no evidence of actual child molestation, but correspondence which indicated that the defendant was moving that way, the court of appeals affirmed a sentence of 87 months incarceration. A sentence of 76 months incarceration was affirmed in a case where the defendant was convicted of possession of 8178 images (some sadomasochistic), 3083 text files and 80 video files. The court of appeals affirmed a 55-month sentence (high end of the guideline range) involving 20000 images of child pornography, some sadistic. . . [159]

In addition to their written opinions and sentencing memoranda in specific cases, federal judges have also spoken out publicly against the sentencing structure in child pornography possession cases. For example, in 2009, the U.S. Sentencing Commission held several public hearings in various parts of the country, and numerous federal trial and appellate court judges offered testimony.

Federal District Judge Robin J. Cauthron testified:

The Guideline sentences for child pornography cases are often too harsh where the defendant's crime is solely possession unaccompanied by an indication of "acting out" behavior on the part of the defendant. It is too often the case that a defendant appears to be a social misfit looking at dirty pictures in the privacy of his own home without any real prospect of touching or otherwise acting out as to any person. As foul as child pornography is, I am unpersuaded by the suggestion that a direct link has been proven between viewing child porn and molesting children.

I have two specific suggestions: (a) keep the Guidelines in this area flexible, recognizing that a broad range of conduct is encompassed within them, some of which is truly evil deserving very harsh penalties and some of which is considerably less so; and (b) consider whether the enhancement for use of a computer makes sense. As widespread as computer use is now, enhancing for use of a computer is a little like penalizing speeding but then adding an extra penalty if a car is involved.[160]

Federal District Judge Jay Zainey testified that he was not defending those who possess what he called "filth" but sometimes found prison terms in child pornography cases to be "too harsh."[161]

Chief District Court Judges James Carr and Gerald Rosen testified that criminal sentences for simple possession of child pornography, as opposed to manufacture or commercial distribution, "may need to be changed."[162] The judges agreed that "many people convicted of the offense are not threats to the community, but rather socially awkward first-time offenders."[163] Judge Carr told the Commission, "I'm of the view that in many instances the sentences are simply too long."[164] Judge Rosen "emphasized that he doesn't condone possession of child pornography or understand it, but focused on the unfairness of treating one person sitting in his basement receiving videos over the Internet the same as a commercial purveyor of child pornography."[165] He added that "In some cases, a person who has watched one video gets a maximum sentence that may be higher than someone sentenced for raping a child repeatedly over many years."[166] "The average sentence for possession of child pornography" in his district, he noted, had "more than doubled, from about 50 months to 109 months, between 2002 and 2007."[167]

Judge Frank Easterbrook, Chief Judge of the U.S. Court of Appeals for the Seventh Circuit, testified that child pornography possession laws might be "ripe for review."[168] He told the Commission that "it gives him pause when he sifts through a stack of sentences that includes a bank robber getting a 10-month sentence and a person convicted of downloading child pornography receiving a 480-month sentence."[169] "One wonders if we aren't facing some unreasonable and unjustifiable disparities," Judge Easterbrook concluded.[170]

Finally, Julia O'Connell, Federal Public Defender for the Eastern and Northern Districts of Oklahoma, testified before the Commission on November 19, 2009. Though she is not a federal judge, she summarized the thinking of many federal judges:

> Judges are appropriately concerned that guideline sentences . . . do not reflect the low risk of recidivism associated with most child pornography possessors, but instead focus on factors that bear little, if any, explicable relationship to the purposes of sentencing. . .
>
> As the Commission knows, the guideline range for a typical child pornography offender easily reaches or exceeds the statutory maximum . . . Depending on the circumstances, these sentences can exceed sentences for actual sex with a child. Those who express concern about the severity of the child pornography guidelines legitimately question the value of such lengthy sentences for offenders who have no prior history of abusing or attempting to abuse a child and are not likely to do so in the future. In my experience, the vast majority of child pornography defendants have no criminal history whatsoever. It is not surprising that judges across the country question the need for severe sentences for first-time offenders, and in particular, offenders who are not likely to re-offend. I share the view that the child pornography guidelines are unreasonably harsh, and urge the Commission to revise them to provide punishment proportional to the offense and the risk to public safety.[171]

Conclusion And Recommendations

It is difficult to disagree with federal judges and others who have called for more rational criminal sentencing of those convicted of possessing child pornography. There is no doubt that images of children being sexually abused are an abomination and have no legitimate place in civilized society. Moreover, there is reason to believe that those who knowingly possess these images may be at least marginally contributing to this scourge. But there is also no evidence that the extremely harsh punishments being meted out to these offenders do anything to reduce the amount of child pornography that is available today or the abuse of children in making these repugnant images.

It appears that the sentences the federal courts, and some state tribunals, impose for possession of child pornography are based largely upon visceral moral outrage over the content of child pornography and the unproven belief that any person who would possess and view such images has or soon will sexually abuse a child.

The gut reaction of most people to the very idea of child pornography—which they will never see and can only imagine, if they dare—is fully understandable. But does it make sense to routinely sentence those who possess child pornography to serve two decades in prison? Does it make sense to impose a 200-year (i.e., life) sentence with no hope of parole or pardon on a 52-year-man for possessing child pornography? For a number of reasons, the answer to these questions is "no."

Consider first the notion of proportionality, a principle fundamental to punishment in our system of justice. It is rare for a person convicted of molesting a child to be sentenced to 20 years in prison. Indeed, in many states, 20 years is the maximum sentence possible for having sexual contact with a young child. For example, in Alabama sexual contact between an adult and a child under 11 carries a penalty ranging from 2 to 20 years; in Texas, the same sentencing range governs sexual contact with a minor as old as 16. In Arizona, where Morton Berger was sentenced to 200 years in prison for possessing child pornography, he would have been subject to a "presumptive term of imprisonment" of 17 years had he been convicted instead of actual "molestation of a child."[172]

But in many states, the criminal penalties for having sexual contact with a child are much less than 20 years. A study released by the U.S. Department of Justice in 2003 examined the sentences imposed upon and time served by 3,104 child molesters in 13 states.[173] The mean sentence was 88.1 months; the median sentence was 66 months. Upon release, 5.7 percent of these offenders had served 6 months or less; 12.6 percent had served 7 to 12 months; 20.8 percent had served 13 to 18 months; 7.2 percent had served 25 to 30 months; 11.2 percent had served 31 to 36 months; 19.7 percent had served 37 to 60 months; and only 12.8 percent had served 61 months or more.

In 2008, a federally sponsored study of 550 released sex offenders in New Jersey, 80 percent of whom were child molesters, reported that the mean length of sentence was 104.4 months and the mean time served was 56.2 months.[174] And, in 2007, the Georgia Department of Corrections reported that, since that state toughened its sentences for child molesters, "[T]he average sentence received for a new conviction on aggravated child molestation ['an offense of child molestation which act physically injures the child or involves an act of sodomy'] has jumped from about 12 years to about 19 years. In contrast, the average sentences received for child molestation [doing 'any immoral or indecent act to or in the presence of or with any child under the age of 16 years with the intent to arouse or satisfy the sexual desires of either the child or the person'] only went from about 6 years to about 7 years."[175]

In recent years, a number of other states have also increased the sentences they impose upon child molesters, particularly those who rape or otherwise sexually penetrate children, but many still impose sentences on child contact sex offenders that are much less severe than those meted out to child pornography possessors. For example, in New York sexual contact with a child under the age of 11 years carries a maximum penalty of 7 years in prison[176]; in Utah such contact with a child under 14 carries a sentence of 1 to 15 years[177]; and in Missouri such contact with a minor under the age of 17 is only a misdemeanor and carries a maximum sentence of 1 year in jail.[178]

Treating possession of child pornography as a crime much more serious than actually having sexual contact with a child implies, if not asserts, that the indirect harm of the former is greater than the direct harm of the latter. Even taking into account the generalized harm child pornography does to society as a whole, it is difficult to fathom how that harm could be greater than the direct harm done to the child victims of hands-on sex offenses.

At a more practical level, a sentencing structure that punishes images of child sexual abuse more harshly than child sexual abuse itself creates perverse incentives for pedophiles and other individuals sexually attracted to children: Gratify your sexual needs by viewing pornographic images of children and risk two decades or more behind bars; sexually abuse a child (short of penetration) and risk a relative "slap on the wrist."

The notion that penalties for possession of child pornography should be much less severe than those imposed for hands-on child sex offenses is neither new nor untested. In England and Wales, where both real and virtual (i.e., computer-generated) child pornography is outlawed, many individuals found in possession of child pornography receive cautions (warnings that become part of the individual's criminal record but do not result in conviction). From 1998 to 2004, for example, 624 child pornography possessors were cautioned in England and Wales, while 1,831 were formally prosecuted and 1,267 were convicted.[179]

Individuals in England and Wales charged with possession of child pornography face a maximum sentence of 5 years in prison, while those who create, distribute, show, advertise, or possess child pornography with intent to distribute it may be sentenced to a maximum of 10 years in prison.[180]

It appears, however, that the English and Welsh courts are much more lenient than American federal courts in their sentencing for possession of child pornography. There, the courts are guided in sentencing by five categories based upon the nature of the images depicted:

(1) images depicting erotic posing with no sexual activity;
(2) sexual activity between children, or solo masturbation by a child;
(3) non-penetrative sexual activity between adults and children;
(4) penetrative sexual activity between children and adults;
(5) sadism or bestiality.[181]

As the Court of Appeal of England and Wales explained in *Regina v. Oliver* et al.:

[A] fine will normally be appropriate in a case where the offender was merely in possession of material solely for his own use, including cases where material was down-loaded from the internet but was not further distributed, and either the material consisted entirely of pseudo-photographs, the making of which had involved no abuse or exploitation of children, or there was no more than a small quantity of material at Level 1. A conditional discharge may be appropriate in such a case if the defendant pleads guilty and has no previous convictions...

[A] community sentence may be appropriate in a case where the offender was in possession of a large amount of material at Level 1 and/or no more than a small number of images at Level 2, provided the material had not been distributed or shown to others. For an offender with the necessary level of motivation and co-operation, the appropriate sentence would be a community rehabilitation order with a sex offender programme. [T]he custody threshold will usually be passed where any of the material has been shown or distributed to others, or, in cases of possession, where there is a large amount of material at Level 2, or a small amount at Level 3 or above. A custodial sentence of up to six months will generally be appropriate in a case where (a) the offender was in possession of a large amount of material at Level 2 or a small amount at Level 3; or (b) the offender has shown, distributed, or exchanged indecent material at Level 1 or 2 on a limited scale, without financial gain. A custodial sentence of between six and twelve months will generally be appropriate for (a) showing or distributing a large number of images at Level 2 or three; or (b) possessing a small number of images at Levels 4 or 5.

In relation to more serious offences, a custodial sentence between twelve months and three years will generally be appropriate for (a) possessing a large quantity of material at Levels 4 or 5, even if there was no showing or distribution of it to others; or (b) showing or distributing a large number of images at Level 3; or (c) producing or trading in material at Levels 1 to 3. Sentences longer than three years should be reserved for cases where (a) images at Levels 4 or 5 have been shown or distributed; or (b) the offender was actively involved in the production of images at Levels 4 or 5, especially where that involvement included a breach of trust, and whether or not there was an element of commercial gain; or (c) the offender had commissioned or encouraged the production of such images...

Sentences approaching the ten-year maximum will be appropriate in very serious cases where the defendant has a previous conviction either for dealing in child pornography, or for abusing children sexually or with violence. Previous such convictions in less serious cases may result in the custody threshold being passed and will be likely to give rise to a higher sentence where the custody threshold has been passed... [182]

Adopting a sentencing structure and guidelines such as these in the United States would not only show greater respect for the principle of proportionality by rationalizing sentences imposed for possession for child pornography and those imposed for child molestation, but would also save the government millions of dollars, money that could be spent in efforts more likely to affect the creation and spread of child pornography via the Internet.

The costs of confining individuals convicted of possessing child pornography in federal prisons are staggering. According the U.S. Government, in fiscal year 2008, the annual, per-inmate cost of federal imprisonment was $25,894.50.[183] One source outside the federal government estimates that the current annual cost per inmate is close to $30,000.[184] Another reports that "Depending upon whose numbers one wishes to use, the cost to the country to incarcerate our huge federal population runs approximately $30,000 to $40,000 per inmate per year."[185]

As noted earlier in this chapter, between 1997 and 2007 the average sentence for child pornography offenders convicted in federal courts increased from 20.59 months to 91.30 months of confinement. Assuming a $2,500-a-month average cost of confinement for federally convicted child pornography offenders, which now (considering the effects of inflation) is probably realistic, and applying the 2007 sentencing data released by the federal government, the average total cost per offender would be $228,250 (91.30 × $2,500).

Federal data also indicate that, in fiscal year 2007, federal courts sentenced 1,084 defendants convicted of child pornography possession. Thus, applying the projected average total cost of confinement for these offenders (computed immediately above), the estimated total cost of confining these offenders (i.e., those sentenced in just 1 year) for the duration of their sentences is nearly a quarter of a billion dollars (i.e., $247 million).

The annual number of child pornography possession convictions in the federal justice system continues to grow rapidly. In recent years there has been a 15 percent annual average increase in sex offenses handled by the federal courts, and child pornography offenses have accounted for 82 percent of this growth.[186] The cost of federal incarceration also continues to rise. According to the U.S. General Accounting Office, the annual budget for the Federal Bureau of Prisons nearly doubled during one recent 10-year period.[187] Thus, this quarter of a billion dollars figure seems bound to grow as both federal child pornography possession convictions and the cost of federal incarceration increase.

Clearly, one way, if not the only practical way, to reduce the staggering costs of federal incarceration for those convicted of possessing child pornography is to decrease the criminal penalties for this offense. But criminal sanctions for possession of child pornography should be reduced not simply to save money but rather to use portions of their cost more productively in the government's efforts to combat the production and distribution of these images of child sexual abuse.

To get an idea of how some portion of that quarter of a billion dollars could be spent annually in ways that are likely to be more productive than simply tacking additional years onto the sentences imposed upon those convicted of possessing child pornography, consider the Innocent Images National Initiative (IINI).

The IINI is a federal law enforcement program directed by the FBI's Cyber Program. IINI is focused on "organizations, enterprises, and communities that exploit children for profit or personal gain."[188] IINI targets "major distributors of child pornography... who appear to have transmitted a large volume of child pornography via an online computer on several occasions to several other people" as well as "producers of child pornography."[189] As part of this program, the FBI recently initiated the Innocent Images International Task Force, in which "investigators from more than five countries are assigned to the Innocent Images program within the US [and help] the FBI address this global crime problem [with a] focus on several large international cases draw[ing] upon extensive resources."[190]

In fiscal year 2008, IINI was funded at $60.8 million, or less than one quarter of what the U.S. government committed to spend on the incarceration of child pornography possessors convicted in that year alone.[191]

In fiscal year 2008, IINI set a target of "rescuing" 120 children who were identified as victims of child pornography.[192] "Rescuing" was defined as "bring[ing] the child to safety away from the control or influence of the person(s) exploiting him or her."[193] IINI exceeded this target by more than 50 percent, "rescuing" 187 children.[194]

In the same fiscal year, IINI set a target of shutting down 1,000 child pornography websites or web hosts. IINI exceed that goal as well, forcing the shutdown of 1,474 websites or web hosts featuring child pornography.[195]

Clearly, given the nature of child pornography and the role the Internet plays in its distribution, government efforts to combat it must employ many different tactics. The investigation, conviction, and incarceration of those who possess child pornography is certainly one valid if not vital approach to the problem. However, child pornography is a blight that transcends international borders and is unlikely to be significantly reduced by punishing a small number of individual possessors to lengthy prison terms in the United States. Any substantial reduction in the production and marketing of child pornography will require more sophisticated, internationally cooperative efforts such as those employed by IINI and its international task force, aimed at large-scale producers and distributors as well as Internet service providers who are aware that their services are being used to transmit images of child sexual abuse but do nothing to stop such commerce.

If Congress were to follow the lead of England and Wales, thereby imposing a maximum sentence of 5 years in prison for possession of child pornography, even if every convicted offender received the maximum sentence, the average cost of incarceration for these offenders would be reduced by approximately one third, thereby enabling the federal government to invest approximately $80 million or more per year in programs such as IINI and its international task force that not only target producers of child pornography but also rescue some of their child victims.

4

Internet Sex Offenders

The Internet provides opportunities for many sex offenders to sexually exploit children and adolescents. These offenders use the World Wide Web to locate and then abuse vulnerable youngsters. In some instances, the abuse is limited to exposing victims to sexually explicit chats, e-mail, instant messages, or other forms of written communication. In some cases, offenders send sexually explicit images (adult and/or child pornography) to their targets and/or solicit sexually explicit photos of their targets. Offenders sometimes utilize "webcams" to expose themselves to their targets in real time and/or seek sexual exposure from targets. Some offenders also use the online contacts they make with children and adolescents to attempt to arrange in-person meetings. Some attempts are successful and culminate in sexual contact between the perpetrator and victim. In many cases, the offender's effort to meet a young victim in person fails because the intended target, believed by the offender to be a child or adolescent, is in fact an adult posing as a youth as part of a law enforcement or vigilante "sting" operation.

Nature And Scope Of The Problem

A handful of studies, including federally funded surveys of youth and law enforcement, conducted over the past decade help shed light on the extent to which, and ways in which, children and adolescents are sexually victimized via the Internet.

Youth Internet Safety Survey I

Between August 1999 and February 2000, Finkelhor, Mitchell, and Wolak interviewed "a nationally representative sample of 1,501 youth ages 10 to 17 who use the Internet regularly."[1] Nineteen percent of these youngsters reported having "received an unwanted sexual solicitation or approach in the last year,"[2] while 3 percent reported receiving an "aggressive sexual solicitation" via the Internet during that same time period.[3] Sexual solicitations and approaches were defined as "[r]equests to engage in sexual activities or sexual talk or give personal sexual information that were unwanted or, whether wanted or not, made by an adult."[4] Aggressive sexual solicitations were defined as "[s]exual solicitations involving offline contact with the perpetrator through regular mail, by telephone, or in person or attempts or requests for offline contact."[5]

According to Finkelhor et al., "More than three quarters of targeted youth (77%) were age 14 or older… Only 22% were ages 10 to 13, but this younger group was disproportionately distressed. They reported 37% of the distressing episodes, suggesting that younger youth have a harder time shrugging off such solicitations."[6] In 65 percent of the reported incidents, "the youth met the person who solicited them in a chat room; in 24% of episodes the meeting occurred through Instant Messages."[7]

Finkelhor et al. further indicated that "many of the sexual solicitations appear to be propositions for 'cybersex'—a form of fantasy sex, which involves interactive chat-room sessions where the participants describe sexual acts and sometimes disrobe and masturbate"[8] but that "[i]n 10% of incidents, the perpetrators asked to meet the youth somewhere, in 6% the youth received regular mail, in 2% a telephone call, in 1% money or gifts. In one instance, the youth received a travel ticket."[9]

Significantly, however, only two of the reported incidents resulted in relationships that "may have had sexual aspects."[10] "One was the romantic relationship between a 17-year-old male and the woman in her late twenties. His parents knew about the relationship. The second friendship involved a man in his thirties who traveled to meet a 16-year-old girl. While she stated the relationship was not sexual, he did want to spend the night with her."[11]

As regards the offenders in these reported incidents, 97 percent were individuals the targets met online. Most of the offenders were reported to be youths themselves or young adults. Twenty-four percent of sexual solicitations and 34 percent of aggressive solicitations were committed by adults, most of whom were said to be 18 to 25 years old; a quarter of the aggressive solicitations were reported to have come from females. Only roughly 4 percent of the offenders "were known to be older than 25."[12] The report cautioned, however, that "In almost all of the cases where the youth gave an age or gender for a perpetrator, the youth had never met the perpetrator in person, thus leaving the accuracy of the identifying information in question."[13]

National Juvenile Online Victimization Study

As a result of a national survey of 2,574 enforcement agencies, Wolak, Mitchell, and Finkelhor estimated that there had been "2,577 arrests for Internet sex crimes against minors in the 12 months starting July 1, 2000."[14] Since this is an estimate of arrests, not offenses, it almost assuredly understates the true incidence of these offenses. Also, however, it appears that arrests for Internet-related sex offenses against children constitute an extremely small percentage of child sex offenses. As these researchers observed, their "rough estimate… from the FBI's National Incident Based Reporting System (NIBRS) suggests that there were approximately 65,000 arrests in the year 2000 for all types of sexual assaults against minors [and] Internet crimes were still a small fraction of this total…"[15]

Thirty-six percent of these 2,577 arrests were for possession, distribution, and/or trade of child pornography only. Thirty-nine percent involved crimes with identified victims, including production of child pornography. Twenty-five percent of these arrests involved solicitations made to undercover law enforcement officers posing as minors. In approximately half of the arrests involving crimes against identified victims, the offender utilized the Internet to initiate a relationship with the victim. When the Internet was used to initiate a relationship, "only 5% of offenders pretended to be teens when they met potential victims online."[16] Also, according to the researchers, "[O]ffenders rarely deceive victims about their sexual interests. Sex is usually broached online, and most victims who meet offenders face to face go to such meetings expecting to engage in sexual activity."[17]

Also noteworthy are the study's findings that (1) "73% of victims who had face-to-face encounters with offenders did so more than once"[18]; (2) "[i]n 89% of cases with face-to-face meetings, offenders had sexual intercourse, oral sex, or other form of penetrative sex with victims"[19]; and (3) some victims who attended face-to-face meetings were given illegal drugs or alcohol (40 percent), exposed to adult or child pornography (23 percent and 15 percent, respectively), or photographed in sexual poses (21 percent).[20]

Virtually all (99 percent) of the offenders in these cases were men, 92 percent were non-Hispanic whites, 3 percent were 17 or younger, 11 percent were 18 to 25, 45 percent were 26 to 39, and 41 percent were 40 or older. About 11 percent were "known to be violent in any manner"[21] and some 10 percent "had prior arrests for sexually offending against minors."[22] However, only "5% used threats or violence"[23] and none abducted a victim.

Two thirds (67 percent) of all of these offenders possessed child pornography: "By definition, all the C[hild] P[ornography] Possession arrests involved this crime, but, in addition, 52% of the Identified-Victim cases involved offenders who possessed child pornography, as did 41% of the cases involving Solicitations to Undercover Law Enforcement."[24] About 20 percent of all of these offenders either took or convinced victims to take "suggestive or explicit photographs" of themselves or their friends, while 18 percent "sent photos of themselves in sexual poses to victims."[25]

Almost all (99 percent) of the victims in the Internet sex crimes in this study were 13 to 17 years old and none were younger than 12. Nearly half (48 percent) were 13 or 14 years old.

Youth Internet Safety Survey II

In a follow-up to the earlier-described 2000 youth survey, from March to June 2005 Wolak, Mitchell, and Finkelhor interviewed another sample of 1,500 American youths between the ages of 10 and 17.[26] As opposed to 2000, when 19 percent of respondents reported having been sexually solicited online, only 13 percent reported having had such an experience within the preceding year. At the same time, the number of surveyed youths reporting aggressive solicitations rose from 3 to 4 percent. Yet the percentage of youths who found these incidents distressing rose from about 25 percent in the initial survey to around 34 percent in the follow-up.

Again, the vast majority of online sexual solicitation targets were older juveniles: 81 percent were 14 or older, while "no 10-year-olds and only 3% of 11-year-olds were solicited."[27] Furthermore, "aggressive and distressing solicitations were... concentrated among older youth with 79% of aggressive incidents and 74% of distressing incidents happening to youth ages 14 and older."[28]

In "aggressive solicitation incidents" three quarters of the offenders asked their targets to meet them in person; 34 percent telephoned the target; 18 percent came to the target's home; 12 percent gave money, gifts, or other items to the target; 9 percent contacted the target by offline mail; and 3 percent purchased travel tickets for the target.[29]

Overall, with regard to offenders, the survey found that only 14 percent were previously known to their targets; 86 percent initially met their targets online. Seventy-three percent of the offenders were men. Unlike the earlier survey, in which 24 percent of the solicitors were said to be 18 or older, respondents in the 2005 study reported that 28 percent of solicitors were 18 or older. Forty-three percent of all solicitations and 44 percent of "aggressive solicitations" were reported to have been made by people under the age of 18. Sixteen percent of those making "aggressive solicitations" were reported to be females,

64 percent of whom were under 18 and 36 percent of whom were 18 to 24 years old.

As in the earlier survey, researchers learned that few targets of online sexual solicitations met their solicitors in person and even fewer had actual sexual contact with adults who solicited them:

> In YISS-2, 4% of youth had formed close online relationships with adults (age 18 or older) they met online, and of those youth, 29% had face-to-face meetings with the adults they met online. Most of these relationships seemed benign; however, of the 58 youth who had close online relationships with adults, 8 told interviewers about relationships that had sexual aspects. These included the adult asking the youth for sexually explicit photographs of themselves, sending the youth sexually explicit photographs, having some degree of sexual physical contact with the youth, or acting in some other way that showed a sexual interest in the youth. All of these close online relationships involved adults who were 5 or more years older than the youth. Four (4) youth (7%) had "physical contact [they] would call sexual" during face-to-face meetings with adults they met online. These youth were all 17 years of age, and the adults were all in their early 20s. All 8 of these cases were counted as solicitations because of the sexual component, whether or not a youth was disturbed by the sexual aspect in the relationship.[30]

U.S. Bureau of Prisons' Sex Offender Treatment Study

This research, published by Malesky in 2007, surveyed 31 male inmates in the Federal Bureau of Prisons' Sex Offender Treatment Program, all of whom had committed or attempted to commit contact sex offenses against minors they initially met and communicated with online.[31] Survey participants were all volunteers drawn from a "highly intensive and very demanding" sex offender treatment program at the Butner Federal Correctional Facility in North Carolina, a program in which sex offenders "often are very motivated to stop their sexually abusive behaviors."[32] Twenty-two of these inmates (71 percent) reported having had sexual contact with at least one victim.

While the results of this small sample survey may not be representative of online sex offenders more generally, they do offer some additional insights into offenses committed against youngsters by offenders who use the Internet to seek their victims.

As found in the Youth Internet Safety Survey I described earlier, chat rooms were the most frequently used online means of access to victims used by the 31 Butner inmates. Twenty-five of them (81 percent) reported visiting chat rooms to identify and contact potential victims; 15 (48.4 percent) said they utilized minors' online profiles; and 3 (9.7 percent) reported screening youths' bulletin board postings for possible victims.

The Butner inmates were also asked, "What initially attracted you to a particular child/adolescent online that you wanted to establish a relationship with for sexual purposes?"[33] Qualitative analyses of their responses revealed three "central themes":

> First, a minor mentioning sex in any fashion online (e.g., in a child's online profile, screen name, posting, e-mail) appeared to serve as an impetus for the participant to contact the minor. Second, participants indicated that when they met a child online who appeared "needy" or "submissive" they would try to initiate an online relationship with the child. For example, one participant stated, "Neediness is very apparent when a child will do anything to keep talking to you. Also, that they are always online shows a low sense of parental contact or interest in the child." Third, the minor's screen name, especially if it was "young sounding," appeared to motivate some participants to contact these children. One participant wrote, "They usually had their age as pat [sic] of their id., e.g., LINDA14." [34]

Asked what they had done once they established online contact with a would-be minor victim, 29 percent of participants reported having represented themselves as minors. Nearly all participants (97 percent) acknowledged engaging in sexually explicit online conversations with their victims, and more than half (52 percent) reported sending the victim child pornography via the Internet.

Federal And State Law

Online solicitations of minors for sex violate the criminal law, regardless of whether they culminate in any in-person contact.

Statutory Rape Laws

Offenders who have nonconsensual sexual contact with minors are subject to prosecution for rape, sodomy, and/or sexual abuse, depending on the nature of the contact. Adults who have consensual sexual contact with minors, regardless of how they met them, are generally open to prosecution for statutory rape. In 2008, Wolak et al. estimated that "25% of the sex crimes committed against minors and reported to the police involve statutory rape" and that "Internet-initiated sex crimes would have accounted for approximately 7% of all statutory rapes."[35]

While the ages of consent in the United States vary from 15 to 18, every American jurisdiction has a statutory rape law that criminalizes sexual acts between adults and minors, even when the minor victim consents or even initiates the sexual contact.[36] Under these laws, minors are presumed to be incapable of consent by virtue of their immaturity.

Statutory rape laws generally consider not only the age of the minor but also that of the perpetrator, and there is often a specified age difference that is required for conviction. Under New York law, for example, third-degree rape occurs when anyone age 21 or older has sexual intercourse with someone under age 17; second-degree rape occurs when anyone age 18 or older engages in sexual intercourse with someone under age 15, although the fact that the offender was less than 4 years older than the victim at the time of the act is an affirmative defense; and first-degree rape occurs when anyone has sexual intercourse with someone who is less than age 11, or less than age 13 if the perpetrator is 18 or older.[37]

Statutory rape is generally a strict liability offense and any mistake, even a reasonable one, regarding the victim's age is usually not a defense. Criminal sanctions for statutory rape range from as little as 6 months in jail to as much as life in prison. As a practical matter, while there have been some notorious exceptions, statutory rape sentences are generally relatively lenient. For example, in New York, rape in the second degree, which includes "[b]eing 18 years or older [and] engaging in sexual intercourse with another person less than 15 years (except where defendant was less than 4 years older than the victim)," carries a penalty of 2 to 7 years in prison.[38] However, in some states, individuals convicted of statutory rape may be required to register as sex offenders and/or be subject to civil confinement when they have completed their incarceration.

Enticement Statutes

Until recently, in most jurisdictions, adults who unwittingly solicited sex from undercover police operatives, thinking that they were communicating with a minor, could be punished, at worst, for attempted statutory rape. To prove attempt, however, prosecutors had to meet a high evidentiary burden. In many jurisdictions, for example, to convict a defendant of attempted statutory rape the prosecutor must prove beyond a reasonable doubt that the defendant's act(s) constituted a "substantial step"[39] toward commission of the crime or were "strongly corroborative of the actor's criminal purpose"[40] to commit the crime.

To lessen that prosecutorial burden and ensure punishment for this class of offenders (which, by estimates noted earlier, may account for as many as a quarter of all arrests for sex offenses against minors), some states and the federal government have enacted statutes making it a criminal offense to persuade, induce, entice, coerce, or attempt to persuade, induce, entice, or coerce a minor into sexual activity. The effect is to lessen the burden on prosecutors, who "need only prove that the defendant knowingly used a computer to communicate with a person the defendant believed to be a minor and that the defendant intended on engaging in sexual activity with the minor."[41]

Minnesota law, for example, provides that "A person 18 years of age or older who uses the Internet or a computer, computer program, computer network, or computer system to commit any of the following acts, with the intent to arouse the sexual desire of any person, is guilty of a felony and may be sentenced… to imprisonment for not more than three years, or to payment of a fine of not more than $5,000, or both."[42] Acts covered by the statute are "(1) soliciting a child or someone the person reasonably believes is a child to engage in sexual conduct; (2) engaging in communication relating to or describing sexual conduct with a child or someone the person reasonably believes is a child; or (3) distributing any material, language, or communication, including a photographic or video image, that relates to or describes sexual conduct to a child or someone the person reasonably believes is a child."[43]

Federal law is similar but more straightforward and harsh: "Whoever, using the mail or any facility or means of interstate or foreign commerce, or within the special maritime and territorial jurisdiction of the United States knowingly persuades, induces, entices, or coerces any individual who has not attained the age of 18 years, to engage in prostitution or any sexual activity for which any person can be charged with a criminal offense, or attempts to do so, shall be fined under this title and imprisoned not less than 10 years or for life."[44]

When this statute was first enacted in 1996, it called for a maximum sentence of 10 years in prison. In 1998, in "response to requests of victim parents and law enforcement to address public safety issues involving the most vulnerable members of our society, our children,"[45] Congress increased the maximum sentence to 15 years. In 2003, Congress raised the maximum sentence to 30 years and established a mandatory minimum sentence of 5 years.[46] In 2006, Congress passed the Adam Walsh Child Protection and Safety Act, which increased the mandatory minimum sentence to 10 years and the maximum sentence to life in prison.[47]

While Congress was busy increasing the punishment for enticement, the federal courts were giving this statute a broad interpretation. To begin with, these tribunals have held that a defendant may be convicted of enticement of a minor not only for communicating with an actual child but also for attempting to do so, as in so-called Internet sting cases where the defendant has communicated with an adult law enforcement decoy, believing the officer to be a minor. The federal courts have routinely rejected defenses of impossibility and entrapment raised by defendants who never communicated with a minor but were caught in an online sting operation.

Travel Statutes

Federal law also criminalizes "travel[ing] with intent to engage in illicit sexual conduct"[48] and attempting or conspiring to do so. Specifically, the law states that "A person who travels in interstate commerce or travels into the United States, or a United States citizen or an alien admitted for permanent residence in the United States who travels in foreign commerce, for the purpose of engaging in any illicit sexual conduct with another person shall be fined under this title or imprisoned not more than 30 years, or both... Whoever attempts or conspires to [do so] shall be punishable in the same manner as a completed violation..."[49]

Federal courts have also given these travel statutes a liberal interpretation. For instance, they have held that it is no defense that the "minor" the defendant crossed state lines to have sex with did not exist but was an online adult law enforcement decoy. As one court put it, "the relevant concern is [the defendant's] intent rather than the true age or identity of his intended victim."[50]

Pornography Statutes

Federal law also criminalizes efforts to get a minor to engage in sexual conduct for purposes of creating or transmitting a visual representation (i.e., photo or video) of such conduct, with the knowledge that such representation will be transmitted via interstate means, including the Internet:

> Any person who employs, uses, persuades, induces, entices, or
> coerces any minor to engage in, or who has a minor assist any other

person to engage in, or who transports any minor in or affecting interstate or foreign commerce, or in any Territory or Possession of the United States, with the intent that such minor engage in, any sexually explicit conduct for the purpose of producing any visual depiction of such conduct or for the purpose of transmitting a live visual depiction of such conduct, shall be [fined . . . and imprisoned not less than 15 years nor more than 30 years] if such person knows or has reason to know that such visual depiction will be transported or transmitted using any means or facility of interstate or foreign commerce or in or affecting interstate or foreign commerce or mailed, if that visual depiction was produced or transmitted using materials that have been mailed, shipped, or transported in or affecting interstate or foreign commerce by any means, including by computer, or if such visual depiction has actually been transported or transmitted using any means or facility of interstate or foreign commerce or in or affecting interstate or foreign commerce or mailed. . . .

[B]ut if such person has one prior conviction under this chapter . . . or under the laws of any State relating to aggravated sexual abuse, sexual abuse, abusive sexual contact involving a minor or ward, or sex trafficking of children, or the production, possession, receipt, mailing, sale, distribution, shipment, or transportation of child pornography, such person shall be fined under this title and imprisoned for not less than 25 years nor more than 50 years, but if such person has 2 or more [such] prior convictions[,] such person shall be fined under this title and imprisoned not less than 35 years nor more than life. . .[51]

U.S. Sentencing Guidelines

As noted in the preceding chapter, criminal sentencing in the federal courts is heavily influenced by the U.S. Sentencing Guidelines. The Guidelines detail presumptive sentences based upon the conduct associated with the offense and the defendant's criminal history. Various specified aspects of the conduct involved in the criminal offense may enhance the sentence imposed. With regard to defendants who have offended or attempted to offend sexually against minors, several such factors may substantially enhance the severity of criminal punishment. The Guidelines provide, for example, that punishment should be enhanced when "the offense involved the knowing misrepresentation of a participant's identity to persuade, induce, entice, or coerce a minor to engage in prohibited sexual conduct"[52] or "the offense involved the use of a computer or an interactive computer service to persuade, induce, entice, or coerce a minor to engage in prohibited sexual conduct..."[53]

For instance, under the Guidelines, a defendant who was convicted of or pleaded guilty to persuading, inducing, enticing, or coercing or attempting to persuade, induce, entice, or coerce a minor to engage in sexual activity would warrant a presumptive sentence of 97 to 121 months in prison. However, if the defendant's criminal conduct was found to have involved "the knowing misrepresentation of a participant's identity to persuade, induce, entice, or coerce a minor to engage in prohibited sexual conduct, or to facilitate trans-portation or travel, by a minor or a participant, to engage in prohibited sexual conduct,"[54] the presumptive sentence jumps to 121 to 151 months. Similarly, if the defendant's offense involved "the use of a computer or an interactive computer service to persuade, induce, entice, or coerce a minor to engage in prohibited sexual conduct, or to facilitate transportation or travel, by a minor or a participant, to engage in prohibited sexual conduct,"[55] the presumptive sentence would also leap from 97 to 121 months to 121 to 151 months. Significantly, if both of these elements were part of the defendant's offense (e.g., he sexually solicited a minor or a decoy posing as a minor online and lied about his age), the presumptive sentence under the Guidelines would soar from 97 to 121 months to 151 to 188 months. To put it another way, the pre-sumptive sentence to be imposed under the Guidelines will be increased by almost 25 percent if one of these factors is associated with the offense, and by over 55 percent if both are.

Another section of the Guidelines significantly enhances the sentence imposed upon an Internet sex offender if he "unduly influenced a minor to engage in prohibited sexual conduct."[56] The Guidelines do not define the term "unduly influenced," but specify that "In determining whether [this factor] applies, the court should closely consider the facts of the case to determine whether a participant's influence over the minor compromised the voluntari-ness of the minor's behavior. In a case in which a participant is at least 10 years older than the minor, there shall be a rebuttable presumption... that such participant unduly influenced the minor to engage in prohibited sexual conduct. In such a case, some degree of undue influence can be presumed because of the substantial difference in age between the participant and the minor."[57]

Federal courts have held that "undue influence" may be found even where no victim was influenced because the defendant was soliciting not a minor but an undercover officer posing as a minor online. In one leading case, *United States v. Root*, a federal appellate court upheld a significant enhancement to the sentence of John Allen Root, who was convicted of one count of attempting to persuade a minor to engage in criminal sexual activity and one count of traveling in interstate commerce for the purpose of engaging in a criminal sexual act with a minor, after he conversed online with a police decoy pretending to be 13-year-old "Jenny" and then traveled to meet "her."[58] In explaining the application of the "undue influence" enhancement in this case, the court held that:

> Root's own words . . . provided more than sufficient evidence to support the district court's finding of undue influence. We look to facts related to the three types of power the Sentencing Commission stated sex offenders frequently use to manipulate minors. First, Root displayed increased knowledge to influence Jenny. When Jenny told Root in her instant messages that she was not sexually experienced and was not familiar with some of the terms Root was using in his messages, he described a variety of sexual activities in detail to her—including masturbation, ejaculation, orgasms, cunnilingus, fellatio, manual penetration and sexual intercourse. Root also said he had participated in these activities before, they would "feel good," and they would not cause pain or pregnancy (because he was "fixed").
>
> Second, Root used persuasive powers to influence Jenny. He said girls Jenny's age—13—engaged in the sexual acts he had described and invited her to perform, which he described as "playing." He told her she was at an age when she needed to "learn some things," but that he would "love to teach you some of these things" and "experiment with you." He also promised he would be "gentle" and "patient." And Root explained to her that although he could "get in a lot of trouble" for meeting Jenny and engaging in sexual acts, everything would be OK because he "trusted" her not to tell anyone about it. Moreover, Root's conversations with Jenny are peppered with reassuring comments about Jenny's appearance, personality and his interest in her. He also made statements to bolster Jenny's self-confidence, commenting on her sexual vitality and responding to her statements of nervousness. All of these messages were phrased by Root to win over the insecure teenager portrayed by Agent Howell. Ultimately, he said he would truly like Jenny—"especially if you f--- me."
>
> Third, Root used superior resources to influence Jenny. He used his office computer to conduct his instant message sessions with her

and send his picture to her. He planned to, and did, drive his late-model Dodge sedan across three states to meet Jenny after taking a day off from work. He told her that after her mother dropped her off at the Mall of Georgia on December 22, they could see a movie together, stating that Jenny did not need to worry about how much money to bring. And he said she could come inside his car to engage in sex acts while listening to music on his car CD player.

Given that the primary focus is on Root's own conduct, his argument that a 13-year-old girl would have been repulsed by Root's statements instead of being lured in is unpersuasive. In any event, we cannot find fault with the district court's conclusion on the record before us that Root's conduct was not so off-putting as to be repulsive to a 13-year-old, and thus not undue influence. The district court reviewed the transcripts of the conversations between Root and Jenny, heard testimony from the task force agents who portrayed Jenny and interviewed Root, and considered whether a child of this age could be enticed by Root's words. It is entirely plausible and reasonable to believe that due to Root's steady stream of reassuring, knowledgeable and skillful manipulation, an unwilling child of 13 would be convinced to follow along the primrose path he set out for Jenny. . . [59]

Law Enforcement

At 13 you decided to be a rock star. At 16 you decided to be a quarterback. At 25 you married the girl of your dreams. So when DID you decide to become a sex predator? It doesn't matter who you are. It doesn't matter what you've achieved. Download sexual images of children or entice a minor online, and you have committed a serious federal crime. You will go to prison and it will ruin your life. Exploiting a minor is a major offense.

Text of a public service announcement from the U.S. Department of Justice[60]

If you use the Internet to solicit sex from a person you believe is a minor, will you go to prison? Based on a review of such cases reported by federal law enforcement officials during the first quarter of 2009, the answer is clearly "yes," especially if you are caught and charged by federal rather than state authorities. Consider, for example, the following cases.

In a Texas case, a 55-year-old man was sentenced to more than 24 years in federal prison (292 months) for enticing a minor to engage in sex.[61] This man had carried on a number of lengthy chats via instant messaging with what he thought was a 13-year-old girl but was actually an undercover police officer. After the officer repeatedly denied being a law enforcement operative, the man used graphic sexual detail to tell the "girl" what he wanted to do with her. During one online conversation, he also used a webcam to display himself masturbating. At some point he gave the decoy his home telephone number. Another officer, posing as the girl, called the man and arranged to meet him. When he arrived for the meeting he was arrested.

In a Georgia case, a 63-year-old man was sentenced to serve 15 years and 8 months in federal prison (to be followed by a lifetime of supervised release) for using a computer to attempt to entice a child for sexual activity, even though there was no child and he never believed that he was communicating with a child.[62] The man approached an undercover FBI agent in a chat room dealing with sex with children and expressed an interest in having sex with the agent's fictitious 11-year-old daughter. The two exchanged online messages for several days, arranging for the man to meet the agent and the child at a mall. When the man drove to the mall he was arrested.

In Nevada, a 45-year-old man was sentenced to 7 years and 8 months in prison, to be followed by a lifetime of supervised release, on a charge that he traveled from Illinois to Georgia, intending to have sex with an 11-year-old girl he met online.[63] The "girl" was actually a police officer. Shortly after meeting the "girl" in a teen chat room, the man engaged her in sexually explicit conversations. The "girl" repeatedly told him that she was 11, had never had a boyfriend, had never had sex, and was worried that her parents would learn that she was communicating with him. After about 2 months of online communication, the man asked the "girl" to meet him so that they could go to a motel, have sex, and move to California, where they would eventually marry. When the "girl" agreed, the man drove from his home, checked into a motel, and was arrested shortly thereafter in possession of condoms and lingerie he had told the "girl" he would bring with him.

While, as these cases illustrate, defendants convicted of soliciting or attempting to solicit sex from minors online are routinely incarcerated for long periods of time, there is no way of knowing what percentage of all such online sex offenders are convicted, arrested, or even reported to authorities. As the above-described cases suggest, it appears that many if not most cases that result in apprehension and conviction involve the use of decoy or sting operations. It is also impossible to readily determine how many such cases are, like those above, prosecuted in federal court, where harsh penalties are the norm, as opposed to state courts, in which offenders seem much more likely to receive only modest sentences. Consider, for example, the following cases, all of which involved sentences handed down in state courts around the same time as those in the federal cases just cited.

In Maine, a 45-year-old man repeatedly contacted a 14-year-old middle school student via the Internet, asking the boy for sex.[64] The man contacted the boy after viewing his MySpace pages and solicited sex from him via AOL Instant Messenger. The boy told a school police officer about the communications, at which point the officer assumed the boy's online identity and continued communicating with the man. The decoy made it clear that he was 13 years old, but the man continued to communicate about sex, ultimately asking to meet the "boy" for sex. When the "boy" agreed, the man showed up at the arranged meeting place and was arrested and charged with attempted gross sexual assault, a felony carrying a potential sentence of 10 years. With the agreement of prosecutors, the man pleaded guilty to attempting to engage in a sex act in a public place and was sentenced to serve 30 days in jail and a year of probation. He was not required to register as a sex offender or to refrain from using a computer.

In California, a 45-year-old man logged into an adult gay chat room and began communicating with an undercover decoy claiming to be a 13-year-old boy.[65] In subsequent online chats between the two, he discussed masturbation, fellatio, and anal sex with the "boy" in graphic terms, sent him two photographs of the naked lower half of his body, and asked to meet the "boy" for sex. When the man drove to the agreed-upon meeting site, he was greeted by police, drove away, and was apprehended about 20 minutes later. Charged in state court with attempting lewd acts on a child younger than 14 and attempting to distribute harmful matter to a minor, both felonies, he was allowed by prosecutors to plead guilty to attempting to distribute harmful matter to a minor over the Internet and soliciting a lewd act in a public place, both misdemeanors. As a result, he was sentenced to 90 days of home confinement, 100 hours of community service, and 3 years of probation.

In Oregon, a 48-year-old man who was involved with a Christian youth organization twice tried to arrange meetings for sex with what he thought were underage girls.[66] In both instances, he communicated online with a police officer who first posed as an 11-year-old and then as a 13-year-old. Charged under state law with two counts of online sexual corruption of a child in the first degree, five counts of online sexual corruption of a child in the second degree, and two counts of luring a minor, he was allowed to plead guilty to online corruption of a child and sentenced to 60 days in jail and 5 years of probation, the conditions of which included entering a treatment program for sex offenders and having no unauthorized contact with minors.

In Michigan, a 41-year-old man used instant messaging to contact a police decoy he believed to be a 14-year-old girl.[67] Over the course of several IM chats, the man asked the "girl" if she wanted to see his webcam. He used his webcam to expose himself to "her" and to send "her" live images of him masturbating. Following his arrest, he was charged in state court with two felonies: accosting and soliciting a minor for immoral purposes and use of a computer communicating with another to commit a crime. Facing a possible 4-year prison sentence on the former charge and a 10-year sentence on the latter, he was allowed to plead guilty to accosting a child for immoral purposes and sentenced to time served while awaiting trial (109 days), 2 months of house arrest, and 5 years of probation. He was also barred from using a computer or being within 500 feet of locations regularly frequented by children.

In Hawaii, a 29-year-old man contacted a 15-year-old girl online through MySpace.[68] The girl said she was 16 and the man, who had prior convictions for indecent exposure, open lewdness, and harassment by stalking, claimed to be 18. The man arranged to meet the girl in person, had sexual intercourse with her in the back seat of his pickup truck, and was arrested after she informed her parents of the act. After pleading guilty in state court to second-degree sexual assault, third-degree sexual assault, and first-degree electronic enticement of a minor, he was given the minimum sentence possible under state law: 1 year in jail and 5 years of probation.

In California, a 32-year-old high school teacher posted a profile on an Internet social networking site, claiming to be a 15-year-old boy. [69] His profile also claimed 120 "friends," all but one or two of whom were 13- to 17-year-old girls. Using the same website, he "friended" a 14-year-old girl. After several online and telephone chats with the girl, he convinced her to meet him outside her home in the middle of the night. When they met, they talked for about 10 minutes before he began touching her breasts and genitals. Initially the girl resisted these advances, but she eventually "gave up" and engaged in several acts of unprotected sex. The man then took the girl to his home, where they engaged in two more acts of unprotected sex. At about 6:30 a.m. the man directed the girl to take a shower, drove her to a pharmacy to purchase a so-called morning-after birth control pill, and dropped her off at school. Once the girl informed her parents of these events, police began searching for the man. Using the girl's username and password, they logged on to the social networking site and made an online contact with the man. Thinking that he was chatting with the girl, the man told "her" that she was not pregnant, that she should erase all correspondence between them, and that he wanted to see her again and have further sexual relations. Charged in state court with multiple sex crimes, he was allowed to plead no contest to four of the nine charges against him and was sentenced to 1 year in jail, to be followed by 3 years of probation and lifetime registration as a sex offender.

Vigilante Enforcement

While criminal penalties for online solicitation of sex with a minor obviously vary tremendously, depending upon whether the solicitor is prosecuted in state or federal court, these penalties are not the only punishment meted out to these offenders. Private vigilante groups and some commercial media outlets have run their own sting operations and used them to expose offenders to the public. Some of the individuals caught in these private sting operations have been prosecuted, but others have not.

To Catch a Predator

The best-known vigilante sting operations aimed at snaring adults who seek to use the Internet to troll for sex with minors are those sponsored by the National Broadcasting Company (NBC) and a private nonprofit organization known as Perverted Justice.

NBC produced a "Dateline" program called "To Catch a Predator," in which adult decoys posing as teenagers engaged in online dialogues with adult men they encountered in chat rooms on the Internet.[70] Over a period of about 4 years, these sting operations resulted in the arrests of 256 men, less than half of whom were ever convicted of a crime.[71] Recently, a federal district court judge succinctly summarized the television program's *modus operandi*:

> ["To Catch a Predator"] uses "decoys" posing as teenagers on-line
> to "lure," with the promise of sex, individuals suspected of being
> sexual predators to a "sting house." There, the decoy—who is an
> adult actor posing as a young teenager supposedly alone at home—
> invites the individual into the house. After a few moments, the
> decoy leaves and the host of the show, NBC correspondent Chris
> Hansen, appears. Hansen confronts the individual and starts asking
> questions, such as "why are you here?" In some instances, the
> individual immediately tries to run out of the house. Surprisingly,
> however, in many instances the individual answers Hansen's

questions and allows himself to be interviewed by Hansen, who is armed with a transcript of the on-line chat. It is apparent that most of these individuals believe that Hansen—who does not identify himself at first—is a police officer or the "father" of the decoy. At some point, Hansen will announce: "I'm Chris Hansen with Dateline NBC."

Upon exiting the house, the men are arrested by the police. Several police officers display guns, force the men to the ground face down, and then handcuff them. The men are taken to the police station where they are processed, photographed, and interviewed by a police officer, and they are eventually arraigned in court.

All of these events—the arrival at the sting house, the initial entry into the house, the first meeting with the decoy, the conversation with Hansen, the arrest outside, the processing and interview at the police station, and the arraignment in court—are captured on camera, with video and sound equipment, including hidden cameras, provided by NBC. . .

To increase ratings, Dateline seeks "to sensationalize and enhance the entertainment value" of the confrontations, and accordingly it encourages the police officers "to give a special intensity to any arrests, so as to enhance the camera effect." Indeed, the "mainstay of the show is public humiliation" of the individuals who are lured to the sting houses by the promise of sex with a minor.

In producing "To Catch a Predator," Dateline provides equipment, money, services, and other things of value to local police departments. In return, local law enforcement agrees to participate in the show, permits Dateline to videotape arrests in "dramatically-staged scenarios," provides Dateline with confidential data, and permits Hansen to interview suspects even before detectives interview them. Dateline has produced "Predator" segments in, among other places, Riverside County, California; Greenville, Ohio; Fort Myers, Florida; Petaluma, California; Long Beach, California; and Flagler Beach, Florida.[72]

In one episode of "To Catch a Predator," the NBC sting led not to an arrest but to the death of the perpetrator.[73] In the fall of 2006, with the consent of city officials, NBC set up a sting operation in Murphy, Texas. In one 4-day period, 24 men were ensnared by the operation. All but one showed up at the "sting house," were filmed, and were arrested by waiting police officers.

In every case the charges were eventually dropped by the local prosecutor's office. Meanwhile, however, NBC personnel asked the local police to seek an arrest and search warrant for the one man who failed to show up at the "sting house" as planned. The plan was for NBC cameras to be rolling when those warrants were executed at the man's home.

The man in question was Louis William Conradt, Jr., a 56-year-old local assistant district attorney who had previously served for five terms (20 years) as the district attorney in another nearby county. Conradt had communicated via online messaging with a decoy posing as a 13-year-old boy, whom Conradt ultimately agreed to meet at the NBC "sting house."

According to a transcript of Conradt's online communications with the decoy, Conradt claimed to be a 19-year-old college student. The two openly discussed sexual matters before agreeing to meet for sex. During the online chats, Conradt sent the decoy sexually explicit photographs. He claimed that these were photos of himself, but they were not. Below are some sexually explicit excerpts from the chats between Conradt (Inxsoo) and the decoy (NoOneZero93):

NoOneZero93 [6:41 PM]: is that ur cock?
Inxsoo [6:41 PM]: yes
NoOneZero93 [6:41 PM]: it looks huge

* * *

Inxsoo [8:18 PM]: have you j/o today
NoOneZero93 [8:18 PM]: 3 times
Inxsoo [8:18 PM]: me too
Inxsoo [12:32 PM]: how big are you

* * *

NoOneZero93 [12:32 PM]: 5 but im still growin
Inxsoo [12:32 PM]: nice
Inxsoo [12:32 PM]: i want to see
NoOneZero93 [12:32 PM]: come over

* * *

inxsoo2000 [11/04/06 7:07:22 PM]: i want to feel your cock
noonezero93 [11/04/06 7:07:32 PM]: its right here
inxsoo2000 [11/04/06 7:07:33 PM]: do you shoot alot?
noonezero93 [11/04/06 7:07:38 PM]: not telling!!
inxsoo2000 [11/04/06 7:08:06 PM]: you're so cute
noonezero93 [11/04/06 7:08:49 PM]: well i just wish u had not said
    ud come over then not call

noonezero93 [11/04/06 7:08:50 PM]: or nothing
inxs002000 [11/04/06 7:09:18 PM]: i know, i'm sorry
inxs002000 [11/04/06 7:09:27 PM]: i'll have to make it up somehow
noonezero93 [11/04/06 7:09:31 PM]: you should
noonezero93 [11/04/06 7:09:39 PM]: and you know how
inxs002000 [11/04/06 7:09:45 PM]: maybe you can fuck me several times[74]

Conradt also communicated with the decoy several times by telephone and agreed to meet him. Within days of Conradt's failure to arrive at the sting house as he had agreed, NBC cameras and about 10 crew members were poised at his home to witness the execution of arrest and search warrants. At least five police officers, including the chief of police, were present and their vehicles lined the residential street. Two officers, one with his gun drawn, approached Conradt's home and knocked on the door. When police received no response, they brought in a SWAT team that included "at least seven more officers, carrying large rifles, some wearing visored helmets."[75]

The SWAT team opened a locked sliding door and entered Conradt's home, calling out "Terrell Police" and "Search Warrant."[76] Conradt entered the room, said "I'm not gonna hurt anyone," and then shot himself with a handgun.[77] Police reported to NBC personnel that Conradt had shot himself, one officer reportedly telling a producer, "That'll make good TV."[78] NBC cameras recorded the scene as emergency medical technicians removed Conradt from the home and took him via helicopter to a Dallas hospital, where he was pronounced dead within the hour. NBC was also provided with photographs of Conradt's body, his gun, and the death scene, in addition to an audiotape of his last words.

NBC later ran an episode of "To Catch a Predator" featuring the case, including much of what has just been described. The show's host interviewed the local police chief, who confirmed that Conradt's three computers had been seized for forensic analysis. When asked what could be on these computers, the chief said, "Unfortunately, and I'm just surmising or guessing here, too, there's going to be something that's way worse than the chats or the pictures he had already sent."[79] The program's coverage of this case segment concluded with shots of Conradt's sister addressing the Murphy Town Council shortly after Conradt's death and denouncing "reckless actions of a self-appointed group acting as judge, jury, and executioner, that was encouraged by an out-of-control reality show."[80]

Subsequently, Conradt's sister brought a $105 million federal lawsuit against NBC alleging, among other complaints, that the network and its employees intentionally inflicted emotional distress on her brother, thereby creating a substantial risk that he would commit suicide. NBC moved to dismiss the lawsuit for "failure to state a claim upon which relief may be granted."[81] NBC argued that it had no duty to protect Conradt from suicide, that neither the network nor the police violated Conradt's constitutional right against unreasonable searches and seizures, and that what it did in this case was not "extreme and outrageous"[82] as required to support a claim of intentional infliction of emotional distress in the state of Texas. Holding that Conradt's sister was entitled to have at least some of her complaints heard by a jury, a U.S. District Court Judge concluded that:

> Although many of plaintiff's claims will be dismissed, the principal claims survive, for if the allegations of the amended complaint are proven, a reasonable jury could find that NBC crossed the line from responsible journalism to irresponsible and reckless intrusion into law enforcement. Rather than merely report on law enforcement's efforts to combat crime, NBC purportedly instigated and then placed itself squarely in the middle of a police operation, pushing the police to engage in tactics that were unnecessary and unwise, solely to generate more dramatic footage for a television show. On the facts alleged in the amended complaint, for example, a reasonable jury could find that there was no legitimate law enforcement need for a heavily armed SWAT team to extract a 56-year-old prosecutor from his home when he was not accused of any actual violence and was not believed to have a gun, and that this was done solely "to sensationalize and enhance the entertainment value" of the arrest. A reasonable jury could find that by doing so, NBC created a substantial risk of suicide or other harm, and that it engaged in conduct so outrageous and extreme that no civilized society should tolerate it.[83]

Four months after the judge's ruling, NBC settled the lawsuit for an undisclosed amount of money. The attorney representing Conradt's sister announced that "the matter has been amicably resolved to the satisfaction of both parties."[84]

Perverted Justice

Online sex offender sting operations are also conducted by individuals and organizations, such as Perverted Justice. A Florida court recently described this organization as follows:

> . . . Perverted Justice [is] an online watchdog [that] enlists the help of approximately 250 unpaid volunteers, some of whom enter

online chat rooms as decoys with underage profiles. The decoys wait for adults within the chat rooms to contact them and solicit sexual activity. Other volunteers, also posing as minors, speak with suspects on the telephone to verify their identities. Perverted Justice electronically records and stores the chat logs and telephone conversations, then notifies the police of suspects and their alleged offenses. Once a suspect requests a meeting with a decoy for sexual activity, the decoy directs the suspect to a location where the suspect is apprehended by law enforcement.[85]

According to Perverted Justice, between 2004 and 2010, its sting operations resulted in the prosecution of over 500 online offenders.[86] Among the most recent of those offenders was Jerald D'Souza, a 50-year-old California man who engaged in online communications with a Perverted Justice volunteer decoy, "an FBI confidential informant."[87] D'Souza identified himself online as "peter2033" and the decoy identified herself as "shy_aimee," a 13-year-old girl. Portions of the first instant messaging "conversation" between D'Souza and the decoy went as follows:

peter2033 [12/28/08 4:59:16 AM]: do like older guys?
shy_aimee [12/28/08 4:59:36 AM]: oh ya
peter2033 [12/28/08 4:59:41 AM]: thats cool
peter2033 [12/28/08 4:59:56 AM]: have ever had sex with some one?
shy_aimee [12/28/08 4:59:57 AM]: :)
shy_aimee [12/28/08 5:00:10 AM]: no
peter2033 [12/28/08 5:00:15 AM]: r u curious?
shy_aimee [12/28/08 5:00:18 AM]: but I no how to kiss
peter2033 [12/28/08 5:00:24 AM]: ok
peter2033 [12/28/08 5:00:30 AM]: like smooching?
shy_aimee [12/28/08 5:00:51 AM]: tongue kissing :">
peter2033 [12/28/08 5:00:57 AM]: i love it too

* * *

peter2033 [12/28/08 5:01:26 AM]: I also love tokiss girls clit
peter2033 [12/28/08 5:01:33 AM]: and lick pussy
shy_aimee [12/28/08 5:01:39 AM]: whats a clit?

* * *

peter2033 [12/28/08 5:02:22 AM]: do u finger ur pussy?
shy_aimee [12/28/08 5:02:46 AM]: no Imma scared to
peter2033 [12/28/08 5:02:56 AM]: nothing toscared
peter2033 [12/28/08 5:03:04 AM]: i can teach u if u wanna

* * *

peter2033 [12/28/08 5:05:28 AM]: as we chat u touch ur pussy
shy_aimee [12/28/08 5:05:41 AM]: oh
* * *
peter2033 [12/28/08 5:06:47 AM]: this is only between me and u
peter2033 [12/28/08 5:06:56 AM]: ok
shy_aimee [12/28/08 5:06:57 AM]: ok I like secrets
peter2033 [12/28/08 5:07:28 AM]: if possible after we know better i
will try to meet u some time
peter2033 [12/28/08 5:07:41 AM]: and then we can have real sex
* * *
peter2033 [12/28/08 5:43:57 AM]: do u wanna swwe some porn
movie clips?
peter2033 [12/28/08 5:44:03 AM]: see*
shy_aimee [12/28/08 5:44:25 AM]: ok
* * *
peter2033 [12/28/08 6:06:54 AM]: r u seeing it?
shy_aimee [12/28/08 6:07:05 AM]: ya
peter2033 [12/28/08 6:07:07 AM]: ok
peter2033 [12/28/08 6:07:46 AM]: these all things I will be doing it
withu
* * *
peter2033 [12/28/08 6:15:40 AM]: continue watching it and touch
ur pussy
shy_aimee [12/28/08 6:16:37 AM]: later
peter2033 [12/28/08 6:16:41 AM]: as u ok
shy_aimee [12/28/08 6:16:41 AM]: I gota get sleep now[88]

In further instant messages with the decoy, D'Souza engaged in what appeared to be lengthy monologues regarding his fantasies:

shy_aimee [12/29/08 4:14:50 AM]: tell me what you wanna do
when we meet
peter2033 [12/29/08 4:15:10 AM]: first I will kiss u
peter2033 [12/29/08 4:15:19 AM]: and love u so much
peter2033 [12/29/08 4:15:27 AM]: and hold u very tight
peter2033 [12/29/08 4:15:32 AM]: and hug u
peter2033 [12/29/08 4:15:48 AM]: then we will have shower
together
* * *
peter2033 [12/29/08 4:16:33 AM]: as we take showe I will kneel
down

peter2033 [12/29/08 4:16:52 AM]: and lift ur legs to my shoulder

peter2033 [12/29/08 4:16:59 AM]: and i kiss ur pussy

peter2033 [12/29/08 4:17:07 AM]: i kiss ur clit

peter2033 [12/29/08 4:17:17 AM]: and slowly finger in ur pussy

peter2033 [12/29/08 4:17:28 AM]: as u widen ur pussy

peter2033 [12/29/08 4:17:34 AM]: and start moaning

* * *

peter2033 [12/29/08 4:17:46 AM]: i finger more deeper in ur pussy

peter2033 [12/29/08 4:19:40 AM]: as u get hot and horny I suck ur clit

peter2033 [12/29/08 4:19:52 AM]: and my tongue goes in to ur pussy

* * *

peter2033 [12/29/08 4:23:05 AM]: as u get more horny

peter2033 [12/29/08 4:23:29 AM]: i will turn u back

peter2033 [12/29/08 4:23:44 AM]: and first i use the condome

peter2033 [12/29/08 4:23:57 AM]: and penentrate my dick in ur back

peter2033 [12/29/08 4:24:07 AM]: and stroke in ur backhole

* * *

peter2033 [12/29/08 4:27:06 AM]: as we enjoy the passion of love u insert my dick in ur pussy

peter2033 [12/29/08 4:27:18 AM]: and u widen ur legs more

peter2033 [12/29/08 4:27:31 AM]: and i isert it more deeper in ur pussy

* * *

peter2033 [12/29/08 4:29:06 AM]: i stroke more harder

peter2033 [12/29/08 4:29:14 AM]: and u bounce up and down

peter2033 [12/29/08 4:29:17 AM]: more faster

peter2033 [12/29/08 4:29:24 AM]: and more deeper i push

peter2033 [12/29/08 4:29:25 AM]: in

peter2033 [12/29/08 4:29:26 AM]: out

peter2033 [12/29/08 4:29:28 AM]: in

peter2033 [12/29/08 4:29:29 AM]: out

peter2033 [12/29/08 4:29:30 AM]: in

peter2033 [12/29/08 4:29:31 AM]: out

peter2033 [12/29/08 4:29:34 AM]: more deeper

peter2033 [12/29/08 4:29:38 AM]: and more faster . . .[89]

After a month and a half of chatting with "Aimee" online, D'Souza arranged to meet her. When he arrived at the agreed-upon location, he had in his possession liquor, condoms, pornography, a laptop with a webcam, and various gifts. He was arrested and charged in federal court with using means of interstate commerce (i.e., the Internet) to attempt to commit criminal sex acts with a minor. In 2009, D'Souza pled guilty and was sentenced to 10 years in prison (the minimum sentence allowed by law) to be followed by 10 years of post-release supervision.[90]

Nature Of The Offenders

As noted in the previous chapter dealing with child pornography, some current data, though limited, suggest that "online offenders," including child pornography offenders and those who use the Internet to solicit sex from minors, may constitute a distinct group of offenders unlikely to commit other sexual crimes. As indicated there, recent meta-analyses have found a number of distinct differences between "online" and "offline" offenders. For example, "online offenders" have been found to have had substantially less prior criminal involvement than "child molesters"[91] and "recidivism rates [that] appear to be quite low."[92] "Online offenders" also appear to show more victim empathy, more sexual deviancy, fewer cognitive distortions, slightly less emotional identification with children, and less of a tendency to engage in "impression management" than "offline offenders."[93] Moreover, they may have "greater self-control and less impulsivity than offline offenders" as well as "more psychological barriers to acting on their deviant interests."[94]

Of course, once an offender soliciting sex from a minor online succeeds in meeting the youth and having any sort of sexual encounter, that offender is no longer "merely" an "online offender." There are few if any data to suggest that such an offender is different from other offenders who have unlawful sexual relations with minors. However, Wolak et al. make the point that these luring offenders and their offenses "more often fit a model of statutory rape—adult offenders who meet, develop relationships with, and openly seduce underage teenagers—than a model of forcible sexual assault or pedophilic child molesting."[95]

Wolak et al. have also sought to determine whether suspects caught in law enforcement Internet sting operations (i.e., those who thought they were soliciting a minor but were actually communicating with an undercover police officer) "pose a significant threat to youth."[96] In so doing, they examined a subsample of cases from the National Juvenile Online Victimization Survey, the federally sponsored study of Internet sex crimes against minors that was mentioned earlier in this chapter.

Mitchell, Wolak, and Finkelhor reported that, based upon the National Juvenile Online Victimization Survey data they reviewed, 13 percent of the offenders arrested in sting operations had previously committed sex crimes against victims they had identified online. They also reported that there were many differences between offenders caught in stings and those who had offended against actual juveniles. Sting offenders were significantly older, more affluent, more likely to be employed, more likely to be living with a minor at the time of the offense, less likely to have demonstrated deviant or violent behavior in the past, and less likely to have been previously arrested for a sexual or nonsexual offense. Forty-one percent of sting offenders and 39 percent of the hands-on offenders had possessed child pornography, a between-group difference that was not statistically significant. In an effort to understand these differences, Mitchell et al. speculated that for sting offenders:

> [P]roblematic Internet use may have contributed or been a factor in the engagement of these crimes, tentatively supported by their lower amount of criminal history. It is also possible that some of these offenders had impulse control issues that were exacerbated by the overwhelming amount of material, particularly sexual material and interaction, available on the Internet. Some may also have been naive or new offenders who had not developed the experience or grooming skills necessary to advance sexual or romantic relationships with teenagers . . . but some did have histories of child sexual assault and other kinds of deviant sexual behavior. Some may have offended before and never been caught. It is possible that they were less likely to be caught because they were more educated and employed and therefore less suspect.[97]

Conclusion And Recommendations

The best available data, derived from the federally funded Youth Internet Safety Surveys and National Juvenile Online Victimization Study, suggest that online sexual offenses constitute an extremely small percentage of all sex crimes against juveniles. These data suggest that while 13 percent of American youths might be expected to be sexually solicited online in a given year, less than a third of those will be asked to meet the adult solicitor, less than a third of those asked will in fact meet the solicitor, and those who do will be mainly older teenagers who are often meeting solicitors who are in their early 20s. These data also suggest, however, that when a youngster who has been sexually solicited online meets the solicitor, sexual contact will occur in the vast majority of cases.

The federal data are troubling because it appears that a fair number of American children are being approached sexually online and thus being put at risk for at least some degree of emotional harm. But these data also suggest that in those relatively rare cases in which these youngsters are victimized by hands-on sexual abuse, it is primarily in the form of what would otherwise be referred to as statutory rape—voluntary sexual contact which is by law deemed nonconsensual because of the age and immaturity of one of the parties.

This is not to say that statutory rape is a victimless crime or an offense that does no harm to juveniles: Statutory rape is a crime in every American jurisdiction in part because of the near-universal belief that even willingly engaging in sex with an adult is potentially detrimental to the interests of a minor. Adults, even young adults, who are found to have had voluntary sexual relations with minors are routinely punished, albeit generally not too severely, by the criminal law. Yet, in federal courts today, adults who commit the same offenses with youngsters contacted via the Internet, are severely punished— that is, generally sentenced to 10 or more years in prison. Moreover, even those who use the Internet in unsuccessful attempts to have sex with minors (or adults pretending to be minors) receive similarly harsh federal sentences. Those prosecuted in state courts for the very same criminal acts are generally punished much less severely.

What is there about statutory rape or attempted statutory rape using the Internet that makes these offenses so much worse than ordinary statutory rape or attempted statutory rape, and compels the federal government to make the punishments imposed for the former set of crimes so much greater than those imposed for the latter?

The most obvious answer seems to be that the online offenders trolling the Internet for underage sex partners probably have a much greater chance of succeeding in that quest than do offenders who rely upon other means to meet potential victims. Offenders using the Internet may have almost instant access to hundreds, even thousands of potential victims, and can make their initial approaches anonymously, with only a relatively small investment of time and energy, and with little likelihood of being apprehended by authorities. If one youngster rebuffs their online advances, they can immediately (and with just a few keystrokes) move on to another. On the other hand, more typical statutory rape offenders must make their initial advances in person, risk face-to-face rejection if not immediate arrest, and generally have to either quickly seduce their victims or invest a good deal of time developing a relationship that may or may not culminate in sexual relations.

Also, online offenders pollute the Internet and make it less safe and desirable for use by children and adolescents. Even if they never succeed at having sex with a minor approached online, or indeed never intend to do so but simply wish to act out their fantasies in a form of "cybersex," these offenders risk corrupting or emotionally harming all youths they sexually solicit. And because of the omnipresence of the Internet, the number of youngsters at risk for such harm is astronomical.

There can be little if any doubt that the government has a strong and legitimate interest in protecting minors from exposure to the possible emotional harm that may accrue from unwanted online sexual solicitation by adults. But the punishment for inflicting that potential harm should fit the crime.

Criminal punishments are generally based upon several justifications: general deterrence, incapacitation, rehabilitation, retribution, and denunciation. It is difficult to see how any one or even all of these justifications support imposing a prison sentence of "not less than 10 years or for life"[98] upon an individual convicted of using the Internet to solicit sex from a minor. Such a sentence appears particularly draconian when compared to much more lenient sentences imposed for the same criminal conduct in many state courts and for much more serious offenses ranging from statutory rape to some forms of hands-on child sexual abuse.

Even if one regards online solicitation as an attempt to commit statutory rape, which it usually is, the penalty should be not be greater than that imposed upon offenders who succeed in committing statutory rape. And the penalty surely should not be greater than that imposed upon offenders who actually molest children.

A fairer and more sensible approach to criminal sentencing for offenders who use the Internet to solicit sex from minors would be to punish them for what they have actually done, not what we believe they might do or what they may have done but the government cannot prove (e.g., possession of child pornography).

All adults who solicit sex from minors online should be charged with criminal online sexual solicitation of a child, an offense grounded in the theory that such solicitation is, by itself, a social harm that must be deterred. Given the likelihood but not certainty of harm involved in the commission of such an offense, and the relatively limited magnitude of such harm in any given instance, this offense should be a misdemeanor and thus carry at most a sentence of

1 year of incarceration to be followed by a period of probation. However, again to make the punishment fit the crime, solicitations of multiple children should each be considered separate offenses, and penalties should be upgraded for persistent offenders who do not appear to be deterred by a misdemeanor conviction.

Offenders whose solicitations rise to the level of attempted statutory rape should also be punished for that offense. Here, too, criminal penalties should be harsher for repeat offenders.

There remain, however, questions regarding the legality and wisdom of using online sting operations that result in the arrest of adults who sexually solicit adult decoys posing as children. Numerous defendants who have been caught in online sex solicitation stings have attempted to raise a defense of entrapment—that is, they claim that government agents unlawfully lured them into committing the offense. Generally, however, the defense of entrapment "is designed to prevent the police from luring individuals into committing crimes they would probably not otherwise commit."[99] Depending upon the jurisdiction, the defense does not apply where (1) the defendant was predisposed to commit the crimes ("ready and willing" to commit the crime "whenever opportunity was afforded")[100] or (2) neither the police nor their agents encouraged commission of the offense "by (a) making knowingly false representations designed to induce the belief that such conduct is not prohibited; or (b) employing methods of persuasion or inducement that create a substantial risk that such an offense will be committed by persons other than those who are ready to commit it."[101] Given that the bulk of arrested online child solicitation offenders appear to have been trolling the Internet for minors with whom they could "chat" if not interact sexually, entrapment is not a defense likely to exculpate many, if any, of them.

It should also be noted that there is no defense of private entrapment. Thus, those solicitors caught in online vigilante sting operations, not tied in any way to law enforcement, may not raise a defense of entrapment, even if they are induced by the decoy to commit the offense. As one federal judge famously observed, "A person hired to commit a crime cannot defend on the ground that the hirer offered him so much money that it broke down his resistance. Such a plea is actually an argument for a heavier sentence, in order to offset the inducement."[102]

A second line of defense sometimes raised in these cases is impossibility— that is, the claim that since there was never any "minor," only an adult decoy, the crime "attempted" was impossible to commit. In many if not most jurisdictions, the courts and legislatures have rejected such a defense. The modern rule is that a defendant is guilty of attempting to commit a crime when he "purposely engages in conduct which would constitute the crime if the attendant circumstances were as he believes them to be."[103] Since most of these offenders appear to believe that they are soliciting minors when they are, in fact, engaged in dialogues with adult decoys, "impossibility" is no defense.

It might be argued that, legality aside, there is something fundamentally wrong or unfair with sting operations such as those conducted against individuals attempting to sexually engage with minors online. Those who make this argument might well use the Conradt case as exhibit number one. As the court held in the civil lawsuit that arose from the consequences of that sting operation, a jury might well have reasonably found that NBC's conduct in the matter was "so outrageous and extreme that no civilized society should tolerate it."[104]

However, that extreme case appears to have pushed, if not exceeded, the bounds of decency and fairness, and it did so not in the name of protecting children but rather for the sake of entertainment and commercial gain. In the more typical instance in which an online solicitor is caught in a sting operation, such as the D'Souza case described earlier, the offender clearly demonstrates his willingness to meet a minor in person and, in all likelihood, attempt to have sex with the minor absent police intervention.

Offenders such as D'Souza pose a risk to vulnerable children and adolescents simply by virtue of their willingness to engage in sexually explicit online conversations ("chats"), which, as his case demonstrates, can be "so outrageous and extreme that no civilized society should tolerate [them]."[105]

Undercover sting operations may be either investigatory or deterrent in nature. As Hay has observed, in the former sort of sting "the government is trying to catch and punish wrongdoers" while in the latter "the government wants to sow distrust among crooks so that (ideally) every crook is afraid that his confederates or victims are agents."[106] Moreover, as Hay adds, "[T]he government sometimes widely publicizes the existence of sting operations. Such announcements would be inexplicable if the government's objective were solely to identify wrongdoers. If the police simply wanted to catch actual or potential [offenders], it would hardly do to say publicly that it was sending out agents to transact with them, for this would scare many [of them] away. But scaring them away may be precisely the point. If so, advertising the existence of undercover operations makes eminent sense."[107]

Through programs such as "To Catch a Predator," other media accounts, and even government press releases on these operations, the general public has been made abundantly aware of their existence. Thus, stings of this sort, even when they do not culminate in an arrest, may have some deterrent effect simply because they are now widely known to exist. As such, these sting operations serve as a warning to solicitors that they never know with whom they are conversing online when they make sexual overtures to someone they believe is a child or underage adolescent.

Whether these sting operations are a cost-effective means of deterring online sexual advances toward minors is an empirical question that has yet to be answered, and may well never be answered. However, despite the possibility of their abuse when conducted by the wrong people for the wrong reasons (as in the case of Louis William Conradt), when these sting operations are conducted solely by private individuals or organizations who later report their findings to the police, very little in the way of government financial support is required. Thus, at least for now, there is no strong argument to be made against them.

EPILOGUE

Over the past two decades or so, federal, state, and local governments have waged what some have called a "war on sex offenders." Legislators and policymakers have developed a variety of new or recycled laws aimed at reducing the threat these offenders pose to the public. This volume has examined four major examples of these laws: sex offender civil commitment statutes; sex offender registration, reporting, and restriction acts; child pornography laws; and Internet child luring offenses.

For the most part, while these legal initiatives have enjoyed great popular and political support, there is little evidence that any of them have had a significant effect, if any effect, in reducing sex crimes. Indeed, it has been argued plausibly that some of them, particularly sex offender registration, reporting, and restriction acts, may have actually increased the likelihood that convicted sex offenders will recidivate.

The financial cost of these laws and policies has been staggering and continues to grow at a time when the nation faces its greatest economic crisis since the Great Depression. Billions of taxpayer dollars are being spent on these programs each year while, at the same time, governments at all levels are imposing draconian funding cuts on vital programming in education, mental health care, child welfare, law enforcement, corrections, and even national security. Sadly, if the goal has been to reduce the incidence of sexual offending, it appears fair to say that much of the money that funds the implementation of these sex offender laws and policies is simply wasted.

But the cost of these laws is far more than financial. To uphold many of these laws against constitutional and other legal challenges, courts, including the U.S. Supreme Court, have been forced to strain or ignore numerous fundamental principles of American jurisprudence in ways that threaten the rights not only of sex offenders but all citizens.

The new wave of sex offender laws and policies in this country has also imposed an enormous cost on psychology, psychiatry, and the other mental health professions. Not only is much of today's sex offender law at odds with empirical evidence from the social sciences, but the policies and programs mandated by this body of law have spawned a huge and often lucrative job market for psychologists, psychiatrists, and other mental health experts, without whose professional input many such policies and programs could not be implemented. As a result, many mental health professionals, all of whom are trained in the social sciences, have been offered a choice between empiricism and employment. In the short run the payoff, especially for some individual practitioners, has been great, but in the long run, the damage done to their professions and the people who would be served by them may prove to be much greater.

Sexual offending is a scourge that will never be eradicated but clearly can be (and has been) reduced. Indeed, the best available data suggest that the incidence of sexual offending had been decreasing for some time prior to America's new wave of sex offender laws. Maintaining the costly current "war on sex offenders" may ultimately prove to have some marginal impact in further reducing the incidence of sexual offending in this country. But, as has been suggested if not established in this volume, even a cursory cost–benefit analysis indicates that any positive results have been rather limited and, for the most part, not justified by the heavy costs imposed by continuing this "war" in its current mode.

This volume does not advocate giving up efforts to even further reduce sexual offending, but proposes modifying this "war" in sensible ways. Today, America needs sex offender laws and policies that are evidence-based and cost-effective, that respect the nation's historic and fundamental commitment to civil liberties, and that do not threaten to make a mockery of psychology, psychiatry, and other mental health professions. The reforms to sex offender law and policy recommended in this book—some modest, others radical— will face great resistance in many quarters. Sex offenders have no organized lobby, and rare is the state legislator or member of Congress who will vote for, much less propose, repeal of sex offender laws that, while costly and largely ineffective, are popular and widely assumed to be helpful. Judges are unlikely to rule against these laws and policies, given that the U.S. Supreme Court has already found, albeit by the narrowest of margins, that they are constitutional. Even mental health experts, who are trained social scientists, are likely to split over the kinds of reforms suggested here. It is difficult to picture, for example, psychologists who now earn their living developing checklists that purport to predict sex offender recidivism, doing evaluations and testifying in sex offender civil commitment trials, and/or training others who do so, encouraging state legislatures to put them out of work.

Ultimately, if these laws and policies are to be reformed, as suggested in this book or otherwise, the initiative will likely have to come from three sources: (1) psychologists and other social scientists who continue to conduct and/or disseminate research of the sort reviewed in this volume; (2) taxpayers who demand less costly government programs proven to be effective; and (3) citizens who are unwilling to trade their civil liberties for the illusion of greater public safety.

NOTES

PREFACE

1. New York State Office of Mental Health, Report to the Governor and the Legislature Pursuant to Article 10 of New York State Mental Hygiene Law (January 28, 2008), 1, http://www.omh.state.ny.us/omhweb/statistics/forensic/(accessed May 2, 2010)
2. *Ibid.*, 3.
3. *Ibid.*, 1.
4. Personal communication, Jim Hayes, Member, New York State Assembly, 148th District (March 25, 2010).
5. Ibid.
6. Ibid.
7. Associated Press, "Paterson Says Deficit Up to $10 Billion Over Next 2 Years," October 29, 2009, http://www.1010wins.com/pages/5555261.php?contentType=4 &contentId=4957569 (accessed May 2, 2010).
8. Phil Fairbanks, ""Everything" on table, comptroller says, as state budget gap widens," *Buffalo News*, August 8, 2008, D5.

INTRODUCTION

1. Yung, "The Emerging Criminal War on Sex Offenders," *Harvard Civil Rights–Civil Liberties Law Review* (forthcoming, 2010).
2. Federal Bureau of Investigation, "Crime in the United States 2008," http://www.fbi.gov/ucr/cius2008/offenses/violent_crime/forcible_rape.html (accessed May 2, 2010).
3. "National Crime Victimization Survey Resource Guide," http://www.icpsr.umich.edu/NACJD/NCVS/ (accessed May 2, 2010).
4. U.S. Bureau of Justice Statistics, "Terms & Definitions: Victims," http://bjs.ojp.usdoj.gov/index.cfm?ty=tdtp&tid=9 (accessed May 2, 2010).
5. U.S. Bureau of Justice Statistics, "National Crime Victimization Survey Violent Crime Trends, 1973-2008," http://bjs.ojp.usdoj.gov/content/glance/tables/viortrdtab.cfm (accessed May 2, 2010).
6. Katrina Baum, U.S. Bureau of Justice Statistics, "Special Report: National Crime Victimization Survey, Juvenile Victimization and Offending, 1993–2003," http://bjs.ojp.usdoj.gov/content/pub/pdf/jv003.pdf (accessed May 2, 2010).

7. David Finkelhor and Lisa Jones, "Why Have Child Maltreatment and Child Victimization Declined?" *Journal of Social Issues* (2006): 685–716, 685.

8. *Ibid.*, 687.

9. *Ibid.*, 688.

10. Callie Marie Rennison and Michael R. Rand, U.S. Bureau of Justice Statistics, "Criminal Victimization 2002," 11, http://bjs.ojp.usdoj.gov/index.cfm?ty=pbdetail&iid=1056 (accessed May 2, 2010).

11. Ibid.

12. Howard N. Snyder, U.S. Bureau of Justice Statistics, "Sexual Assault of Young Children as Reported to Law Enforcement: Victim, Incident, and Offender Characteristics," http://eric.ed.gov/ERICWebPortal/contentdelivery/servlet/ERICServlet?accno=ED446834 (accessed May 2, 2010).

13. Matthew R. Durose, Patrick A. Langan, and Erica L. Schmitt, U.S. Bureau of Justice Statistics, "Recidivism of Sex Offenders Released from Prison in 1994" (2003), http://bjs.ojp.usdoj.gov/index.cfm?ty=pbdetail&iid=1136 (accessed May 2, 2010).

14. Alan R. McKelvie, "Recidivism of Alaska Sex Offenders," *Alaska Justice Forum* (2008): 14–15, http://justice.uaa.alaska.edu/forum/25/1-2springsummer2008/g_recidivism.html (accessed May 2, 2010); California Sex Offender Management Board, "Recidivism of Paroled Sex Offenders—A Five (5) Year Study" (2008), www.karenfranklin.com/Five%20year%20recidivism%20study%20CDCR%206-16-08.doc (accessed May 2, 2010); California Sex Offender Management Board, "Recidivism of Paroled Sex Offenders—A Ten (10) Year Study" (2008), http://cfcoklahoma.org/New_Site/index.php?option=com_fireboard&Itemid=0&func=view&catid=87&id=&id=1492&catid=87 (accessed May 2, 2010).

15. Yung, *supra* note 1.

CHAPTER 1: CIVIL COMMITMENT OF SEX OFFENDERS

1. *Kansas v. Hendricks,* Brief for the Petitioner, Supreme Court of the United States, 1995 U.S. Briefs 1649; 1996 U.S. S. Ct. Briefs LEXIS 448.

2. Ibid.

3. Ibid.

4. Ibid.

5. Ibid.

6. Ibid.

7. Ibid.

8. Ibid.

9. Ibid.

10. Ibid.

11. Ibid.

12. Ibid.

13. Ibid.

14. Ibid.

15. Monica Davey and Abby Goodnough, "Doubts Rise as States Hold Sex Offenders After Prison," *New York Times*, March 4, 2007, http://www.nytimes.com/2007/03/04/us/04civil.html (accessed May 2, 2010).

16. Eric Weslander, "Notorious sex offender is moving to Lawrence, State won't reveal address, citing privacy of convict," *Lawrence Journal World News*, April 1, 2005, http://www.lansingcurrent.com/news/2005/jun/09/sex_offender/ (accessed May 2, 2010).

17. *See* Eric Weslander, "Questions Persist About Sex Predator," *Lawrence Journal World News*, June 5, 2005, http://www2.ljworld.com/news/2005/jun/05/predator/?city_local (accessed May 2, 2010); Lisa Scheller, "Notorious sex offender moves into, out of county, official says SRS "snuck in" convict, files temporary restraining order," *Lansing Current*, June 9, 2005, http://www.lansingcurrent.com/news/2005/jun/09/sex_offender/ (accessed May 2, 2010).

18. *Board of Commissioners of Leavenworth County v. Whitson and Whitson*, 281 Kan. 678, 690 (Kansas 2006) [citations omitted].

19. *Ibid.*, 681.

20. *Ibid.*, 690.

21. *Ibid.*, 689.

22. Davey and Goodnough, *supra* note 15.

23. *See* Washington State Institute for Public Policy, "Comparison of State Laws Authorizing Involuntary Commitment of Sexually Violent Predators: 2006 Update, Revised," http://www.wsipp.wa.gov/rptfiles/07-08-1101.pdf (accessed May 2, 2010).

24. Tamara Rice Lave, "Only Yesterday: The Rise and Fall of Twentieth Century Sexual Psychopath Laws," 69 *Louisiana Law Review* 549, 549 (2009).

25. Estelle B. Freedman, ""Uncontrolled Desires": The Response to the Sexual Psychopath, 1920–1960," *Journal of American History* (1987): 83–106, 92.

26. Edwin H. Sutherland, "The Sexual Psychopath Laws," *Journal of Criminal Law and Criminology* (1950): 543–554, 544.

27. Ibid.

28. Freedman, *supra* note 25, 83–84.

29. Paul W. Tappan, "Sentences for Sex Criminals," *Journal of Criminal Law, Criminology, and Police Science* (1951): 332–337, 335.

30. W.P. Beazell, *The Problem of Sex Offenses in New York City: A Study of Procedure Affecting 2022 Defendants Made by the Staff of the Citizen's Committee on the Control of Crime in New York* (February 15, 1939).

31. Paul W. Tappan, *The Habitual Sex Offender* (1950): 37.

32. Paul W. Tappan, "Some myths about the sex offender," *Federal Probation* (June 1955): 7.

33. American Psychiatric Association, *Dangerous Sex Offenders: A Task Force Report of the American Psychiatric Association* (1999): 11.

34. Group for the Advancement of Psychiatry, *Psychiatry and Sex Psychopath Legislation: The Thirties to the Eighties* (1977): 843.

35. George Santayana, *The Life of Reason* (1906): 35.

36. Barry Siegel, "Locking Up "Sexual Predators"; A Public Outcry in Washington State Targeted Repeat Violent Sex Criminals. A New Preventive Law Would Keep Them in Jail Indefinitely," *Los Angeles Times*, May 10, 1990, A1.
37. Jerry Seper, "System fails to stop repeat offenders," *Washington Times*, December 15, 1993, A7.
38. James Wallace, Two People, One a "Monster"; A Tragic Obsession Drove Him," *Seattle Post-Intelligencer*, January 1, 1993, A1.
39. Washington Revised Code 71.09.020(1) *et seq.* (1994).
40. Ibid.
41. John Q. La Fond, *Preventing Sexual Violence* (2005): 133.
42. *Ibid.*, 134.
43. Ibid.
44. Ibid.
45. *Young v. Weston*, 898 F. Supp. 744, 747 (1995) [citations omitted].
46. Ibid.
47. *Ibid.*, 748–749.
48. *Ibid.*, 751–753.
49. *Ibid.*, 752.
50. 521 U.S. 346 (1997).
51. *In the Matter of the Care and Treatment of Leroy Hendricks*, 912 P.2d 129, 136–138 (1996) [citations omitted].
52. *Kansas v. Hendricks*, 521 U.S. 346, 356–160 (1997) [citations omitted].
53. *Ibid.*, 362.
54. Ibid.
55. 534 U.S. 407 (2002).
56. *Ibid.*, 412.
57. Ibid.
58. *Ibid.*, 423.
59. Texas Health and Safety Code, Sec. 841 (Vernon, 1999).
60. *Supra* note 23.
61. Davey and Goodnough, *supra* note 15.
62. American Psychiatric Association, *Diagnostic and Statistical Manual of Mental Disorders, Fourth Edition* (1994).
63. Eric S. Janus and Robert A. Prentky, "Sexual Predator Laws: A Two-Decade Retrospective," *Federal Sentencing Reporter* (December 2008): 90–97, 93.
64. American Psychiatric Association, *supra* note 62, 649–650.
65. La Fond, *supra* note 41, 140.
66. *Supra* note 55, 412 [citations omitted].
67. *See* Thomas Zander, "Civil commitment without psychosis: the law's reliance on the weakest links in psychodiagnosis," *Journal of Sex Offender Civil Commitment* (2005): 17–82; Michael B. First and Robert L. Halon, "Use of DSM Paraphilia Diagnoses in Sexually Violent Predator Commitment Cases," *Journal of the American Academy of Psychiatry and Law* (2008): 443–454.

68. Dean R. Cauley, "The diagnostic issue of antisocial personality disorder in civil commitment proceedings: A response to DeClue," *Journal of Psychiatry & Law* (2007): 475–497, 488.

69. See, e.g., Jack Vognsen and Amy Phenix, "Antisocial Personality Disorder Is Not Enough: A Reply to Sreenivasan, Weinberger, and Garrick," *Journal of the American Academy of Psychiatry and the Law* (2004): 440–442, 442.

70. Cauley, *supra* note 68, 490.

71. Association for the Treatment of Sexual Abusers, Brief *Amicus Curiae, Kansas v. Hendricks,* 1996 U.S. S. Ct. Briefs LEXIS 553 (1996): 14.

72. American Psychiatric Association, *supra* note 62, 528.

73. Janus and Prentky, *supra* note 63, 94.

74. 2006 Mass. Super. LEXIS 77 (2006): 1–11.

75. *Ibid.,* 3.

76. *Ibid.,* 4.

77. Ibid.

78. *Ibid.,* 5.

79. 842 A.2d 448 (2004); 912 A.2d 213 (2006).

80. *Ibid.,* 216.

81. 842 A.2d 448, 453.

82. Ibid.

83. Ibid.

84. 912 A.2d 213, 224–225.

85. *Ibid.,* 225.

86. *U.S. v. Shields,* 2008 U.S. Dist. LEXIS 13837 (2008): 1–7, 4.

87. *See, generally,* Karen Franklin, "Hebephilia: Quintessence of Diagnostic Pretextuality," *Behavioral Sciences and the Law* (forthcoming, 2010).

88. Ray Blanchard, Amy D. Lykins, Diane Wherrett, Michael E. Kuban, James M. Cantor, Thomas Blak, Robert Dickey, and Philip E. Klassen, "Pedophilia, Hebephilia, and the DSM-V," *Archives of Sexual Behavior* (2009): 335–350.

89. *Supra* note 86, 4.

90. Ibid.

91. American Psychiatric Association, *supra* note 62, 522–523.

92. *Ibid.,* 525–532.

93. *Ibid.,* 532.

94. *Supra* note 86, 5.

95. *Ibid.,* 6.

96. *U.S. v. Graham,* 2010 U.S. Dist. LEXIS 12198 (2010): 1–46, 13.

97. *Ibid.,* 13.

98. *Ibid.,* 14.

99. *Ibid.,* 27.

100. *See, generally,* Raymond A. Knight, "Is a Diagnostic Category for Paraphilic Coercive Disorder Defensible?" *Archives of Sexual Behavior* (2010): 419–426.

101. *Supra* note 96, 16.

102. *Ibid.,* 31.

103. *Ibid.*, 36.
104. Ibid.
105. Ibid.
106. *Ibid*, 39.
107. *Ibid.*, 40.
108. Matthew R. Durose, Patrick A. Langan, and Erica L. Schmitt, U.S. Bureau of Justice Statistics, "Recidivism of Sex Offenders Released from Prison in 1994" (2003), http://bjs.ojp.usdoj.gov/index.cfm?ty=pbdetail&iid=1136 (accessed May 2, 2010).
109. Alan R. McKelvie, "Recidivism of Alaska Sex Offenders," *Alaska Justice Forum* (2008): 14–15, http://justice.uaa.alaska.edu/forum/25/1-2springsummer2008/g_recidivism.html (accessed May 2, 2010).
110. Lisa L. Sample and Timothy M. Bray, "Are Sex Offenders Different? An Examination of Rearrest Patterns," *Criminal Justice Policy Review* (March 2006): 83–102.
111. California Sex Offender Management Board, "Recidivism of Paroled Sex Offenders—A Five (5) Year Study" (2008), www.karenfranklin.com/Five%20year%20recidivism%20study%20CDCR%206-16-08.doc (accessed May 2, 2010); California Sex Offender Management Board, "Recidivism of Paroled Sex Offenders—A Ten (10) Year Study" (2008), http://cfcoklahoma.org/New_Site/index.php?option=com_fireboard&Itemid=0&func=view&catid=87&id=&id=1492&catid=87 (accessed May 2, 2010).
112. R. Karl Hanson and Monique T. Bussiere, "Predicting Relapse: A Meta-Analysis of Sexual Offender Recidivism Studies," *Journal of Consulting and Clinical Psychology* (1998): 348–362, 351.
113. *Ibid.*, 350.
114. *Ibid.*, 351.
115. Andrew J. R. Harris and R. Karl Hanson, "Sex Offender Recidivism: A Simple Question," *Public Safety and Emergency Preparedness Canada* (2004): 1–23. http://www.publicsafety.gc.ca/res/cor/rep/2004-03-se-off-eng.aspx (accessed May 2, 2010).
116. *Ibid.*, 8.
117. *Ibid.*, 11.
118. Eric S. Janus and Robert A. Prentky, "Forensic Use of Actuarial Risk Assessment with Sex Offenders: Accuracy, Admissibility and Accountability," *American Criminal Law Review* (2003): 1443–1499, 1454.
119. Robert P. Archer, Jacqueline K. Buffington-Vollum, Rebecca Vauter Stredny, and Richard W. Handel, "A Survey of Psychological Test Use Patterns Among Forensic Psychologists," *Journal of Personality Assessment* (2006): 84–94, 87.
120. "Static-99 Clearinghouse," http://www.static99.org/ (accessed May 2, 2010).
121. Ibid.
122. Ibid.
123. *See* R. Karl Hanson and David Thornton, "Static 99: Improving Actuarial Risk Assessments for Sex Offenders "(1999), http://www.courtdiagnostic.

com/Static%2099-02.pdf (accessed May 2, 2010); R. Karl Hanson and David Thornton, "Improving Risk Assessments for Sex Offenders: A Comparison of Three Actuarial Scales," *Law and Human Behavior* (2000): 119–136.

124. R. K. Hanson, R. A. Steffy, and R. Gauthier, "A Comparison of Child Molesters and Nonsexual Criminals: Risk Predictors and Long-Term Recidivism," *Journal of Research in Crime and Delinquency* (1995): 325–337, 335.

125. Ibid.

126. "STATIC-99 Coding Form," http://www.static99.org/ (accessed May 2, 2010).

127. Ibid.

128. "STATIC-99 Recidivism Percentages by Risk Level," http://www.static99.org/pdfdocs/originalestimates.pdf (accessed May 2, 2010).

129. Leslie Helmus, R. Karl Hanson, and David Thornton, "Reporting Static-99 in Light of New Research on Recidivism Norms" (2009): 1–8, http://www.static99.org/pdfdocs/forum_article_feb2009.pdf (accessed May 2, 2010).

130. *Ibid.*, 7.

131. Ibid.

132. Report on file with the author.

133. Ibid.

134. 889 N.Y.S.2d 369, 390–391 (2009).

135. Amy E. Amenta, Laura S. Guy, and John F. Edens, "Sex Offender Risk Assessment: A Cautionary Note Regarding Measures Attempting to Quantify Violence Risk," *Journal of Forensic Psychology Practice* (2003): 39–50, 45.

136. *People v. Curtis*, 2006 Cal. App. Unpub. LEXIS 9862 (2006), 1–11, 8; *People v. Magpie* (2006) Cal. App. Unpub. LEXIS 5307 (2006): 1–22, 11.

137. *State v. Benjamin*, 2005 Ohio App. LEXIS 2218 (2005): 1–14, 11.

138. *People v. Evans*, 2005 Cal. App. Unpub. LEXIS 7485 (2005): 1–18, 6; 132 Cal. App. 4th 950 (2005): 952.

139. *People v. McKee*, 160 Cal. App. 4th 1517, 1552 (2008).

140. *People v. Evans, supra* note 138, 4.

141. *People v. Myers*, 2005 Cal. App. Unpub. LEXIS 4872 (2005): 1–18, 8.

142. *People v. Therrian*, 113 Cal. App. 4th 609, 612 (2003).

143. *People v. Calderon*, 2009 Cal. App. Unpub. LEXIS 1427 (2009): 1–27, 13.

144. *State v. Medina*, 2006 Ohio App. LEXIS 5761 (2006): 1–14, 11.

145. *Commonwealth v. Barker*, 4 Pa. D. & C.5th 340, 350 (2005).

146. *State v. Guidroz*, 2004 Tex. App. LEXIS 2872 (2004): 1–5, 2.

147. *Matter of Van Grinsven*, 711 N.W.2d 587, 600 (North Dakota, 2006).

148. *State v. Thomas*, 2005 Ohio App. LEXIS 1533 (2005): 1–34.

149. *Ibid.*, 7.

150. *Ibid.*, 8 [emphasis added].

151. Ibid.

152. *People v. Calhoun*, 2006 Cal. App. Unpub. LEXIS 4361 (2006): 1–29, 25.

153. *State v. Stanfield*, 862 N.Y.S.2d 818, 818 (2008).

154. *State v. Morales*, 795 N.E.2d 145, 147 (2003).

155. *People v. Ayala*, 2004 Cal. App. Unpub. LEXIS 2007 (2004): 1–20, 4.

156. *People v. Badura*, 2006 Cal. App. Unpub. LEXIS 9280 (2006): 1–19, 10–11.

157. *Supra* note 142, 612.
158. *People v. Black*, 557 F. Supp. 2d 1100, 1105 (2008).
159. *Matter of Anderson*, 730 N.W.2d 570, 581 (2007).
160. *U.S. v. McIlrath*, 512 F.3d 421, 424–425 (2008) [citations omitted].
161. *Supra* note 134, 392–394 [citations omitted].
162. Stephen D. Hart, Christine Michie, and David J. Cooke, "Precision of actuarial risk assessment instruments: Evaluating the "margins of error" of group v. individual predictions of violence," *British Journal of Psychiatry* (2007): 60–65, 60.
163. Ibid.
164. *Ibid.*, 64.
165. *Ibid.*, 60.
166. *Supra* note 50, 371.
167. W. Lawrence Fitch, "Sex Offender Commitment in the United States," *Journal of Forensic Psychiatry* (1998): 237–240, 240.
168. Center for Sex Offender Management, "The Comprehensive Approach to Sex Offender Management" (2008): 1–12, 5, http://www.csom.org/pubs/Comp_Approach_Brief.pdf (accessed May 2, 2010).
169. *See, generally,* Fabian M. Saleh, "Pharmacological Treatment of Paraphilic Sex Offenders," in Fabian Saleh, Albert K. Grudzinskas, John M. Bradford, and Daniel J. Brodsky, *Sex Offenders: Identification, Risk Assessment, Treatment and Legal Issues* (2009): 189–207.
170. *McKune v. Lile*, 536 U.S. 24 (2002).
171. *Ibid.*, 31.
172. Ibid.
173. *Ibid.*, 32.
174. *Ibid.*, 33.
175. Ibid.
176. *Ibid.*, 33–36 [citations omitted].
177. *Supra* note 168.
178. Jill S. Levenson and David S. Prescott, "Treatment Experiences of Civilly Committed Sex Offenders: A Consumer Satisfaction Survey," *Sexual Abuse: A Journal of Research and Treatment* (2009): 6–20, 6–7.
179. Howard Barbaree, "Evaluating Treatment Efficacy with Sexual Offenders: The Insensitivity of Recidivism Studies to Treatment Effect," *Sexual Abuse: A Journal of Research and Treatment* (1997): 111–128, 112.
180. R. Karl Hanson, Ian Broom, and Marylee Stephenson, "Evaluating Community Sex Offender Treatment Programs: A 12-Year Follow-Up of 724 Offenders," *Canadian Journal of Behavioural Science* (2004): 87–96, 87.
181. Robert Prentky and Barbara Schwartz, "Treatment of Adult Sex Offenders Treatment of Adult Sex Offenders," *Applied Research Forum* (December 2006): 1–10, 2, http://new.vawnet.org/Assoc_Files…/AR_SexOffendTreatment.pdf (accessed May 2, 2010).
182. R. Karl Hanson, Arthur Gordon, Andrew J. R. Harris, Janice K. Marques, William Murphy, Vernon L. Quinsey, and Michael C. Seto, "First Report of

the Collaborative Outcome Data Project on the Effectiveness of Psychological Treatment for Sex Offenders," *Sexual Abuse: A Journal of Research and Treatment* (2002): 169–194.

183. *Ibid.*, 181.

184. Ibid.

185. Marnie E. Rice and Grant T. Harris, "The size and sign of treatment effects in sex offender therapy," *Annals of the New York Academy of Sciences* (2003): 428–440, 440.

186. Friedrich Losel and Martin Schmucker, "The effectiveness of treatment for sexual offenders: A comprehensive meta-analysis," *Journal of Experimental Criminology* (2005): 117–146.

187. *Ibid.*, 117.

188. Ibid.

189. Gregory DeClue, "Should states require special certification for psychologists who work with sex offenders?" *WebPsychEmpiricist* (2006): 1–10, 6–7, http://www.wpe.info/papers_table.html (accessed May 2, 2010).

190. *Supra* note 41, 79.

191. DeClue, *supra* note 189, 7.

192. Davey and Goodnough, *supra* note 15.

193. Texas Department of State Health Services Council on Sex Offender Treatment, "Civil Commitment of the Sexually Violent Predator—Inpatient vs. Outpatient SVP Civil Commitment," http://www.dshs.state.tx.us/csot/csot_ccinout.shtm (accessed May 2, 2010).

194. Davey and Goodnough, *supra* note 15.

195. Ibid.

196. Robert Prentky and Ann Wolbert Burgess, "Rehabilitation of Child Molesters: A Cost-Benefit Analysis," *American Journal of Orthopsychiatry* (1990): 108–117, 109.

197. Washington State Institute for Public Policy, *supra* note 23.

198. New York State Office of Mental Health, Annual Report on the Implementation of Mental Hygiene Law Article 10 Sex Offender Management and Treatment Act of 2007 (January 2009), www.omh.state.ny.us/omhweb/resources/.../ 2008_SOMTA_Report.pdf (accessed May 2, 2010).

199. Personal communication, Jim Hayes, Member, New York State Assembly, 148th District (March 25, 2010).

200. Davey and Goodnough, *supra* note 15.

201. Molly T. Geissenhainer, "The $62 Million Question: Is Virginia's New Center to House Sexually Violent Predators Money Well Spent?" *University of Richmond Law Review* (2008): 1301–1336.

202. "Bill stuck on sex offender funding," *Minneapolis Star Tribune*, March 9, 2010, http://www.startribune.com/politics/state/87182192.html (accessed May 2, 2010).

203. Rocco LaDuca, "$30M later, Mid-State facility not yet housing sex offenders," *Utica Observer-Dispatch*, http://www.uticaod.com/news/x512367636/-30M-later-Mid-State-facility-not-yet-housing-sex-offenders (accessed May 2, 2010).

204. New York State Assembly Codes Committee, "Memorandum (Assembly Bill 6162)," www.communityalternatives.org/pdf/Civil%20Commitment%20Codes. doc (accessed May 2, 2010).

205. *Ibid.*, 7.

206. Davey and Goodnough, *supra* note 15.

207. American Psychiatric Association, *Dangerous Sex Offenders* (1999): 173–174.

208. Ibid.

209. Order, New York State Administrative Board of the Courts, November 10, 2009.

210. Charles Piller and Lee Romney, "State pays millions for contract psychologists to keep up with Jessica's Law," *Los Angeles Times*, August 10, 2008, A1, http://www.latimes.com/news/local/la-me-jessica10-2008aug10,0,969181. story?page=1 (accessed May 2, 2010).

211. Ibid.

212. National Association of State Mental Health Program Directors, *A Tool Kit for the SMHA Commissioners and Directors: Legislation for the Psychiatric Commitment of Sexually Violent Predators* (1997): 1.

213. Ron Donate and Martin Shanahan, "The Economics of Child Sex-Offender Rehabilitation Programs: Beyond Prentky & Burgess," *American Journal of Orthopsychiatry* (2001): 131–139, 132.

214. *Ibid.*, 131.

215. Council on Sex Offender Treatment, "Civil Commitment of the Sexually Violent Predator—Texas Sexually Violent Predator Act," http://www.dshs.state. tx.us/csot/csot_ccact.shtm (accessed May 2, 2010).

216. Ibid.

217. *Supra* note 197.

218. Ibid.

219. *Supra* note 215.

220. *Supra* note 207, 170.

221. Leslie Huss, "Overview of Texas Sexually Violent Predator Program" (2008), http://www.srskansas.org/.../SPTP_in_Texas_SWAM-2%20-10-09.pdf (accessed May 2, 2010).

222. Sandra Norman-Eady, "Report of the Committee to Study Sexually Violent Persons" (2007), http://www.cga.ct.gov/2007/rpt/2007-R-0684.htm (accessed May 2, 2010).

223. Ibid.

224. Ibid.

225. Ibid.

226. Ibid.

CHAPTER 2: SEX OFFENDER REGISTRATION, NOTIFICATION, AND RESTRICTION LAWS

1. Doug Giles, "A Time to Kill, *Townhall*, April 23, 2005, http://townhall.com/ columnists/DougGiles/2005/04/23/a_time_to_kill?page=full&comments=true (accessed May 4, 2010).

2. 42 U.S.C. § 16913.

3. "Sex Offender Notification and Registration Act (SORNA): Barriers to Timely Compliance by States," Hearing Before the Subcommittee on Crime, Terrorism, and Homeland Security of the Committee on the Judiciary, U.S. House of Representatives, March 10, 2009, 131–132, http://judiciary.house.gov/hearings/hear_090310_1.html (accessed May 4, 2010).

4. http://www.nsopw.gov/Core/Conditions.aspx?AspxAutoDetectCookieSupport=1 (accessed May 10, 2010).

5. *See* http://www.gencourt.state.nh.us/RSA/html/LXII/632-A/632-A-3.htm (accessed May 4, 2010).

6. *See,* e.g., Lisa L. Sample and Mary K. Evans, "Sex Offender Registration and Notification," in Richard G. Wright (Ed.), *Sex Offender Laws: Failed Policies, New Directions* (2009): 211–242, 212; Wayne A. Logan, *Knowledge as Power: Criminal Registration and Community Notification Laws in America* (2009): 205.

7. E. A. Riddle, "Compulsory Registration: A Vehicle of Mercy Discarded," *California Western Law. Review* (1967): 195, 199.

8. Logan, *supra* note 6, 185.

9. Robert L. Jacobson, ""Megan's Laws" Reinforcing Old Patterns of Anti-Gay Police Harassment," *Georgetown Law Journal* (1999): 2431, 2443.

10. Ibid.

11. Ibid.

12. Washington Revised Code § 71.09.010 *et seq.*

13. Dretha M. Phillips, "Community Notification as Viewed by Washington's Citizens" www.wsipp.wa.gov/rptfiles/CnSurvey.pdf (accessed May 4, 2010).

14. Jerry Seper, "System fails to stop repeat offenders," *Washington Times,* December 15, 1993, A7.

15. Richard Meryhew, "Hope keeps search for Jacob going; Ten years and thousands of leads have come and gone, but the abduction of Jacob Wetterling still grips St. Joseph and the investigators who have poured their lives and hearts into the case," *Minneapolis Star Tribune,* October 22, 1999, 1B.

16. Mary Divine, "After 20 years, Minnesota still wonders, Where's Jacob?" *St. Paul Pioneer Press,* October 21, 2009, 1.

17. 42 U.S.C. § 14071 (1994), repealed by 42 U.S.C. § 16901(1) (2006).

18. Ibid.

19. Richard Jerome, Maria Eftimades, "Megan's Legacy; Little Megan Kanka was Brutally Murdered," *People,* March 20, 1995, 46.

21. http://www.megannicolekankafoundation.org/mission.htm (accessed May 4, 2010).

22. Angie Cannon, "Mother Perseveres in Megan's Law Effort," *The Philadelphia Inquirer,* May 15, 1996, B1.

23. Ibid.

24. New Jersey Statutes Annotated § 2C:7-2b(3).

25. *Doe v. Poritz,* 142 N.J. 1, 14-17 (1995) [citations omitted].

26. 42 USCS § 14071.

27. Human Rights Watch, *No Easy Answers for Sex Offenders* (2007), 25, www.hrw.org/en/reports/2007/09/11/no-easy-answers (accessed May 4, 2010).

28. Ibid.

29. Ibid.

30. "The President's Radio Address," August 24, 1996, http://www.presidency.ucsb.edu/ws/index.php?pid=53230 (accessed May 4, 2010).

31. 42 USCS § 14071.

32. 64 Fed. Reg. 572, 581 (1999).

33. *Connecticut Department of Safety v. Doe*, 538 U.S. 1, 3 (2003).

34. *Ibid.*, 4.

35. *Ibid.*, 5 [citations omitted].

36. Ibid.

37. *Doe v. Lee* et al., 132 F. Supp. 2d 57 (2001).

38. *Doe v. Connecticut Department of Safety*, 271 F.3d 38 (2001).

39. *Ibid.*, 62.

40. *Ibid.*, 57.

41. *Supra* note 33, 6.

42. 538 U.S. 84 (2002).

43. *Rowe v. Burton*, 884 F. Supp. 1372 (1994).

44. *Doe v. Otte*, 259 F.3d 979 (2001).

45. *Supra* note 42, 93–94.

46. Pub. L. No. 104-236, 110 Stat. 3093 (1996) (codified at 42 U.S.C. § 14072).

47. Pub. L. No. 109-248, 120 Stat. 587 (2006) (codified at 42 U.S.C. § 1690).

48. *See* "Congress Reaches Agreement on Hatch's Sex Offender Bill," *States News Service*, July 20, 2006.

49. 42 U.S.C. § 16902.

50. National Conference of State Legislatures, "Cost-Benefit Analyses of SORNA Implementation," (2010), http://www.ncsl.org/?tabid=19499 (accessed May 4, 2010).

51. http://www.nsopw.gov/Core/Conditions.aspx (accessed May 4, 2010).

52. *Supra* note 3, 46.

53. 971 A.2d 401 (2008).

54. Ibid.

55. Lane DeGregory, "Miami sex offenders limited to life under a bridge," *St. Petersburg Times*, August 16, 2009, http://www.tampabay.com/features/humaninterest/miami-sex-offenders-limited-to-life-under-a-bridge/1027668 (accessed May 4, 2010).

56. "Sex Offenders," *ABC News, World News Tonight*, June 7, 2006.

57. *See, e.g.*, Tex. Govt. Code Ann. § 508.187 (Vernon 2009); Bridget Brown, "Ordinances will affect most sex offenders," *The Facts*, May 10, 2006, http://thefacts.com/news/article_08e43fef-41bd-54b1-bd42-52221ecce527.html (accessed May 4, 2010); Carol Christian, "New law limits where sex offenders can reside: Violators can be fined $500 per day of offense," *The Houston Chronicle*, April 16, 2009, 1; Texas Department of Safety, "Frequently Asked Questions,"

http://www.txdps.state.tx.us/administration/crime_records/pages/faq.htm (accessed May 4, 2010).

58. Loretta Kalb, "Libraries plan sex-offender response," *Sacramento Bee*, August 29, 2006, B2.

59. Wendy Koch, "Developments bar sex offenders," *USA Today*, June 15, 2006, http://www.usatoday.com/news/nation/2006-06-15-sex-offenders-barred_x.htm (accessed May 4, 2010); "A Closer Look: Sex Offenders," *ABC News, World News Tonight*, March 7, 2007.

60. Ibid.

61. Koch, *supra* note 59.

62. *See* Joseph L. Lester, "The Legitimacy of Sex Offender Residence and Employment Restrictions," 40 *Akron Law Review* 339 (2007).

63. Ibid.

64. Alayna DeMartini, "Some sex offenders can live by schools: 2003 law doesn't apply if crimes were before then," *Columbus Dispatch*, August 11, 2008, http://www.dispatch.com/live/content/local_news/stories/2008/08/11/School_zone.ART_ART_08-11-08_A1_B0B08Q8.html?sid=101 (accessed May 4, 2010).

65. Ibid.

66. California Department of Corrections and Rehabilitation, "Jessica's Law," http://www.cdcr.ca.gov/Parole/Sex_Offender_Facts/Jessicas_Law.html (accessed May 4, 2010).

67. Katharine Mieszkowski, "Tracking sex offenders with GPS," *Salon*, December 19, 2006, http://www.salon.com/news/feature/2006/12/19/offenders (accessed May 4, 2010).

68. *Doe v. Miller*, 298 F. Supp. 2d 844 (2004).

69. *Doe v. Miller*, 405 F.3d 700, 706 (2005).

70. *Doe v. Miller*, *supra* note 68, 873–874.

71. *Ibid.*, 775–876.

72. *Doe v. Miller*, *supra* note 69, 710–716 [citations omitted].

73. *Weems v. Little Rock Police Department*, 453 F.3d 1010 (2006).

74. *Ibid.*, 1016.

75. *Ibid.*, 1014.

76. *Ibid.*, 1015.

77. *Ibid.*, 1016–1017.

78. *Doe v. Schwarzenegger*, 476 F. Supp. 2d 1178 (2007).

79. W. Somerset Maugham, *A Writer's Notebook* (1949): 72.

80. *Doe v. Poritz*, *supra* note 25, 13.

81. *Supra* note 69, 716.

82. Washington State Institute for Public Policy, "Does Sex Offender Registration and Notification Reduce Crime? A Systematic Review of the Research Literature" (June 2009), www.wsipp.wa.gov/rptfiles/09-06-1101.pdf (accessed May 4, 2010).

83. *Ibid.*, 3.

84. J.J. Prescott and Jonah E. Rockoff, "Do Sex Offender Registration and Notification Laws Affect Criminal Behavior?" *National Economic Bureau of Research*

Working Paper No. 13803 (February 1, 2008), www.gsb.columbia.edu/.../prescot t%20rockoff%20meglaw%20jan%2010.pdf (accessed May 4, 2010).

85. Federal Bureau of Investigation, "National Incident-Based Reporting System," http://www.fbi.gov/ucr/faqs.htm (accessed May 4, 2010).

86. Prescott and Rockoff, *supra* note 84, 1.

87. L. Shao, L. and J. Li, "The Effect of Sex Offender Registration Laws on Rape Victimization," Unpublished Manuscript (2006).

88. Washington State Institute for Public Policy, *supra* note 82, 5.

89. Amanda Agan, "Sex offender registries: Fear without function?" Unpublished manuscript (2008).

90. *Ibid.*, 54.

91. Naomi J. Freeman, "The Public Safety Impact of Community Notification Laws: Rearrest of Convicted Sex Offenders," *Crime and Delinquency* (OnlineFirst, published on May 18, 2009 as doi:10.1177/0011128708330852).

92. *Ibid.*, 9.

93. *Ibid.*, 18.

94. Robert Barnoski, "Sex Offender Sentencing in Washington State: Has Community Notification Reduced Recidivism?" (2005), http://www.wsipp. wa.gov/pub.asp?docid=05-12-1202 (accessed May 4, 2010).

95. *Ibid.*, 1.

96. *Supra* note 82, 3.

97. Kristin Zgoba, Philip Witt, Melissa Dalessandro, and Bonita Veysey, "Megan's Law: Assessing the Practical and Monetary Efficacy" (December 2008), www.ncjrs.gov/pdffiles1/nij/grants/225370.pdf (accessed May 4, 2010).

98. *Ibid.*, 2.

99. Annie K. Yessine and James Bonta, "Tracking High-Risk, Violent Offenders: An Examination of the National Flagging System," *Canadian Journal of Criminology and Criminal Justice* (2006), 573–607.

100. *Ibid.*, 596.

101. Ibid.

102. Ibid.

103. *Ibid.*, 599.

104. Geneva Adkins, David Huff, and Paul Stageberg, *The Iowa Sex Offender Registry and Recidivism* (December 2000), publications.iowa.gov/1516/1/ SexOffenderReport.pdf (accessed May 4, 2010).

105. *Ibid.*, 21.

106. Jeffrey C. Sandler, Naomi J. Freeman, and Kelly A. Socia, "Does a Watched Pot Boil? A Time-Series Analysis of New York State's Sex Offender Registration and Notification Law," *Psychology, Public Policy, and Law* (2008), 284–302.

107. *Ibid.*, 297.

108. Ibid.

109. *Ibid.*, 284.

110. *Report on Safety Issues Raised by Living Arrangements for and Location of Sex Offenders in the Community* (March 15, 2004), dcj.state.co.us/ors/pdf/ docs/FullSLAFinal.pdf (accessed May 4, 2010).

111. *Ibid.*, 3.
112. *Ibid.*, 22.
113. *Ibid.*, 30.
114. *Ibid.*, 37.
115. Grant Duwe, William Donnay, and Richard Tewksbury, "Does Residential Proximity Matter? A Geographic Analysis of Sex Offense Recidivism," *Criminal Justice and Behavior* (2008), 484–504.
116. *Ibid.*, 489.
117. *Ibid.*, 494.
118. *Ibid.*, 497.
119. *Ibid.*, 498.
120. Ibid.
121. *Ibid.*, 501.
122. Jill S. Levenson and Leo P. Cotter, "The Impact of Sex Offender Residence Restrictions: 1,000 Feet From Danger or One Step From Absurd?" *International Journal of Offender Therapy and Comparative Criminology* (2005), 168–178, 170.
123. *Ibid.*, 174.
124. Michael Chajewski and Cynthia Calkins Mercado, "An Evaluation of Sex Offender Residency Restriction Functioning in Town, County, and City-Wide Jurisdictions," *Criminal Justice Policy Review* (2009), 44–61.
125. *Ibid.*, 59.
126. Ibid.
127. Ibid.
128. Paul A. Zandbergen and Timothy C. Hart, "Reducing Housing Options for Convicted Sex Offenders: Investigating the Impact of Residency Restriction Laws Using GIS," *Justice Research and Policy* (Fall 2006): 1–24.
129. *Ibid.*, 1.
130. Ibid.
131. Ibid.
132. *Supra* note 33, 109.
133. *E.B. v. Verniero*, F.3d 1077, 1102 (1997).
134. Human Rights Watch, *supra* note 27, 87–88.
135. Ibid.
136. *Ibid.*, 7.
137. "Murdered in the United States—2008: Registered Sex Offenders & Others" (February 18, 2009), http://sexoffenderresearch.blogspot.com/search/label/%28...Advocacy%20-%20RSOs%20Murdered (accessed May 4, 2010).
138. National Alliance to End Sexual Violence, *Legislative Analysis: The Adam Walsh Child Protection and Safety Act of 2006*, www.naesv.org/Policypapers/Adam_Walsh_SumMarch07.pdf (accessed May 4, 2010).
139. Justice Policy Institute, *What Will it Cost States to Comply with the Sex Offender Registration and Notification Act?* (August 2008), www.justicepolicy.org/images/.../08-08_FAC_SORNACosts_JJ.pdf (accessed May 4, 2010).
140. National Conference of State Legislatures, *supra* note 50.

141. Justice Policy Institute, *supra* note 139.

142. Ibid.

143. Ibid.

144. Ibid.

145. Christopher Dela Cruz, "Report finds Megan's Law fails to reduce sex crimes, deter repeat offenders in N.J.," *Newark Star-Ledger*, February 7, 2009, http://www.nj.com/news/index.ssf/2009/02/study_finds_megans_law_fails_t_1.html (accessed May 4, 2010).

146. Marcus Nieto and David Jung, *The Impact of Residency Restrictions on Sex Offenders and Correctional Management Practices: A Literature Review* (2006), http://www.google.com/search?sourceid=navclient&ie=UTF-8&rlz=1T4GGLL_enUS365US365&q=Hastings+Law+School+Public+Law+Research+Institute++%2488.4+million+per+year+monitor+sex+offenders+GPS (accessed May 4, 2010), 5.

147. Ibid.

148. John Simerman, "State spends millions on rents for paroled sex offenders, sometimes illegally," *Contra Costa Times*, January 17, 2009.

149. James E. Larsen, Kenneth J. Lowrey and Joseph W. Coleman, "The effect of proximity to a registered sex offender's residence on single-family house selling price," *Appraisal Journal* (2003): 253–266.

150. "Sex offenders hurt property values, Wright State University study shows," April 12, 2002, http://www.wright.edu/cgi-bin/cm/news.cgi?action=news_item&id=310 (accessed May 4, 2010).

151. Leigh Linden and Jonah E. Rockoff, *There Goes the Neighborhood? Estimates of the Impact of Crime Risk on Property Values from Megan's Laws.* Paper presented at American Law & Economics Association Annual Meetings (2007), law.bepress.com/cgi/viewcontent.cgi?article=1931&context=alea (accessed May 4, 2010).

152. *Ibid.*, 11.

153. *Ibid.*, abstract.

154. Human Rights Watch, *supra* note 27, 9.

155. 42 USCS § 16918(b).

156. http://www.nsopw.gov/Core/Conditions.aspx (accessed May 4, 2010).

CHAPTER 3: POSSESSION OF CHILD PORNOGRAPHY

1. 134 P.3d (2006).

2. Ariz. Rev. Stat. § 13-3553(A)(2).

3. Ariz. Rev. Stat. § 13-3551(11).

4. *State v. Berger,* 103 P.3d 298 (2004); 134 P.3d 378 (2006) (affirmed); *Berger v. Arizona,* 549 U.S. 1252 (2007) (cert. denied).

5. 134 P.3d 378, 385 (2006) [citations omitted].

6. Susan J. Creighton, *Child Pornography: Images of the Abuse of Children* (November 2003), 1–7, 1, http://www.nspcc.org.uk/Applications/Search/Search.aspx (accessed May 4, 2010).

7. S. Rep. No. 95–438, p. 5 (1977).
8. *Sexual Exploitation of Children,* Hearings before the Subcommittee on Select Education of the House Committee on Education and Labor, 95th Cong., 1st Sess., 41–42 (1977).
9. *New York v. Ferber,* 458 U.S. 747 (198).
10. *Ibid.,* 750.
11. *People v. Ferber,* 52 N.Y.2d 674, 678 (1981).
12. *Ibid.,* 681.
13. *Ibid.,* 687.
14. *Supra* note 11.
15. *Ibid.,* 756.
16. *Ibid.,* 758 [citations omitted].
17. *Ibid.,* 759–760 [citations omitted].
18. *Stanley v. Georgia,* 394 U.S. 557 (1969).
19. *Ibid.,* 565.
20. *Osborne v. Ohio,* 495 U.S. 103,107 (1990).
21. *Ibid.,* 106.
22. *Ibid.,* 108–110.
23. 18 U.S.C.S. § 2256(8)(B).
24. *Ashcroft v. Free Speech Coalition,* 535 U.S. 234 (2002).
25. *Ibid.,* 246.
26. *Ibid.,* 250.
27. Ibid.
28. U.S. Department of Justice, Child Exploitation and Obscenity Section, *Citizen's Guide to United States Federal Child Exploitation Laws,* http://www.justice.gov/criminal/ceos/citizensguide_porn.html (accessed May 4, 2010).
29. Ibid.
30. Ibid.
31. Associated Press, "Connecticut Judge Lets Child Porn Defendant Walk, No Jail Time," October 10, 2006, http://www.foxnews.com/story/0,2933,219159,00.html?sPage=fnc/us/lawcenter (accessed May 4, 2010).
32. United States Attorney, District of Connecticut, "Avon Man Sentenced to More than Three Years for Possessing Child Pornography" (Press Release, November 12, 2008), http://newhaven.fbi.gov/dojpressrel/2008/nh111208.htm (accessed May 4, 2010).
33. 18 USCS § 2252.
34. Ibid.
35. Ibid.
36. Ibid.
37. *U.S. v. Skotzke,* 2007 U.S. Dist. LEXIS 39352, 1 (2007).
38. *Ibid.,* 11–13.
39. Statement of B. Todd Jones (U.S. Attorney, District of Minnesota), U.S. Sentencing Commission Regional Hearing on the State of Federal Sentencing, October 20, 2009, www.ussc.gov/AGENDAS/20091020/Jones_testimony.pdf (accessed May 4, 2010).

40. 18 USCS § 2252.

41. Ibid.

42. See U. S. Sentencing Commission, *The History of the Child Pornography Guidelines,* October 2009, http://docs.google.com/viewer?a=v&q=cache:Ww OlNPEfqZYJ:www.ussc.gov/general/20091030_History_Child_Pornography_ Guidelines.pdf+%22history+of+child+pornography+sentencing+guidelines% 22&hl=en&gl=us&pid=bl&srcid=ADGEESgCRwdNj1sWJ79xCC1WIlIfEJb SSuxirhMy37N99x7B8UU4e1qfVZhrHXxvRBDKR4GJvS8AFw6ig 6-mTONXHZIhnWMUUZX0GcxJgur_lSl5EVEFbnt9kT2yF9UJtl- aooipnWwu&sig=AHIEtbQUKp31-to_lQG3tWVWblyyEDkEew (accessed May 4, 2010).

43. 543 U.S. 220 (2005).

44. *U.S. v. Ontiveros,* 2008 U.S. Dist. LEXIS 58774, 1-2 (2008).

45. *Ibid.,* 2.

46. 18 U.S.C. § 3553.

47. Troy Stabenow, "Deconstructing the Myth of Careful Study: A Primer on the Flawed Progression of the Child Pornography Guidelines," updated January 1, 2009, http://www.fd.org/pdf_lib/child%20porn%20july%20revision.pdf (accessed May 4, 2010).

48. *U.S. v. Moore,* 572 F.3d 489 (2009).

49. *Ibid.,* 490.

50. 2009 *Federal Sentencing Guidelines Manual,* Chapter 2, Part G, www.ussc. gov/2009guid/2g2_2.htm (accessed May 4, 2010).

51. Ibid.

52. Ibid.

53. Ibid.

54. *U.S. v. Moore,* supra note 48.

55. *U.S. v. Griffin,* 482 F.3d 1008 (2007).

56. *Ibid.,* 1008.

57. *Ibid.,* 1010–1013.

58. *U.S. v. Freeman,* 578 F.3d 142 (2009).

59. *Ibid.,* 144.

60. *U.S. v. Lee,* 2009 U.S. App. LEXIS 6452 (2009).

61. *Ibid.,* 6452.

62. Troy Stabenow, "Deconstructing the Myth of Careful Study: A Primer on the Flawed Progression of the Child Pornography Guidelines" (July 3, 2008), 23, http://mow.fd.org/3%20July%202008%20Edit.pdf (accessed May 4, 2010).

63. *U.S. v. Comstock,* 551 F.3d 274, 277 (2009).

64. *U.S. v. Comstock,* 2010 U.S. LEXIS 3879 (2010).

65. *U.S. v. Smathers,* 2009 U.S. App. LEXIS 24965 (2009) [citations omitted].

66. 18 USCS § 2259.

67. 18 USCS § 2251.

68. 18 USCS § 2259.

69. Ibid.

70. Ibid.

71. 18 USCS § 2253.

72. Ashlee Clark, "Lexington house forfeited in child-porn case," *Lexington Herald-Leader*, October 21, 2009, http://www.kentucky.com/2009/10/21/984943/lexington-house-forfeited-in-child.html#ixzzonkdmTjOT (accessed May 4, 2010).

73. U.S. Immigration and Customs Enforcement, "Dallas man sentenced to 10 years on child pornography conviction; Repeat offender was also ordered to forfeit his home to the government," February 20, 2008, http://www.ice.gov/pi/news/newsreleases/articles/080220dallas.htm (accessed May 4, 2010).

74. Ibid.

75. Mark Hansen, "A Reluctant Rebellion," *American Bar Association Journal* (June 2009), 54, http://www.abajournal.com/magazine/article/a_reluctant_rebellion/ (accessed May 4, 2010).

76. *U.S. v. Ontiveros, supra* note 44, 8.

77. *Ibid.*, 5.

78. *U.S. v. Polizzi*, 549 F. Supp. 2d 308, 347–349 (2008).

79. John Shiffman, "Porn suspect accused of smashing hard drive; The instructor at several local colleges took out his hammer when the FBI called, authorities said," *The Philadelphia Inquirer*, March 3, 2007, B02.

80. *U.S. v. Vosburgh*, 2010 U.S. App. LEXIS 8140, 8140 (2010).

81. Declan McCullagh, "FBI posts fake hyperlinks to snare child porn suspects," CNET, March 20, 2008, http://news.cnet.com/8301-13578_3-9899151-38.html (accessed May 4, 2010).

82. *Ibid.; U.S. v. Vosburgh, supra* note 80; John Shiffman, "Guilty verdict in child-porn case," *The Philadelphia Inquirer*, November 7, 2007, B04.

83. Ibid.

84. *U.S. v. Vosburgh, supra* note 80.

85. United Nations, *Report of the Special Rapporteur on the sale of children*, July 13, 2009.

86. Addiction & Industry Pornography Statistics (citing ProtectKids.com. National Society for the Prevention of Cruelty to Children, Oct. 8, 2003), http://www.docstoc.com/docs/36085476/Addiction-and-Industry-Pornography-Statistics/(accessed May 4, 2010).

87. Richard Wortley and Stephen Smallbone, "Child Pornography on the Internet," May 2006, http://purl.access.gpo.gov/GPO/LPS70983 (accessed May 4, 2010), 12.

88. *Ibid.*, 9–10.

89. J. Wolak, D. Finkelhor, and K. Mitchell, "The varieties of child pornography production," in E. Quayle and M. Taylor (Eds.), *Viewing child pornography on the Internet: Understanding the offense, managing the offender, helping the victims* (2005): 31–48, 37–38, http://www.unh.edu/ccrc/national_juvenile_online_victimization_publications.html (accessed May 4, 2010).

90. J. Wolak, D. Finkelhor, and K. Mitchell, "Child Pornography Possessors Arrested in Internet-Related Crimes: Findings from the National Juvenile Online Victimization Study" (2005): 5-6, www.missingkids.com/en_US/publications/NC144.pdf (accessed May 4, 2010).

91. L. Webb, J. Craissati, and S. Keen, "Characteristics of Internet Child Pornography Offenders: A Comparison with Child Molesters," *Sex Abuse* (2007): 449–465.

92. Matt D. O'Brien and Stephen D. Webster, "The Construction and Preliminary Validation of the Internet Behaviours and Attitudes Questionnaire (IBAQ)," *Sex Abuse* (2007): 237–256.

93. J. Endrass, F. Urbaniok, L.C. Hammermeister, C. Benz, T. Elbert, A Laubacher, and A. Rossegger, "The consumption of Internet child pornography and violent and sex offending," *BMC Psychiatry* (2009): 9, 43.

94. Michael C. Seto and Angela W. Eke, "The Criminal Histories and Later Offending of Child Pornography Offenders," *Sexual Abuse: A Journal of Research and Treatment* (2005): 201–210.

95. *Ibid.*, 206.

96. *Ibid.*, 207.

97. *Ibid.*, 208.

98. Ibid.

99. Michael C. Seto, James M. Cantor, and Ray Blanchard, "Child Pornography Offenses Are a Valid Diagnostic Indicator of Pedophilia," *Journal of Abnormal Psychology* (2006): 610–615.

100. *Ibid.*, 610.

101. *Ibid.*, 613.

102. Michael L. Bourke and Andres E. Hernandez, "The "Butner Study" Redux: A Report of the Incidence of Hands-on Child Victimization by Child Pornography Offenders," *Journal of Family Violence* (2009): 183–191, 188.

103. *Ibid.*, 186.

104. *Ibid.*, 188.

105. Webb, Craissati and Keen, *supra* note 91, 457.

106. *Ibid.*, 455.

107. Endrass et al., *supra* note 93.

108. *Ibid.*, 1.

109. Ibid.

110. David L. Riegel, "Effects on Boy-Attracted Pedosexual Males of Viewing Boy Erotica," *Archives of Sexual Behavior* (2004): 321–323.

111. *Ibid.*, 321.

112. Ibid.

113. Ibid.

114. *Ibid.*, 322.

115. Ibid.

116. Ibid.

117. Ibid.

118. *Ibid.*, 323.

119. Kelly M. Babchishin, R. Karl Hanson, and Chantal A. Hermann, "The Characteristics of Online Sex Offenders: A Meta-analysis," unpublished paper.

120. *Ibid.*, 2.

121. Ibid.

122. *Ibid.*, 18.
123. Ibid.
124. *Ibid.*, 19.
125. Ibid.
126. *Ibid.*, 20.
127. *Ibid.*, 2.
128. Michael C. Seto, R. Karl Hanson, and Kelly M. Babchishin, "Contact Sexual Offending By Men with Online Sexual Offenses," *Sexual Abuse: A Journal of Research and Treatment* (in press).
129. *Ibid.*, 9–10.
130. *Ibid.*, 10.
131. *Ibid.*, 11.
132. *Ibid.*, 12.
133. Harris Mirkin, "The Pattern of Sexual Politics: Feminism, Homosexuality and Pedophilia," *Journal of Homosexuality* (1999): 1–24.
134. Jodi Wilgoren, "Scholar's Pedophilia Essay Stirs Outrage and Revenge," *New York Times,* April 30, 2002, http://www.nytimes.com/2002/04/30/education/30MISS.html (accessed May 4, 2010).
135. Ibid.
136. Ibid.
137. Harris Mirkin, "The social, political, and legal construction of the concept of child pornography," *Journal of Homosexuality* (2009): 233–267.
138. *Ibid.*, 259.
139. Amy Adler, "The Perverse Law of Child Pornography," *Columbia Law Review* (2001), 209–273.
140. *Ibid.*, 212.
141. *Ibid.*, 212–213.
142. Hansen, *supra* note 75.
143. *U.S. v. Paull,* 551 F.3d 516 (2009).
144. *Ibid.*, 533.
145. *U.S. v. Johnson,* 588 F. Supp. 2d 997 (2008)
146. *Ibid.*, 1002.
147. *Ibid.*, 1002–1004.
148. *Ibid.*, 1001.
149. *Ibid.*, 1001-1007.
150. *Supra* note 44.
151. *Ibid.*, 16–19.
152. *Ibid.*, 13.
153. *U.S. v. Goldberg,* 491 F.3d 668 (2007).
154. *Ibid.*, 669–671.
155. *Ibid.*, 669.
156. *Ibid.*, 671–673.
157. *U.S. v. Goldberg,* 2008 U.S. Dist. LEXIS 35723, 2–4 (2008).
158. *Ibid.*, 3.
159. *Ibid.*, 5–10.

160. Statement of Judge Robin J. Cauthron, U.S. Sentencing Commission Regional Hearing on the State of Federal Sentencing, November 19, 2009, www.ussc.gov/AGENDAS/20091119/Cauthron.pdf (accessed May 4, 2010).

161. U.P.I., "Judges call for child porn sentence leeway," Dec. 23, 2009, http://www.upi.com/Top_News/US/2009/12/23/Judges-call-for-child-porn-sentence-leeway/UPI-64951261588257/(accessed May 4, 2010); Statement of Judge Jay Zainey, U.S. Sentencing Commission Regional Hearing on the State of Federal Sentencing, November 19, 2009, www.ussc.gov/AGENDAS/20091119/Zainey.pdf (accessed May 4, 2010).

162. Lynne Marek, "Sentences for Possession of Child Porn May Be Too High, Judges Say." *The National Law Journal,* September 10, 2009, http://www.law.com/newswire/cache/1202433693658.html (accessed May 4, 2010).

163. Ibid.

164. Ibid.

165. Ibid.

166. Ibid.

167. Ibid.

168. Ibid.

169. Ibid.

170. Ibid.

171. Statement of Julia O'Connell, U.S. Sentencing Commission Regional Hearing on the State of Federal Sentencing, November 19, 2009, www.ussc.gov/AGENDAS/20091119/OConnell.pdf (accessed May 4, 2010).

172. Arizona Revised Statutes §13-604.01.

173. Patrick A. Langan, Erica L. Schmitt, and Matthew R. Durose, U.S. Bureau of Justice Statistics, "Recidivism of Sex Offenders Released from Prison in 1994" (2003), http://bjs.ojp.usdoj.gov/index.cfm?ty=pbdetail&iid=1136 (accessed May 2, 2010).

174. Kristin Zgoba, Philip Witt, Melissa Dalessandro, and Bonita Veysey, "Megan's Law: Assessing the Practical and Monetary Efficacy" (December 2008), www.ncjrs.gov/pdffiles1/nij/grants/225370.pdf (accessed May 4, 2010).

175. Georgia Department of Corrections, Office of Planning, "Offenders in Georgia: Child Sex Offenders," www.dcor.state.ga.us/pdf/CSO.pdf (accessed May 4, 2010).

176. N.Y. Penal Law § 130.65.

177. Utah Code § 76-5-404.1.

178. Missouri Revised Statutes Missouri Revised Statutes § 566.068.

179. Yaman Akdeniz, *Internet Child Pornography and the Law: National and International Responses* (2008): 24.

180. *Ibid.,* 33, 44.

181. *Regina v Oliver,* EWCA Crim 2766, 2 Cr App R (S) 64, [10] (2002).

182. *Ibid.,* [14]–[18].

183. U.S. Courts, "Costs of Imprisonment Far Exceed Supervision Costs," http://www.uscourts.gov/newsroom/2009/costsOfImprisonment.cfm (accessed May 4, 2010).

184. Tom Hayes, "Ozmint: Corrections budget already "to the bone,"" *South Carolina Radio Network*, February 1, 2010, http://www.southcarolinaradionetwork.com/2010/02/01/ozmint-corrections-budget-already-to-the-bone/ (accessed May 4, 2010).

185. Kenny Linn, "Priority for Amendment Cycle Ending May 1, 2009," public comment to the U.S. Sentencing Commission (September 7, 2008), judiciary.house.gov/hearings/pdf/Linn080716.pdf (accessed May 4, 2010).

186. Mark Motivans and Tracey Kyckelhahn, "Federal Prosecution of Child Sex Exploitation Offenders, 2006" (December 2007), http://www.ojp.usdoj.gov/bjs/abstract/fpceo06.htm (accessed May 4, 2010).

187. United States Government Accountability Office, "Cost of Prisons: GAO Report to the Subcommittees on Commerce, Justice, and Science, Senate and House Appropriations Committees," October 5, 2007, www.gao.gov/new.items/d086.pdf (accessed May 4, 2010).

188. Federal Bureau of Investigation, "Innocent Images National Initiative," http://www.fbi.gov/publications/innocent.htm (accessed May 4, 2010).

189. Ibid.

190. U.S. Department of Justice, Federal Bureau of Investigation, "FY 2011 Authorization and Budget Request to Congress" (February 2010), www.justice.gov/jmd/2011justification/office/fy11-fbi-justification.doc (accessed May 4, 2010): 56.

191. U.S. Department of Justice, Federal Bureau of Investigation, "FY2008: Budget Fact Sheet: Crimes Against Children and Obscenity," www.justice.gov/jmd/2008factsheets/pdf/0804_child_crimes.pdf (accessed May 4, 2010).

192. U.S. Department of Justice, Federal Bureau of Investigation, "FY 2010 Authorization and Budget Request to Congress" (February 2009), www.justice.gov/jmd/2010justification/office/fy10-fbi-justification.doc (accessed May 4, 2010): 56.

193. Ibid.

194. Ibid.

195. Ibid.

CHAPTER 4: INTERNET SEX OFFENDERS

1. David Finkelhor, Kimberly J. Mitchell, and Janis Wolak, "Online Victimization: A Report on the Nation's Youth" (June 2000), www.missingkids.com/en_US/publications/NC62.pdf (accessed May 4, 2010).

2. *Ibid.*, 1.

3. Ibid.

4. *Ibid.*, x.

5. Ibid.

6. *Ibid.*, 2.

7. *Ibid.*, 4.

8. *Ibid.*, 3.

9. *Ibid.*, 4.

10. *Ibid.*, 6.
11. Ibid.
12. *Ibid.*, 3.
13. Ibid.
14. Janis Wolak, Kimberly Mitchell, and David Finkelhor, "Internet Sex Crimes Against Minors: The Response of Law Enforcement" (November 2003), www.unh.edu/ccrc/pdf/CV70.pdf (accessed May 10, 2010): 1.
15. Ibid.
16. Janis Wolak, David Finkelhor, Kimberly J. Mitchell, and Michele L. Ybarra, "Online "Predators" and Their Victims: Myths, Realities, and Implications for Prevention and Treatment," *American Psychologist* (2008): 111–128, 112.
17. *Ibid.*, 113.
18. *Ibid.*, 112.
19. Janis Wolak, David Finkelhor, and Kimberly J. Mitchell, "Internet-initiated Sex Crimes against Minors: Implications for Prevention Based on Findings from a National Study," *Journal of Adolescent Health* (2004): 424–433, 430.
20. Ibid.
21. Kimberly J. Mitchell, Janis Wolak, and David Finkelhor, "Internet sex crimes against minors," in K.A. Kendall-Tackett and S. Giacomoni (Eds.), *Victimization of Children and Youth* (2005): 1–17, 7.
22. Ibid.
23. Wolak, Finkelhor, Mitchell, and Ybarra, *supra* note 16, 119.
24. Wolak, Mitchell, and Finkelhor, *supra* note 14, 7.
25. Wolak, Finkelhor, Mitchell, and Ybarra, *supra* note 16, 120.
26. Janis Wolak, Kimberly Mitchell, and David Finkelhor, "Online Victimization of Youth: Five Years Later" (2006), www.unh.edu/ccrc/pdf/CV138.pdf (accessed May 10, 2010).
27. *Ibid.*, 16.
28. Ibid.
29. *Ibid.*, 18.
30. *Ibid.*, 21.
31. L. Alvin Malesky, Jr., "Predatory Online Behavior: Modus Operandi of Convicted Sex Offenders in Identifying Potential Victims and Contacting Minors Over the Internet," *Journal of Child Sexual Abuse* (2007): 23–32.
32. *Ibid.*, 29.
33. *Ibid.*, 26.
34. *Ibid.*, 27–28.
35. Wolak, Finkelhor, Mitchell, and Ybarra, *supra* note 16, 115.
36. *See*, e.g., Sandra Norman-Eady, Christopher Reinhart, and Peter Martino, "Statutory Rape Laws by State," (April 14, 2003)., http://www.cga.ct.gov/2003/ olrdata/jud/rpt/2003-r-0376.htm (accessed May 10, 2010); Asaph Glosser, Karen Gardiner, and Mike Fishman, "Statutory Rape: A Guide to State Laws and Reporting Requirements Prepared for: Office of the Assistant Secretary for Planning and Evaluation, Department of Health and Human Services"

(December 15, 2004), http://www.lewin.com/Lewin_Publications/Human_
Services/StateLawsReport.htm (accessed May 10, 2010).

37. NY Penal Code §§130. 25, 130. 30, and 130. 35.

38. Ibid.

39. *See, e.g., Leaptrot v. State*, 272 Ga. App. 587, 612 S.E.2d 887, 891 (2005).

40. *See, e.g., State v. Falco*, 59 Wash. App. 354, 796 P.2d 796, 798 (1990).

41. Julie Sorenson Stanger, "Salvaging States' Rights To Protect Children from
Internet Predation: State Power To Regulate Internet Activity Under the
Dormant Commerce Clause," *Brigham Young University Law Review* (2005):
191–228, 228.

42. 2009 Minnesota Statutes § 609.352.

43. Ibid.

44. 18 USC § 2422.

45. Committee on the Judiciary, U.S. House of Representatives (105th Congress),
"Report on the Child Protection and Sexual Predator Punishment Act of 1998,"
http://thomas.loc.gov/cgi-bin/cpquery/T?&report=hr557&dbname=105&
(accessed May 10, 2010).

46. Pub. L. 108-21, Sec. 103(a)(2)(B), (b)(2)(A).

47. Pub. L. 109-248.

48. 18 U.S.C. § 2423.

49. 18 U.S.C. § 2423(b)–(e).

50. *U.S. v. DeBeir*, 186 F.3d 561, 572 (1999).

51. 18 U.S.C. § 2251.

52. Federal Sentencing Guidelines, §2G1.3 (b) (2) (A).

53. *Ibid.,* §2G1.3 (b) (3) (A).

54. *Supra*note 52.

55. *Supra*note 53.

56. Federal Sentencing Guidelines, §2G1.3 (b) (2) (B).

57. Federal Sentencing Guidelines, Application note 3(B).

58. *U.S. v. Root*, 296 F.3d 1222 (2002).

59. *Ibid.,* 1235–1236.

60. U.S. Department of Justice, "Decisions," November 6, 2008,
www.projectsafechildhood.gov/video/psa_expmnr_transcript.pdf (accessed
May 10, 2010).

61. U.S. Immigration and Customs Enforcement, "North Texas Man Sentenced
to More Than 24 Years for Enticing Minor" (Press Release), April 29, 2009,
http://www.ice.gov/pi/nr/0904/090424ftworth.htm (accessed May 10, 2010).

62. U.S. Department of Justice (Office of the U.S. Attorney, Northern District of
Georgia), "North Georgia Man Sentenced to Federal Prison for Enticing a Child"
(Press Release), February 25, 2009, www.justice.gov/usao/gan/press/2009/02-25-
09b.pdf (accessed May 10, 2010).

63. U.S. Department of Justice (Office of the U.S. Attorney, District of Nevada),
"Reno Man Convicted of Using Text Messaging to Entice Teenage Girls to Have
Sex with Him" (Press Release), September 29, 2008, http://lasvegas.fbi.gov/
dojpressrel/pressrel08/lv092908.htm (accessed May 10, 2010).

64. "Orono man gets 30 days in sex case," *Bangor Daily News*, January 22, 2009, B1.

65. CBS News, "News Anchor Gets Probation After Pedophile Sting," December 21, 2007, http://cbs2.com/local/Jim.Philbrick.TV.2.615999.html (accessed May 10, 2010).

66. "Suspected Online Predator Busted in Clackamas County," *Salem News*, October 22, 2008, http://www.salem-news.com/articles/october222008/predator_arrest_10-22-08.php (accessed May 10, 2010); Tom Wolfe, "Medford man sentenced in online sex sting," *The Oregonian*, April 3, 2009, http://www.oregonlive.com/clackamascounty/index.ssf/2009/04/medford_man_sentenced_in_onlin.html (accessed May 10, 2010).

67. Amber Hunt, "Garden City man sentenced in Internet sex case," *Free Press*, May 5, 2009, http://www.freep.com/article/20090505/NEWS04/90505082/(accessed May 14, 2009).

68. "Another Suspected Internet Predator Nabbed," *Hawaii News*, no date, http://www.khnl.com/Global/story.asp?S=4627202 (accessed 5/14/09); "Man Convicted Of Luring Teen For Sex Online: Defendant Had Sex With Girl, 16, After Meeting On MySpace," *Honolulu News*, May 11, 2009, http://www.kitv.com/news/19433227/detail.html (accessed May 10, 2010).

69. Sara Suddes, "DA defends one year sex crimes sentence for former teacher," *Gilroy Dispatch*, May 7, 2009, http://www.gilroydispatch.com/news/255891-da-defends-one-year-sex-crimes-sentence-for-former-teacher (accessed May 10, 2010); Sara Suddes, "High school math teacher arrested for sex crimes with 14-year-old," *Gilroy Dispatch*, February 26, 2009, http://www.gilroydispatch.com/news/254074-high-school-math-teacher-arrested-for-sex-crimes-with-14-year-old (accessed May 10, 2010).

70. Brian Stelter, "'To Catch a Predator' Is Falling Prey to Advertisers' Sensibilities," *New York Times*, August 27, 2007, 1, http://www.nytimes.com/2007/08/27/business/media/27predator.html?pagewanted=print (accessed May 10, 2010).

71. Ibid.

72. *Conradt v. NBC Universal*, 536 F. Supp. 2d 380, 384–385 (2008).

73. *See, generally, Conradt v. NBC Universal, supra* note 72.

74. Complaint, *U.S. v. D'Souza*, U.S. District Court, Eastern District of California (filed February 18, 2009); Transcript of Internet chats, http://www.perverted-justice.com/?archive=Inxs00 (accessed May 10, 2010).

75. *Conradt v. NBC Universal, supra* note 72, 386.

76. Ibid.

77. Ibid.

78. *Ibid.*, 387.

79. Ibid.

80. Ibid.

81. *Ibid.*, 383.

82. Ibid.

83. Ibid.

84. Brian Stelter, "NBC Settles With Family That Blamed a TV Investigation for a Man's Suicide," *New York Times*, June 26, 2008, 3, http://www.nytimes.com/2008/06/26/business/media/26nbc.html (accessed May 10, 2010).

85. *Bist v. State*, 2010 Fla. App. LEXIS 4698, 1–2 (2010).

86. Perverted Justice Foundation, "Frequently Asked Questions," http://www.pjfi.org/?pg=faq (accessed May 10, 2010).

87. Federal Bureau of Investigation, "Dublin Electrical Engineer is Sentenced to 10 Years for Using the Internet to Obtain Sex with a Minor" (Press Release), November 12, 2009, http://sacramento.fbi.gov/dojpressrel/pressrel09/sc111209.htm (accessed May 10, 2010).

88. Transcript of Internet chats, http://www.perverted-justice.com/?archive=peter2033 (accessed May 10, 2010).

89. Ibid.

90. Federal Bureau of Investigation, *supra* note 87.

91. Kelly M. Babchishin, R. Karl Hanson, and Chantal A. Hermann, "The Characteristics of Online Sex Offenders: A Meta-analysis," unpublished paper, 18–19.

92. Michael C. Seto, R. Karl Hanson, and Kelly M. Babchishin, "Contact Sexual Offending By Men with Online Sexual Offenses," *Sexual Abuse: A Journal of Research and Treatment* (in press), 5.

93. Babchishin, Hanson and Hermann, *supra* note 91, 14.

94. *Ibid.*, 15–16.

95. Wolak, Finkelhor, Mitchell, and Ybarra, *supra* note 16, 111.

96. Kimberly J. Mitchell, Janis Wolak, and David Finkelhor, "Police Posing as Juveniles Online to Catch Sex Offenders: Is It Working?" *Sexual Abuse: A Journal of Research and Treatment* (2005), 241–267, 245.

97. *Ibid.*, 260.

98. 18 USC § 2422.

99. Bruce Hay, "Sting Operations, Undercover Agents, and Entrapment," *Missouri Law Review* (2005), 387–431, 399–400.

100. Wayne R. LaFave, *Criminal Law* (2010): 536.

101. Model Penal Code, § 2.13 (1962).

102. *U.S. v. Hollingsworth*, 27 F.3d 1196, 1203 (1994).

103. Model Penal Code § 5.01(1) (1985).

104. *Conradt v. NBC Universal, supra* note 72, 383.

105. Ibid.

106. Hay, *supra* note 99, 395.

107. Ibid.

INDEX